Snowflake Cookbook

Techniques for building modern cloud data warehousing solutions

Hamid Mahmood Qureshi

Hammad Sharif

BIRMINGHAM—MUMBAI

Snowflake Cookbook

Group Product Manager: Kunal Parikh

Publishing Product Manager: Ali Abidi

Commissioning Editor: Sunith Shetty

Acquisition Editor: Ali Abidi

Senior Editor: Roshan Kumar

Content Development Editors: Athikho Rishana, Sean Lobo

Technical Editor: Sonam Pandey

Copy Editor: Safis Editing

Project Coordinator: Aishwarya Mohan

Proofreader: Safis Editing

Indexer: Priyanka Dhadke

Production Designer: Vijay Kamble

First published: February 2021

Production reference: 1230221

Published by Packt Publishing Ltd.
Livery Place
35 Livery Street
Birmingham
B3 2PB, UK.

ISBN 978-1-80056-061-1

www.packt.com

To my father, whose authoring of countless books was an inspiration.

To my mother, who dedicated her life to her children's education and well-being.

– Hamid Qureshi

To my dad and mom for unlimited prayers and (according to my siblings, a bit extra) love. I cannot thank and appreciate you enough.

To my wife and the mother of my children for her support and encouragement throughout this and other treks made by us.

– Hammad Sharif

Contributors

About the authors

Hamid Qureshi is a senior cloud and data warehouse professional with almost two decades of total experience, having architected, designed, and led the implementation of several data warehouse and business intelligence solutions. He has extensive experience and certifications across various data analytics platforms, ranging from Teradata, Oracle, and Hadoop to modern, cloud-based tools such as Snowflake. Having worked extensively with traditional technologies, combined with his knowledge of modern platforms, he has accumulated substantial practical expertise in data warehousing and analytics in Snowflake, which he has subsequently captured in his publications.

I want to thank the people who have helped me on this journey: my co-author Hammad, our technical reviewer, Hassaan, the Packt team, and my loving wife and children for their support throughout this journey.

Hammad Sharif is an experienced data architect with more than a decade of experience in the information domain, covering governance, warehousing, data lakes, streaming data, and machine learning.

He has worked with a leading data warehouse vendor for a decade as part of a professional services organization, advising customers in telco, retail, life sciences, and financial industries located in Asia, Europe, and Australia during presales and post-sales implementation cycles.

Hammad holds an MSc. in computer science and has published conference papers in the domains of machine learning, sensor networks, software engineering, and remote sensing.

I would like to first and foremost thank my loving wife and children for their patience and encouragement throughout the long process of writing this book. I'd also like to thank Hamid for inviting me to be his partner in crime and for his patience, my publishing team for their guidance, and the reviewers for helping improve this work.

About the reviewers

Hassaan Sajid has around 12 years of experience in data warehousing and business intelligence in the retail, telecommunications, banking, insurance, and government sectors. He has worked with various clients in Australia, UAE, Pakistan, Saudi Arabia, and the USA in multiple BI/data warehousing roles, including BI architect, as a BI developer, ETL developer, data modeler, operations analyst, data analyst, and technical trainer. He holds a master's degree in BI and is a professional Scrum Master. He is also certified in Snowflake, MicroStrategy, Tableau, Power BI, and Teradata. His hobbies include reading, traveling, and photography.

Buvaneswaran Matheswaran has a bachelor's degree in electronics and communication engineering from the Government College of Technology, Coimbatore, India. He had the opportunity to work on Snowflake in its very early stages and has more than 4 years of Snowflake experience. He has done lots of work and research on Snowflake as an enterprise admin. He has worked mainly in retail- and **Consumer Product Goods** (CPG)-based Fortune 500 companies. He is immensely passionate about cloud technologies, data security, performance tuning, and cost optimization. This is the first time he has done a technical review for a book, and he enjoyed the experience immensely. He has learned a lot as a user and also shared his experience as a veteran Snowflake admin.

Daan Bakboord is a self-employed data and analytics consultant from the Netherlands. His passion is collecting, processing, storing, and presenting data. He has a simple motto: a customer must be able to make decisions based on facts and within the right context. DaAnalytics is his personal (online) label. He provides data and analytics services, having been active in Oracle Analytics since the mid-2000s. Since the end of 2017, his primary focus has been in the area of cloud analytics. Focused on Snowflake and its ecosystem, he is Snowflake Core Pro certified and, thanks to his contributions to the community, has been recognized as a Snowflake Data Hero. Also, he is Managing Partner Data and Analytics at Pong, a professional services provider that focuses on data-related challenges.

Table of Contents

3

Loading and Extracting Data into and out of Snowflake

4

Building Data Pipelines in Snowflake

5

Data Protection and Security in Snowflake

6

Performance and Cost Optimization

9
Advanced SQL Techniques

10
Extending Snowflake Capabilities

Preface

Understanding a technology for analytics is an important aspect before embarking on delivering data analytic solutions, particularly in the cloud. This book introduces Snowflake tools and techniques you can use to tame challenges associated with data management, warehousing, and analytics.

The cloud provides a quick onboarding mechanism, but at the same time, for novice users who lack the knowledge to efficiently use Snowflake to build and maintain a data warehouse, using trial and error can lead to higher bills. This book provides a practical introduction and guidance for those who have used other technologies, either on-premise or in the cloud for analytics and data warehousing, and those who are keen on transferring their skills to the new technology.

The book provides practical examples that are typically involved in data warehousing and analytics in a simple way supported by code examples. It takes you through the user interface and management console offered by Snowflake and how to get started by creating an account. It also takes you through examples of how to load data and how to deliver analytics using different Snowflake capabilities and touches on extending the capabilities of Snowflake using stored procedures and user-defined functions. The book also touches on integrating Snowflake with Java and Apache Spark to allow it to coexist with a data lake.

By the end of this book, you will be able to build applications on Snowflake that can serve as the building blocks of a larger solution, alongside security, governance, the data life cycle, and the distribution of data on Snowflake.

Who this book is for

The book acts as a reference for users who want to learn about Snowflake using a practical approach. The recipe-based approach allows the different personas in data management to pick and choose what they want to learn, as and when required. The recipes are independent and start by helping you to understand the environment. The recipes require basic SQL and data warehousing knowledge.

What this book covers

Chapter 1, Getting Started with Snowflake, walks you through the process of setting up an account and connecting with Snowflake via its Web UI. The chapter introduces the concept of a virtual warehouse and how a virtual warehouse can be used elastically according to the user's needs around the complexity of user queries. Then the chapter moves onto ecosystem support for Snowflake, showing how Snowflake can be connected and used with different tools using different interfaces.

Chapter 2, Managing the Data Life Cycle, provides a set of recipes that introduce how data can be managed with Snowflake. The chapter talks about typical DBMSes and data warehouse concepts and introduces nuances specific to Snowflake.

Chapter 3, Loading and Extracting Data into and out of Snowflake, guides you on staging and loading data. In this chapter, we explore methods provided by Snowflake to load data into a Snowflake table. We explore the loading of data from familiar cloud sources such as Amazon S3, Azure Blob Storage, and GCP Cloud Storage, and on-premise hosts. The chapter also provides an example of how near-real-time data loading works on Snowflake.

Chapter 4, Building Data Pipelines in Snowflake, explains the capabilities on offer with Snowflake to process a string of SQL statements through the concept of tasks. Tasks allow developers to create data pipelines that process data and perform various functions as they progress through the execution sequence. Tasks combined with the concept of streams enables the user to manage complex orchestration and scheduling patterns. This chapter deals with setting up pipelines using tasks and streams and applying different techniques for transforming data within tasks.

Chapter 5, Data Protection and Security in Snowflake, walks you through handling authentication and authorization on Snowflake. Authentication refers to letting a user connect, and authorization refers to verifying what objects a connected user can access. Snowflake provides granular controls to limit access for out-of-the-box and custom roles. This chapter will help you set up role hierarchies, add custom roles, and set default roles for users.

Chapter 6, Performance and Cost Optimization, enables you to exploit Snowflake's capabilities to optimize queries and performance through various built-in features such as caching, autoscaling, and automatically clustering tables. There is always an opportunity to positively influence the performance by tweaking table structures, introducing physicalization techniques, and optimizing your compute resources to the maximum. In this chapter, we explore some of these techniques, which can be used to make a Snowflake-based data warehouse run more efficiently and therefore at a lower cost. The chapter also explores optimization strategies for reducing unnecessary storage costs.

Chapter 7, Secure Data Sharing, details how to share data with other Snowflake customers as well as non-Snowflake customers. Traditional warehouse solutions share data by extracting the data out and sending it over transport mechanisms, compromising data security and leading to inefficiencies. Another downside to this is that as soon as the data is extracted, it is already out of date. Snowflake overcomes this by providing a unique data sharing solution that ensures reduced costs, reduced operational overhead, and always up-to-date data.

Chapter 8, Back to the Future with Time Travel, equips you to deal with unpleasant data issues such as not determining when data was changed or whether the data has been lost altogether. Snowflake provides a unique way of going back in time through the Time Travel feature. This chapter explores the various applications of the Time Travel feature and combines it with cloning to tackle common data loss and debugging issues.

Chapter 9, Advanced SQL Techniques, provides you with multiple advanced SQL techniques using a Snowflake data warehouse. These SQL techniques are essential from a data warehousing perspective, such as trend analysis, temporal analytics, managing sequences, unique counts, and managing processes as transactions.

Chapter 10, Extending Snowflake's Capabilities, provides you with techniques for extending a Snowflake data warehouse and integrating it to coexist and work with other technologies. The chapter walks you through user-defined functions, through which custom functionality can be achieved. The chapter also involves connecting Snowflake with Apache Spark and demonstrates how to perform data processing on the Spark engine.

To get the most out of this book

You must have some knowledge of SQL, as that is the primary language used in Snowflake. There are a few examples that require knowledge of Java, Spark, and Linux:

Software/Hardware covered in the book	OS Requirements
Web Browser (Chrome, MS Edge, Firefox)	OS (Windows, macOS X, and Linux (any) with UI)
Snowflake Web UI, SnowSQL, SnowPipe	OS (Windows, macOS X, and Linux (any) with UI)
Apache Spark	OS (Windows, macOS X, and Linux (any) with UI)

If you are using the digital version of this book, we advise you to type the code yourself or access the code via the GitHub repository (link available in the next section). Doing so will help you avoid any potential errors related to the copying and pasting of code.

Download the example code files

You can download the example code files for this book from GitHub at `https://github.com/PacktPublishing/Snowflake-Cookbook`.

In case there's an update to the code, it will be updated on the existing GitHub repository.

We also have other code bundles from our rich catalog of books and videos available at `https://github.com/PacktPublishing/`. Check them out!

Download the color images

We also provide a PDF file that has color images of the screenshots/diagrams used in this book. You can download it here: `https://static.packt-cdn.com/downloads/9781800560611_ColorImages.pdf`.

Conventions used

There are a number of text conventions used throughout this book.

`Code in text`: Indicates code words in text, database table names, folder names, filenames, file extensions, pathnames, dummy URLs, user input, and Twitter handles. Here is an example: "We will start by simply selecting all rows from the `QUERY_HISTORY` view."

A block of code is set as follows:

```
CREATE TRANSIENT SCHEMA temporary_data
DATA_RETENTION_TIME_IN_DAYS = 0
COMMENT = 'Schema containing temporary data used by ETL
processes';
```

When we wish to draw your attention to a particular part of a code block, the relevant lines or items are set in bold:

```
USE ROLE ACCOUNTADMIN;
USE SNOWFLAKE;
SELECT QUERY_ID, QUERY_TEXT, EXECUTION_TIME,USER_NAME
FROM SNOWFLAKE.ACCOUNT_USAGE.query_history
ORDER BY EXECUTION_TIME DESC;
```

Any command-line input or output is written as follows:

```
$ mkdir css
$ cd css
```

Bold: Indicates a new term, an important word, or words that you see on screen. For example, words in menus or dialog boxes appear in the text like this. Here is an example: "Select **System info** from the **Administration** panel."

Tips or important notes

Appear like this.

Sections

In this book, you will find several headings that appear frequently (*Getting ready*, *How to do it...*, *How it works...*, *There's more...*, and *See also*).

To give clear instructions on how to complete a recipe, use these sections as follows:

Getting ready

This section tells you what to expect in the recipe and describes how to set up any software or any preliminary settings required for the recipe.

How to do it...

This section contains the steps required to follow the recipe.

How it works...

This section usually consists of a detailed explanation of what happened in the previous section.

There's more...

This section consists of additional information about the recipe in order to make you more knowledgeable about the recipe.

See also

'lhis section provides helpful links to other useful information for the recipe.

Get in touch

Feedback from our readers is always welcome.

General feedback: If you have questions about any aspect of this book, mention the book title in the subject of your message and email us at customercare@packtpub.com.

Errata: Although we have taken every care to ensure the accuracy of our content, mistakes do happen. If you have found a mistake in this book, we would be grateful if you would report this to us. Please visit www.packtpub.com/support/errata, selecting your book, clicking on the Errata Submission Form link, and entering the details.

Piracy: If you come across any illegal copies of our works in any form on the i nternet, we would be grateful if you would provide us with the location address or website name. Please contact us at copyright@packt.com with a link to the material.

If you are interested in becoming an author: If there is a topic that you have expertise in and you are interested in either writing or contributing to a book, please visit authors.packtpub.com.

Reviews

Please leave a review. Once you have read and used this book, why not leave a review on the site that you purchased it from? Potential readers can then see and use your unbiased opinion to make purchase decisions, we at Packt can understand what you think about our products, and our authors can see your feedback on their book. Thank you!

For more information about Packt, please visit packt.com.

1
Getting Started with Snowflake

Snowflake is a cloud analytics solution that uses the cloud's flexibility and cost benefits but does not compromise on providing the user with a database-like environment. It allows the user to manage data using familiar concepts. Moreover, it allows the user to use SQL to query data. This chapter will provide you with an introduction to Snowflake's architecture and its different components. Then, you'll learn how to connect to Snowflake via its Web UI. You will also be introduced to the concept of a Virtual warehouse and how a Virtual warehouse can be used elastically according to the complexity of user queries. Later, we move onto the ecosystem support for Snowflake, explaining how Snowflake can be connected to and used with diverse tools using different interfaces.

The following recipes will be covered in this chapter:

- Creating a new Snowflake instance
- Creating a tailored multi-cluster virtual warehouse
- Using the Snowflake WebUI and executing a query
- Using SnowSQL to connect to Snowflake
- Connecting to Snowflake with JDBC
- Creating a new account admin user and understanding built-in roles

Let's get started!

Technical requirements

For this chapter, you will need access to a modern internet browser (Chrome, Microsoft Edge, Firefox, and so on) and access to the internet in order to provision and connect to your Snowflake instance in the cloud. Since we will be installing the SnowSQL client, administrative (root) access on your machine will be required.

To set up, configure, and compile a sample program that uses the Snowflake JDBC driver, you will need to have the following installed and configured:

- **OpenJDK 1.8+**
- **Maven 2.4+**

You may use Visual Studio IDE for Linux or another IDE of your choice to compile the Java code.

The code for this chapter can be found at `https://github.com/PacktPublishing/Snowflake-Cookbook/tree/master/Chapter01`.

Creating a new Snowflake instance

There are a number of decisions that you need to make when setting up a new Snowflake instance via the Snowflake website at `www.Snowflake.com`. Among those decisions is also the question of what Snowflake edition you should get and which public cloud to host your instance on. Let's get answers to these as we go through the process of creating a new Snowflake instance.

Getting ready

Before starting this process, please have your contact details (name, email, company/business name, country, and so on) ready as you will be using them during the sign-up process. Your email address will be used to send a link to your Snowflake instance, so make sure you have the correct email address ready. You do not need payment information at this stage, but as soon as your trial expires (after 30 days), you will need to provide this.

How to do it...

The steps for this recipe are as follows:

1. Let's start by creating a Snowflake account. Snowflake's website offers an easy-to-use UI for creating and managing your account. It also offers a free-to-use (for 30 days) account that has $400 credit for compute.

2. Navigate to the Snowflake website at www.Snowflake.com and find the **START FOR FREE** button. Then, click on the **START FOR FREE** button on that page to start the provisioning process.

3. You will be navigated to a signup page, prompting you to start your 30-day trial with $400 worth of credit to use. Please fill in the required contact details on this page and continue.

4. The next steps show you the different options that are available regarding the type of instance and choice of the underpinning cloud platform. These two decisions are critical both from a cost perspective as well as in terms of efficiency.

5. On the next screen, you will be prompted to select your Snowflake edition and public cloud provider, as well as the region where you want to host your Snowflake instance. The Snowflake edition you choose mainly depends on your use case. The **Standard** edition is the entry-level edition and provides all the necessary SQL warehouse functionality. However, it does not support multi-cluster virtual warehouses or materialized views and provides only 1 day of *time travel* (Snowflake's way of maintaining versions of data as a result of merging as new data arrives). The **Enterprise** edition is a good choice for most organizations as it supports multi-cluster virtual warehouses, materialized views, and up to 90 days of time travel. As shown in the following screenshot, we have selected **Enterprise**:

Choose your Snowflake edition

○ **Standard**
A strong balance between features, level of support, and cost.

● **Enterprise**
Standard plus 90-day time travel, multi-cluster warehouses, and materialized views.

○ **Business Critical**
Enterprise plus enhanced security, data protection, and database failover/fallback.

Figure 1.1 – Types of instance

Business Critical provides several additional security features and enhanced failovers, thus delivering you better business continuity.

6.   A key thing to note here is that Snowflake is a **Software as a Service (SaaS)**, so regardless of which public cloud platform you choose, you will be accessing your Snowflake instance using a URL and will not necessarily need to log into your cloud provider console. Snowflake offers its service on the three major public cloud vendors: AWS, Microsoft Azure and **Google Cloud Platform (GCP)**. These three platforms offer largely similar capabilities with slight constraints due to the platform architecture.

7.   Which public cloud you choose is important when you take into consideration which public cloud the rest of your applications and data is hosted on. Usually, it would be best to choose the same public cloud and the same region where the rest of your data is hosted, since this will result in lower overall costs and better performance for your organization.

8.   We have decided to AWS as the platform of choice for this book. All of the examples provided work on AWS, unless specified otherwise.

9.   The next step involves activating your account, which involves Snowflake validating the email address that has been provided by the user.

10.   Once you have made that choice, continue to the next screen, when you will see a message stating **Account Setup in Progress**. This will turn into a success message once the instance has been set up. You will receive an activation email so that you can activate the account and set up an initial username and password:

Figure 1.2 – Account setup

11.   In the activation email, you will find an activation link that will activate your account but also present you with a screen where you can create a username and password. This username becomes the Account Administrator for your instance, so please choose this carefully and keep your username and password secure. Once you've set up your username and password, you will be taken to the Snowflake webUI.

How it works...

For almost all public cloud solutions, you need to be logged into the public cloud's administrative portal to provision an instance of a database service. Snowflake takes a different approach as it has been designed to work on different cloud platforms. Snowflake offers a single and consistent entry point to its users, thus reducing the administrative overhead for them. The user is provided with a unique URL that will always end with `Snowflakecomputing.com`. A Snowflake instance can accessed via an account identifier and a web URL that takes the user to the Snowflake WebUI.

Once the instance has been created, theoretically, you do not need to know about or access the underlying public cloud platform at all since all the mapping is managed by Snowflake. However, you should choose the same public cloud and region where most of your data and applications are, since it eases the process of managing costs related to data transfer.

Creating a tailored multi-cluster virtual warehouse

While creating a standard virtual warehouse is a straightforward affair, configuring a virtual warehouse that the standard options have been customized for can be a slightly more involved process. In this recipe, we will create a new multi-cluster virtual warehouse and set the scaling configuration so that the virtual warehouse can scale up and down on demand. We will also configure some advanced parameters to allow a higher number of concurrent queries to be executed.

Getting ready

To create a multi-cluster virtual warehouse, you must have the **Enterprise** or higher edition of Snowflake. If you run the following statements on a lower edition, you will likely receive an error stating `'MULTI_CLUSTER_WAREHOUSES'` not enabled. Your user should have the SYSADMIN role or higher since the SYSADMIN (or the even higher ACCOUNTADMIN) role can create a virtual warehouse.

How to do it...

Log into either the Snowflake WebUI or SnowSQL before proceeding with the following steps:

1. Switch role to the SYSADMIN role (or higher):

    ```
    USE ROLE SYSADMIN;
    ```

2. Create a virtual warehouse that can auto-scale between one and three clusters, depending on the demand:

    ```
    CREATE WAREHOUSE ETL_WH
    WAREHOUSE_SIZE = XSMALL
    MAX_CLUSTER_COUNT = 3
    MIN_CLUSTER_COUNT = 1
    SCALING_POLICY = ECONOMY
    AUTO_SUSPEND = 300 -- suspend after 5 minutes (300
    seconds) of inactivity
    AUTO_RESUME = TRUE
    INITIALLY_SUSPENDED = TRUE
    COMMENT = 'Virtual warehouse for ETL workloads. Auto
    scales between 1 and 3 clusters depending on the
    workload'
    ```

How it works...

Setting MIN_CLUSTER_COUNT and MAX_CLUSTER_COUNT to different values ensures that the multi-cluster virtual warehouse will start with a number of clusters equal to MIN_CLUSTER_COUNT initially. However, it will scale up to MAX_CLUSTER_COUNT if the number of concurrent queries exceeds the server's capacity and queries start to queue.

Setting SCALING_POLICY to ECONOMY (as opposed to STANDARD) ensures that the cluster is only scaled up if there are enough queries to keep the additional cluster busy for at least 6 minutes.

Furthermore, the AUTO_SUSPEND setting ensures that the cluster is suspended automatically after 300 seconds (or 5 minutes) of inactivity.

There's more...

The warehouse's size corresponds to the number of nodes in the virtual warehouse. Each node is a compute unit. The larger it grows, the more nodes there are. The following diagram shows the number of nodes and the respective size of the virtual warehouse:

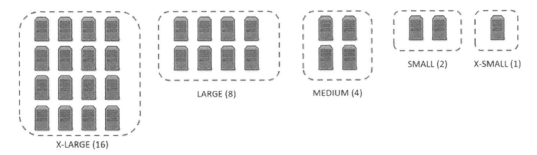

Figure 1.3 – Virtual warehouses' (relative) sizes in terms of nodes

However, more nodes does not always mean faster performance for all queries. Some queries will benefit from a larger virtual warehouse size, while certain queries will not. You will need to do some testing to find the best virtual warehouse size that works for your scenario. Start small and increase its size until you reach a point where no further performance improvement is observed. The following diagram shows how different sizes of Virtual warehouses can be used in different scenarios or for user roles:

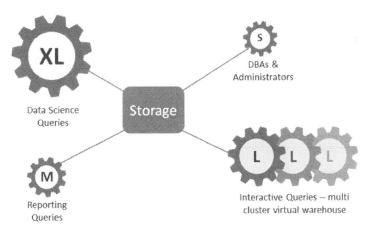

Figure 1.4 – Virtual warehouses' size and use

Virtual warehouses are the compute engines or units of a Snowflake instance. You can have as many virtual warehouses created for a given Snowflake instance and they can be of varying sizes. These warehouses can be suspended when they are not being used and set to auto-resume as soon as a new query is received. This requires a running virtual warehouse instance. This powerful feature allows us to scale in an infinite manner and allows us to assign virtual warehouses to a specific group of queries or users, and then size those virtual warehouses in a dynamic manner as per our needs. We will discuss this in detail in *Chapter 6, Performance and Cost Optimization.*

Using the Snowflake WebUI and executing a query

There are two interactive Snowflake tools that can be used to connect to a Snowflake instance: the *SnowSQL command-line utility* and the *web-based Snowflake WebUI*. The Snowflake WebUI is the most common way to connect to a Snowflake instance, execute queries, and perform administrative functions such as creating new database objects, managing virtual warehouses, managing security, and reviewing the costs associated with your instance. In this recipe, we will connect to our Snowflake instance that we created previously and explore the important components of the Snowflake Web UI. We will then create an empty table and run a test query on top of that table.

Getting ready

You should have received a link to your Snowflake instance in your account activation email. Make sure you have the link and your username and the password handy so that you can log into the Snowflake Web UI.

How to do it...

The steps for this recipe are as follows:

1. Navigate to the Snowflake WebUI using the instance link that you received. The link should look something like the following. Provide your username and password on the login screen and log in. Once you've done this, the Snowflake WebUI will open:

    ```
    jy95958.ap-southeast-2.Snowflakecomputing.com
    ```

2. The Snowflake Web UI is divided into several components, as shown in the following screenshot. We will use some of these components to create a table and perform a simple query:

Figure 1.5 – UI offered by Snowflake

From the preceding screenshot, we can see the following:

- **A**: The **Databases** button shows a list of databases that are available to the selected role and allows you to create new databases if you have the necessary privileges.

- **B**: The **Shares** button shows a list of Snowflake shares that exist in the system and allows you to manage and create new shares if you have the necessary privileges.

- **C**: The **Warehouses** button shows virtual warehouses that are available on the system. You can also create new virtual warehouses from that interface if you have the required privileges.

- **D**: **Worksheets** is the default view that the Snowflake Web UI opens on. Queries are written and executed in Worksheets.

- **E**: The top-right corner of the web UI displays your username and, importantly, your effective role. The role that's selected here determines what user interface elements you have access to. In this example, the selected role is SYSADMIN, due to which the **ACCOUNT** button is not shown. This can only be accessed by an ACCOUNTADMIN role.

- **F**: Understanding the purpose of various selections here is particularly important. The selections that are made here are applied to the corresponding worksheet. The role and virtual warehouses that are selected here determine how your queries will run.

- **G**: This shows the list of databases that are available to the role that's been selected (in **F**).

- **H**: This is the editor where queries are composed and executed.

- **I**: This tab shows the results of the queries that have been run, as well as the queries that are currently executing.

3.   To create a new database, click the **Worksheets** button if it is not already selected. Select a role and a virtual warehouse to run your query. The selected role should have privileges to create a new database (usually, the SYSADMIN role has this privilege). In the new worksheet, enter the following query to create a new database. You should see a success message:

```
CREATE DATABASE COOKBOOK;
```

4.   Create a new table in this newly created database by running the following query:

```
USE DATABASE COOKBOOK;
CREATE TABLE MY_FIRST_TABLE
(
    ID STRING,
    NAME STRING
);
```

5.   Query the newly created table by running a simple SELECT query. You will get zero rows as a result as there is no data in the table, but the query should run successfully:

```
SELECT * FROM MY_FIRST_TABLE;
```

How it works...

The Snowflake Web UI is the central interface for querying and managing your Snowflake instance. The options that are available in the UI depend on what role you have selected in the right-most dropdown of the UI, highlighted as **E** in the preceding screenshot (*UI offered by Snowflake*).

Worksheets can be used to execute SQL. Each worksheet can have its own combination of a selected *role*, *virtual warehouse*, *database*, and *schema*. To execute a query, you should select a valid role and a virtual warehouse and then select the database and schema for the table that you are querying. You can also fully qualify your table if you are querying tables from multiple databases and schemas in a single query; for example, SELECT * FROM <database_name>.<schema_name>.<table_name>;.

Using SnowSQL to connect to Snowflake

Previously, we looked at how Snowflake's Web UI allows users to connect to, manage, and query data stored in Snowflake. In this recipe, you will learn how to install Snowflake's **command-line interface (CLI)** software and use that to connect to a Snowflake instance. You will learn how to achieve this connectivity and look at the steps and required configurations to query data over that connection.

Getting ready

This recipe assumes you are using a Linux machine and have access to the Snowflake Web UI via a compatible browser. Google Chrome is the preferred browser as Snowflake tests the Web UI extensively against Chrome. Since SnowSQL is the command-line interface for Snowflake, you will need to have command-line access to the operating system with `superuser/root/administrative` privileges so that you can install any necessary software.

How to do it...

Note that SnowSQL is being downloaded in the home directory of the `sfuser` user on a `sfchost` Linux host. These names have no significance and are abbreviations for *Snowflake user* and *Snowflake client host*. Any Linux shell commands shown in the following steps are preceded by a `sfcuser@sfchost:~$,` prompt, though this has been omitted for the sake of clarity. Follow these steps:

1. Download the location (URL) from the link provided by Snowflake (for AWS):

    ```
    curl -O https://sfc-repo.Snowflakecomputing.com/snowsql/
    bootstrap/1.2/linux_x86_64/snowsql-1.2.5-linux_x86_64.
    bash
    ```

    You can find the URL that provides the latest version of the SnowSQL download by navigating to `https://sfc-repo.Snowflakecomputing.com/snowsql/index.html` and browsing to find the version of SnowSQL that's the most relevant for you.

2. Confirm that the download is complete by listing the files. You should see the following file among them:

    ```
    snowsql-1.2.5-linux_x86_64.bash
    ```

3. Install SnowSQL by executing the bash script. At this point, the installer shall ask for inputs, such as the location for installing executables. By default, the directory will be `~/bin`; that is, the user's home directory for binaries. Let's stick with the defaults here. The second prompt is for the user profile. Linux will ask you if the `~/.` profile file should be updated with the path to the SnowSQL binary. This is a Y/N question from Linux. Provide `Y` and press *Enter* on the keyboard.

4. Confirm that the installation was a success and check its version. You can do this by executing `snowsql` with the `v` option:

    ```
    snowsql -v
    ```

    This should produce the following output:

    ```
    Version: 1.2.5
    ```

    This means SnowSQL version 1.2.5 has been installed.

5. Now, let's configure SnowSQL. First, let's check the folder structure that has been created by the installer. The installer has created a hidden folder called `snowsql` within the home directory of the user, `/home/sfuser/.snowsql`. The listing for the directory is as follows:

    ```
    1.2.5  autoupgrade  config  log_bootstrap
    ```

    The `config` file contains all the different configurations that are required by SnowSQL to connect to and interact with a SnowSQL cloud instance. It's recommended that the following configurations are edited. The file can be edited in any editor available in the OS. Good old Linux's vi has been used in this recipe.

    The `accountname`, `username` , `password`, `dbname`, `schemaname`, and `warehousename` configurations are contained within the `[connections]` section of the `config` file. This `[connections]` section in the configuration file is the default section for connecting to a Snowflake instance.

6. Now, create a named connection. Creating a named connection can come in handy as it allows you to keep different configurations separate. All the configurations discussed in the preceding step can be put into a connection named `c1r5`:

    ```
    [connections.c1r5]
    accountname = abc12345.ap-southeast-2
    username = jdoe
    password = "password01234"
    dbname = Snowflake_SAMPLE_DATA
    ```

```
schemaname = TPCDS_SF10TCL
warehousename = COMPUTE_WH
```

Please substitute the values for the preceding configurations according to your account setup:

a) `accountname` includes the account name and the region where the Snowflake instance has been configured to run.

b) `username` is the username that was provided at the time of account creation.

c) `password` is the password that was provided at the time of account creation.

Save the file after providing the values for the preceding configurations.

Please note that the `config` file has our password stored in plain text. This is a security vulnerability, and it is recommended to protect the `config` file by limiting its access to the OS user, as follows:

```
chmod 700 ./config
```

7. Connect to the named connection that's been defined; that is, `c1r5`:

```
snowsql -c c1r5
```

The following should appear on your screen, with `<username>` being a placeholder. This will be replaced by your username. The rest of the prompts will be as shown here:

```
* SnowSQL * v1.2.5Type SQL statements or !help
<username>#COMPUTE_WH@Snowflake_SAMPLE_DATA.TPCDS_
SF10TCL>
```

8. Execute a query on the SnowSQL prompt:

```
<username>#COMPUTE_WH@Snowflake_SAMPLE_DATA.TPCDS_
SF10TCL>select count(*) from ITEM;
+----------+
| COUNT(*) |
|----------|
|   402000 |
+----------+
```

The preceding query will produce the following output:

```
1 Row(s) produced. Time Elapsed: 0.661s
```

The query results also inform the user that only one row was returned by the database.

How it works...

Step 1 provides a fully qualified URL so that we can download the bash script from a known location. This has been derived from the following template link:

```
curl -O https://sfc-repo.Snowflakecomputing.com/snowsql/
bootstrap/<bootstrap_version>/linux_x86_64/snowsql-<version>-
linux_x86_64.bash
```

This was derived by plugging in the version (1.2.5) and the bootstrap version (1.2):

- `<version>` can be 1.2.5, where 1, 2, and 5 represent the major, minor, and patch versions for SnowSQL, respectively.
- `<bootstrap_version>` is 1.2, where 1 and 2 are the major and minor versions, respectively, without the patch version.

There's more...

1.2.5 is the version that will be used in this book as it was the latest to be released at the time of writing. If a newer version is available, these values can be updated. You can find the latest releases at `https://docs.Snowflake.com/en/release-notes/client-change-log-snowsql.html`.

Connecting to Snowflake with JDBC

The previous recipe talked about using SnowSQL to connect to Snowflake, which provides more control over how a user can interact with Snowflake. SnowSQL can be used with the Linux shell to automate code execution. But if applications have to be supported with Snowflake serving as a data tier, it will require more granular control over connecting and executing SQL. This recipe demonstrates how to install Snowflake's **Java Database Connectivity** (**JDBC**) driver and how to use that in a Java application to connect to a Snowflake instance. This functionality is captured in a Java app.

Getting ready

Ubuntu Linux 64-bit has been used for this recipe. The JDBC driver will be downloaded in the home directory of the `sfuser` user on a 64-bit Linux host called `sfchost`. These names have no significance and are abbreviations of the Snowflake user and Snowflake client host. Any Linux shell commands shown will be preceded by a `sfcuser@ sfchost:~$,` prompt, though this has been omitted for the sake of clarity. It is also assumed that you have Java installed on your system. Java 1.8+ is required for this recipe.

How to do it...

The following steps will show you how to confirm the different dependencies or requirements for this recipe to work (in particular, Java):

1. As we mentioned previously and toward the start of this chapter, the JDBC driver for Snowflake (`Snowflake-jdbc`) requires the following:

    a) Java 1.8 or higher

    b) A 64-bit OS

    I have OpenJDK installed on my system, as shown in the following screenshot of my Linux Terminal:

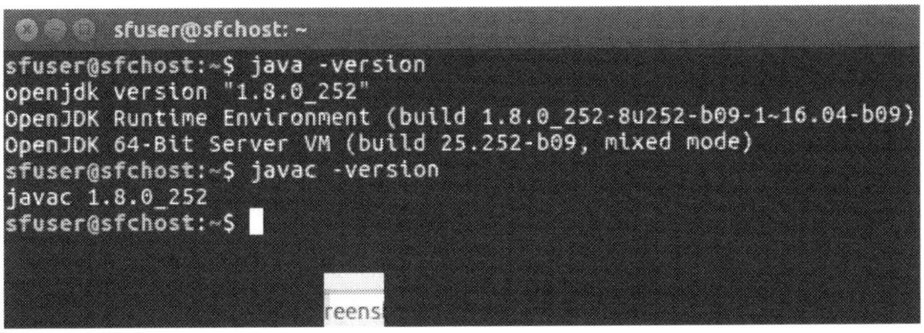

Figure 1.6 – Ubuntu Linux Terminal showing the Java runtime and JDK versions

2. Download the JDBC driver from the `maven` repository at `https://repo1.maven.org/maven2/net/Snowflake/Snowflake-jdbc`. The following screenshot is of the `maven` repository's web page (at the time of writing):

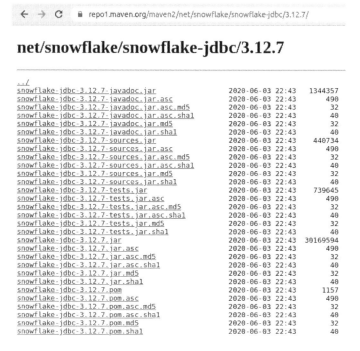

Figure 1.7 – Maven web page listing different Snowflake JDBC driver versions

The latest driver, at the time of writing, is `Snowflake-jdbc-3.12.7.jar`. This file has been downloaded onto my Linux system, in my `Home` directory, as shown in the following screenshot:

Figure 1.8 – Content of the Downloads folder

This JAR file needs to be included when we're creating a Java application so that it can interact with Snowflake. The other way we can include Snowflake JDBC capabilities in a Java application is by creating a *maven* dependency.

This JAR will need to be included in `classpath`. An alternative to downloading and putting the JAR in `classpath` is to use a Java IDE with Maven (which is the preferred approach). Downloading a JAR and making it part of `classpath` is not required in this case as maven takes care of any dependencies. This method has been used for this book. The following dependency will need to be added to maven's `pom.xml` file:

```
<dependency>
<groupId>net.Snowflake</groupId>
<artifactId>Snowflake-jdbc</artifactId>
<version>3.12.7</version>
</dependency>
```

Please note that `<version>3.12.7</version>` may need to be replaced with another/later version.

Now that we have defined the maven dependency, let's move on and define a connection string for the JDBC connection.

3. In the previous setup, we downloaded the JDBC driver. Now, let's create a connection string for the JDBC driver. These settings are required by a Java application to connect to a Snowflake instance. The two main things that are required by a connection are as follows:

a) Account information

b) Credentials

Account information and credentials are compulsory to establish a connection, so we will focus on these. There are other parameters that also help control the behavior of the connection, but they are not mandatory. The basic structure of a connection string for a JDBC connection is as follows:

```
jdbc:Snowflake://<account_info>.Snowflakecomputing.
com/?<connection_params>
```

`<account_info>`is the account identifier and the region where the Snowflake instance is running.

4. To connect to Snowflake, we will develop a Java application that connects to a Snowflake instance. This application will have three main sections. First, it will create different constants that are required for a connection to be created. These were discussed in *step 3*. Then, a function will be created that takes those constants as parameters and creates a JDBC connection. Finally, the main application will receive the connection object and use it to query the database.

5. First, let's create the class and define the different constants we discussed in *step 4*:

```
package c1;

import java.sql.*;
import java.util.Properties;

public class App {
//STEP 1
// JDBC driver class
static final String SF_JDBC_DRIVER = "net.Snowflake.
client.jdbc.SnowflakeDriver";
// Database credentials
static final String ACCOUNT = "xy12345.region123"; //To
be replaced
static final String USER = "xyz"; //To be replaced
static final String PASS = "#############"; //To be
replaced
```

6. Now, let's add the main function to the Java class, which is the entry point for the Java runtime environment:

```
public static void main(final String[] args) {
Connection conn = null;
try {
System.out.println("Creating a new connection ...");
conn = getConnection(ACCOUNT, USER, PASS);
System.out.println("Successfully created a connection
with Snowflake ...");

System.out.println("\nClosing connection ...");
conn.close();
System.out.println("Closed connection.");
```

```
    } catch (final SQLException se) {
    System.out.println("Error connecting to the database");//
    Handle errors for JDBC
    se.printStackTrace();
    }
    }// end main
```

7. Now that we have a main function, we can create a function that manufactures and returns a JDBC connection. The different constants that we created in the previous step must be passed to this function as parameters:

```
    private static Connection getConnection(
    final String par_account,
    final String par_user,
    final String par_password) throws SQLException {
    try {
    Class.forName(SF_JDBC_DRIVER);
    }catch (final ClassNotFoundException ex) {
    System.err.println("Driver class not found");
    }
```

8. Now that we have defined the function parameters, we can define the properties for the connection – the things that are required by the connection so that it can be configured for the user:

```
    // Setup connection properties
    final Properties properties = new Properties();
    properties.put("user", par_user); // replace "" with your
    username
    properties.put("password", par_password); // replace ""
    with your password
```

9. Here, we have defined a properties object that can be used to invoke an instance of our JDBC connection:

```
    // create a new connection
    System.out.println("Creating connection string...");
    final String connectionStr = "jdbc:Snowflake://" + par_
    account + ".Snowflakecomputing.com";
    System.out.println("connectionStr: " + connectionStr + "
```

```
created.");
//return connection object reference
return DriverManager.getConnection(connectionStr,
properties);
}// end getConnection
}//end App
```

This completes the class implementation with the `getConnection` function. This function can be used in different scenarios to execute a query.

How it works...

In this section, we will look at the different steps that are required for a Java application to connect to a Snowflake instance via JDBC connectivity.

Let's focus on the initial part of the application. A public class has been created that defines different constants that can be used to store connection parameters. These are defined with a global scope:

```
static final String SF_JDBC_DRIVER = "net.Snowflake.client.
jdbc.SnowflakeDriver";
// Database credentials
static final String ACCOUNT = "xy12345.region123"; //To be
replaced
static final String USER = "xyz"; //To be replaced
static final String PASS = "##############"; //To be replaced
```

Please note that `SF_JDBC_DRIVER` has a value of `net.Snowflake.client.jdbc.SnowflakeDriver`. This is the fully qualified class name that has been developed by Snowflake, as per the JDBC interface requirements. If the class is not registered, then an exception will be thrown. This will be caught as `classNotFoundException`.

Then, three constants for account, username, and password are declared and initiated with values.

Then comes the entry point into the application. The `main` function is there to run the `getConnection()` function. It starts by declaring a reference that shall point to a connection created by the `getConnection()` function. The `conn = getConnection(ACCOUNT, USER, PASS);` call is used to pass three required pieces of information; that is, the account information, username, and password, respectively:

```
Connection conn = null;
try {
System.out.println("Creating a new connection ...");
conn = getConnection(ACCOUNT, USER, PASS);
System.out.println("Successfully created a connection with
Snowflake ...");
```

The call has been preceded and followed by two printing steps that have been included to make the process verbose for you if you run the code.

Please note that `getConnection()` has been enclosed in a `try` construct. This is because the `getConnection()` function is throwing an exception. The `try` construct is followed by a `catch` clause that is anticipating an `SQLException` object in case the connection fails:

```
catch (final SQLException se) {
System.out.println("Error connecting to the database"); //
Handle errors for JDBC
    se.printStackTrace();
}
```

The `getConnection()` function starts by declaring three parameters for holding the values for account, username, and password.

Looking at at the code for the `getConnection()` function that was added in *step 4* of the *How to do it...* section, the first step is to test whether the driver class has been registered and is available:

```
try {
Class.forName(SF_JDBC_DRIVER);
    }catch (final ClassNotFoundException ex) {
        System.err.println("Driver class not found");
}
```

if the class is not available to the application, this function will throw a `ClassNotFoundException` object.

Next, the function prepares a `java.util.properties` object so that it can hold different configuration parameters for the connection object to be created:

```
final Properties properties = new Properties();
properties.put("user", par_user);
properties.put("password", par_password);
```

The next piece of the following code creates a connection string by making use of the account information that was passed to the function as a function parameter:

```
System.out.println("Creating connection string...");
final String connectionStr = "jdbc:Snowflake://" + par_account
+ ".Snowflakecomputing.com";
System.out.println("connectionStr: " + connectionStr + "
created.");
```

Finally, a reference to a JDBC connection object is created by making a call to the `java.sql.DriverManager` object. This is then returned by the function to the call:

```
return DriverManager.getConnection(connectionStr, properties);
```

There's more...

In older versions of the JDBC driver, there was an error that created Java exceptions that didn't make it very clear about what the cause of the error was. Those errors resulted from inappropriate access to or absence of a folder in Linux systems. This folder is a hidden folder that's created in the home directory of the user and is called `cache`. It is used by the connection object. Please make sure a `~/.cache` folder exists. If the folder is not there or exists with access issues, remove the folder and create a new one with an appropriate level of access to it.

Creating a new account admin user and understanding built-in roles

By default, a new Snowflake instance comes with a single user that has the account administrator (or ACCOUNTADMIN) role. The recommended best practice is to have at least two users with the ACCOUNTADMIN role and to protect the users with **multi-factor authentication** (**MFA**). In this recipe, we will create a new user with the ACCOUNTADMIN role, though enabling MFA will be covered later in *Chapter 5, Data Protection and Security in Snowflake*.

How to do it...

The steps for this recipe are as follows:

1. Log in as an existing user with security administrator privileges. You would normally do this with the username that you created when you activated a new Snowflake instance. Once you've logged in, execute the following query to switch roles to security administrator:

    ```
    USE ROLE SECURITYADMIN;
    ```

2. Create a new user with the default role of ACCOUNTADMIN. Make sure that you set the password to something that is difficult to guess. You can set the username so that it matches the naming standards that your organization uses:

    ```
    CREATE USER secondary_account_admin
    PASSWORD = 'password123'
    DEFAULT_ROLE = "ACCOUNTADMIN"
    MUST_CHANGE_PASSWORD = TRUE;
    ```

3. Make sure that you grant the ACCOUNTADMIN role to the newly created user as well:

    ```
    GRANT ROLE "ACCOUNTADMIN" TO USER secondary_account_
    admin;
    ```

4. Log out and then log in as the newly created user. You will be prompted to change your password since we set the MUST_CHANGE_PASSWORD parameter to TRUE when creating the user.

How it works...

To create a new user and grant them a role, you need a minimum of SECUTRITYADMIN privileges so that we can change our role to SECURITYADMIN. Then, we must use some standard SQL syntax to create a new user, specifying the default role for the new user as ACCOUNTADMIN. However, specifying a default role is not enough as it simply assigns the default role for a user – it is required to grant roles to the user as well.

There's more...

There are five built-in system roles in Snowflake, and you can create new custom roles as well. These built-in roles are set up in a hierarchy. So, the ACCOUNTADMIN role automatically contains other roles. Therefore, if you have a user with the ACCOUNTADMIN role, that user also has access to other roles:

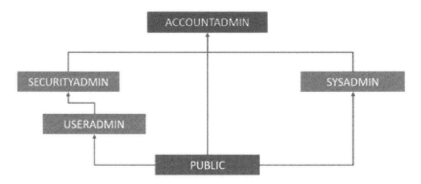

Figure 1.9 – Graphical depiction of the default role hierarchy

If you create new custom roles, it is recommended that you grant those custom roles to the SYSADMIN role since it is a best practice to complete the role hierarchy. Granting new custom roles to the SYSADMIN role ensures that your system administrators have the required privileges to operate on all the objects in the system, regardless of who has created those objects.

2
Managing the Data Life Cycle

This chapter provides a set of recipes that introduce you to data management in Snowflake. The chapter talks about common database concepts and introduces you to nuances specific to Snowflake. We'll look at common operations that are required to manage and structure data in a database. Snowflake is not very different from traditional databases and provides similar capabilities, but since Snowflake has been designed for the cloud from the ground up, it has small configurations that allow control over how data is managed in a database or a table and how temporary data is maintained and destroyed when not required. These capabilities are required when designing an ETL system or structuring data according to a data model.

The following recipes are given in this chapter:

- Managing a database
- Managing a schema
- Managing tables
- Managing external tables and stages
- Managing views in Snowflake

Technical requirements

The chapter assumes that you have a Snowflake account already set up. It also requires you to have access to an Amazon S3 bucket to use to get hold of external data and use it within Snowflake.

The code for this chapter can be found at the following GitHub URL:

`https://github.com/PacktPublishing/Snowflake-Cookbook/tree/master/Chapter02`

Managing a database

In this recipe, we will create a new database with default settings and walk through several variations on the database creation process. The recipe provides details such as how to minimize storage usage when creating databases and how to set up the replication of databases across regions and when to do so.

Getting ready

This recipe describes the various ways to create a new database in Snowflake. These steps can be run either in the Snowflake web UI or the SnowSQL command-line client.

How to do it...

Let's start with the creation of a database in Snowflake:

1. The basic syntax for creating a new database is fairly straightforward. We will be creating a new database that is called `our_first_database`. We are assuming that the database doesn't exist already:

    ```
    CREATE DATABASE our_first_database
    COMMENT = 'Our first database';
    ```

    The command should successfully execute with the following message:

    status

    Database OUR_FIRST_DATABASE successfully created.

    Figure 2.1 – Database successfully created

2. Let's verify that the database has been created successfully and review the defaults that have been set up by Snowflake:

```
SHOW DATABASES LIKE 'our_first_database';
```

The query should return one row showing information about the newly created database, such as the database name, owner, comments, and retention time. Notice that **retention_time** is set to **1** and the **options** column is blank:

name	is_default	is_current	origin	owner	comment	options	retention_time
OUR_FIRST_DATABASE	N	N		SYSADMIN	Our first database		1

Figure 2.2 – Information of the newly created database

3. Let's create another database for which we will set the time travel duration to be 15 days (in order to set the time travel duration above 1 day, you must have at least the Enterprise license for Snowflake):

```
CREATE DATABASE production_database
DATA_RETENTION_TIME_IN_DAYS = 15
COMMENT = 'Critical production database';


SHOW DATABASES LIKE 'production_database';
```

The output of SHOW DATABASES should now show **retention_time** as **15**, indicating that the time travel duration for the database is 15 days:

name	is_default	is_current	origin	owner	comment	options	retention_time
PRODUCTION_DATAB...	N	N		SYSADMIN	Critical production dat...		15

Figure 2.3 – SHOW DATABASES output

4. While time travel is normally required for production databases, you wouldn't normally need time travel and the fail-safe for temporary databases such as databases that are used in ETL processing. Removing time travel and the fail-safe helps in reducing storage costs. Let's see how that is done:

```
CREATE TRANSIENT DATABASE temporary_database
DATA_RETENTION_TIME_IN_DAYS = 0
COMMENT = 'Temporary database for ETL processing';


SHOW DATABASES LIKE 'temporary_database';
```

The output of SHOW DATABASES would show retention_time as zero, indicating that there is no time travel storage for this database, and also the options column would show TRANSIENT as the option, which essentially means that there will be no fail-safe storage for this database.

5. The time travel configuration can also be changed at a later time by altering the database with ALTER:

```
ALTER DATABASE temporary_database
SET DATA_RETENTION_TIME_IN_DAYS = 1;


SHOW DATABASES LIKE 'temporary_database';
```

How it works...

The basic CREATE DATABASE command creates a database with the defaults set at the account level. If you have not changed the defaults, the default for time travel is 1 day, which is the value that appears in retention_time when you run the SHOW DATABASES command. The database will also have a fail-safe enabled automatically. Both these options will cost you in storage, and in certain cases, you might want to reduce those storage costs. As an example, databases that are used for temporary ETL processing can easily be configured to avoid these costs.

A key thing to know about databases and tables used for ETL processing is that the data in those tables will be repeatedly inserted and deleted. If such tables are not specifically configured, you will be unnecessarily incurring costs for the time travel and fail-safe that is stored with every data change that happens for those tables. We will set such databases to be transient (with TRANSIENT) so that the fail-safe option is not the default for the tables in that database. Setting this option does mean that such databases are not protected by fail-safe if a data loss event occurs, but for temporary databases and tables, this should not be an issue. Also, we have set time travel to be zero so that there is no time travel storage as well.

Do note that although we have set the database to have no time travel and no fail-safe, we can still set individual tables within the database to be protected by the fail-safe and time travel. Setting these options at the database level only changes the defaults for the objects created within that database.

Note that there is the ALTER DATABASE command as well, which can be used to change some of the properties after the database has been created. It is a powerful command that allows renaming the database, swapping a database with another database, and also resetting custom properties back to their defaults.

It is important to note that creating a database sets the current database of the session to the newly created database. That would mean that any subsequent **data definition language** (DDL) commands such as CREATE TABLE would create a table under that new database. This is like using the USE DATABASE command.

There's more...

We will cover time travel and fail-safes in much more detail in subsequent chapters. We will also cover in depth how to create databases from shares and databases that clone other databases.

Managing a schema

In this recipe, you will be introduced to the concept of a schema and its uses. A schema is a counterpart of a database, and together, these two define a namespace. There can be multiple schemas in a database, but one schema belongs to a single database. Schemas help in grouping tables and views together that are logically related. We will see how a schema is created and its use. Apart from user-created schemas, we will learn about schemas that are automatically available with a database, including the information schema provided by Snowflake.

Getting ready

The following examples can be run either via the Snowflake web UI or the SnowSQL command-line client.

How to do it...

Let's start with the creation of a user-defined schema in a user-defined database, followed by the listing of schemas:

1. Let's first create a database in which we will test the schema creation:

    ```
    CREATE DATABASE testing_schema_creation;
    ```

    You should see a message stating that a schema was successfully created:

    status

    Database TESTING_SCHEMA_CREATION successfully created.

    Figure 2.4 – Database created successfully

2. Let's check whether the newly created database already has a schema in it:

```
SHOW SCHEMAS IN DATABASE testing_schema_creation;
```

You should see two rows in the result set, which are basically the two schemas that are automatically available with every new database:

Row	created_on	name
1	2020-06-24 0...	INFORMATION_SCHEMA
2	2020-06-24 0...	PUBLIC

Figure 2.5 – Schemas of the new database

3. Let's now create a new schema. The syntax for creating a standard schema without any additional settings is quite simple, as shown in the following SQL code:

```
CREATE SCHEMA a_custom_schema
COMMENT = 'A new custom schema';
```

The command should successfully execute with the following message:

status
Schema A_CUSTOM_SCHEMA successfully created.

Figure 2.6 – New schema successfully created

4. Let's verify that the schema has been created successfully and also look at the default values that were set automatically for its various attributes:

```
SHOW SCHEMAS LIKE 'a_custom_schema' IN DATABASE testing_
schema_creation ;
```

The query should return one row displaying information such as the schema name, the database name in which the schema resides, and the time travel retention duration in days:

created_on	name	is_default	is_current	database_name	owner	comment
2020-09-07 04:0...	A_CUSTOM_SCHE...	N	Y	TESTING_SCHEM...	SYSADMIN	A new custom sc...

Figure 2.7 – Validating the schema

5. Let's create another schema for which we will set the time travel duration to be 0 days and also set the type of the schema to be transient. It is common to use these settings on data for which Snowflake data protection features are not required, such as temporary data:

```
CREATE TRANSIENT SCHEMA temporary_data
DATA_RETENTION_TIME_IN_DAYS = 0
COMMENT = 'Schema containing temporary data used by ETL
processes';
```

The schema creation should succeed with the following message:

status
Schema TEMPORARY_DATA successfully created.

Figure 2.8 – New schema successfully created

6. Let's view what the schema settings are by running a SHOW SCHEMAS command as shown:

```
SHOW SCHEMAS LIKE 'temporary_data' IN DATABASE testing_
schema_creation ;
```

The output of SHOW SCHEMAS is shown here:

created_on	name	is_default	is_current	database_name	owner	comment	options	retention_time
2020-12-29 ...	TEMPORARY_DATA	N	N	TESTING_S...	SYSADMIN	Schema con...	TRANSIENT	

Figure 2.9 – Output of SHOW SCHEMAS

The output should show retention_time as zero or a blank value, indicating that there is no time travel storage for this schema, and also the options column should show TRANSIENT as the option, which essentially means that there will be no fail-safe storage for this schema.

How it works...

The standard CREATE SCHEMA command uses the defaults set at the database level. If you have not changed any of the configuration, the created schema will have fail-safe enabled by default. Also, time travel is enabled for the schema automatically and is set to be 1 day by default. Both these features have costs associated with them and in certain cases, you can choose to turn off these features.

For schemas that will store temporary tables, such as tables used for ETL processing, a schema can be created as a transient schema, which means that there is no fail-safe storage associated with the tables created in the schema, and therefore it would cost less. Similarly, such schemas can also be set to have time travel set to zero to reduce costs further. By default, the time travel for transient schemas is 1 day.

Do note that although we have set the schema to have no time travel and no fail-safe, we can still set individual tables within the schema to be protected by fail-safe and time travel. Setting these options at the schema level sets the default for all tables created inside that schema.

It is important to note that creating a new schema sets the current schema of the session to the newly created schema. The implication of this behavior is that any subsequent DDL commands such as CREATE TABLE would create the table under that new schema. This is like issuing the USE SCHEMA command to change the current schema.

There's more...

Every database in Snowflake will always have a **public** schema that is automatically created upon database creation. Additionally, under every database, you will also find an additional schema called the **information schema**. The information schema implements the SQL 92 standard information schema and adds additional information specific to Snowflake. The purpose of the information schema is to act as a data dictionary containing metadata that you can query to find information such as all the tables in the system, all columns along with their data types, and more. It is possible to add many additional schemas under a given database, which can help you organize your tables in a meaningful structure.

A good example of using databases and schemas to organize your data and your environment would be the approach of setting up production, testing, and development databases using the concept of schemas and databases. This approach is especially required if your organization has a single Snowflake account that is being used for development, testing, and production purposes at the same time. The approach is shown in the following diagram:

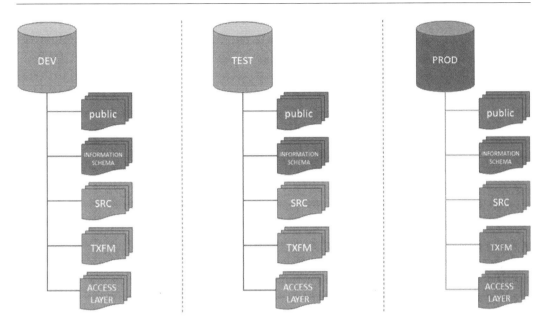

Figure 2.10 – A DEV, TEST, PROD setup using databases and schemas

In this approach, a database is created for each environment, for example, the **PROD** database for production data, the **DEV** database for development data, and so on. Within each database, the schema structures are identical; for example, each database has an **SRC** schema, which contains the source data. The purpose of this approach is to segregate the various environments but keep the structures identical enough to facilitate the development, testing, and productionization of data.

Managing tables

This recipe shows you how to create a table and insert data to explain different behaviors in storing data. Here you will be introduced to the different options that are available from a life cycle perspective, such as tables being permanent, temporary, volatile, and so on. Most of the concepts are not new, so the focus is going to be on the specifics related to Snowflake. We will start with a simple example that creates a table. We shall insert some sample data into it and then try out different variations on creating tables in Snowflake.

Getting ready

The following examples can be run either via the Snowflake web UI or the SnowSQL command-line client.

How to do it...

Let's start by creating a table for storing customer data. We shall start with the DDL statement for creating a table:

1. The following example DDL statement will be executed to create a table called CUSTOMERS in Snowflake:

```
CREATE TABLE customers (
    id              INT NOT NULL,
    last_name       VARCHAR(100)  ,
    first_name      VARCHAR(100),
    email           VARCHAR(100),
    company         VARCHAR(100),
    phone           VARCHAR(100),
    address1        VARCHAR(150),
    address2        VARCHAR(150),
    city            VARCHAR(100),
    state           VARCHAR(100),
    postal_code     VARCHAR(15),
    country         VARCHAR(50)
);
```

The command should successfully execute, generating the following message:

Row	status
1	Table CUSTOMERS successfully created.

Figure 2.11 – Table created successfully

2. To confirm that the table has been generated as per the specification, we can run a DESCRIBE TABLE statement a shown:

```
DESCRIBE TABLE customers;
```

It should generate the following results in the Snowflake web UI:

name	type	kind ↓	null?	default	primary key	unique key	check	expression	comment	name
ID	NUMBER(38,0)	COLUMN	N	NULL	N	N	NULL	NULL	NULL	
LAST_NAME	VARCHAR(100)	COLUMN	Y	NULL	N	N	NULL	NULL	NULL	
FIRST_NAME	VARCHAR(100)	COLUMN	Y	NULL	N	N	NULL	NULL	NULL	
EMAIL	VARCHAR(100)	COLUMN	Y	NULL	N	N	NULL	NULL	NULL	
COMPANY	VARCHAR(100)	COLUMN	Y	NULL	N	N	NULL	NULL	NULL	
PHONE	VARCHAR(100)	COLUMN	Y	NULL	N	N	NULL	NULL	NULL	
ADDRESS1	VARCHAR(150)	COLUMN	Y	NULL	N	N	NULL	NULL	NULL	
ADDRESS2	VARCHAR(150)	COLUMN	Y	NULL	N	N	NULL	NULL	NULL	
CITY	VARCHAR(100)	COLUMN	Y	NULL	N	N	NULL	NULL	NULL	
STATE	VARCHAR(100)	COLUMN	Y	NULL	N	N	NULL	NULL	NULL	
POSTAL_CODE	VARCHAR(15)	COLUMN	Y	NULL	N	N	NULL	NULL	NULL	
COUNTRY	VARCHAR(50)	COLUMN	Y	NULL	N	N	NULL	NULL	NULL	

Figure 2.12 – Output of the DESCRIBE statement

3. Let's assume there was something wrong with a data type; for example, say
    ADDRESS1 and ADDRESS2 were supposed to be stored as a STRING data type. This
    can be addressed using the REPLACE TABLE statement, along with CREATE. This
    will overwrite the existing CUSTOMERS table:

```
CREATE TABLE customers (
    id              INT NOT NULL,
    last_name       VARCHAR(100) ,
    first_name      VARCHAR(100),
    email           VARCHAR(100),
    company         VARCHAR(100),
    phone           VARCHAR(100),
    address1        STRING,
    address2        STRING,
    city            VARCHAR(100),
    state           VARCHAR(100),
    postal_code     VARCHAR(15),
    country         VARCHAR(50)
);
```

4. Let's verify whether the desired change has been successfully applied. For that,
    we can execute the DESCRIBE TABLE statement again as shown:

```
DESCRIBE TABLE customers;
```

It should generate the following result in the Snowflake web UI:

name	type	kind	null?	default	primary key	unique key	check	expression	comment
ID	NUMBER(38,0)	COLUMN	N	NULL	N	N	NULL	NULL	NULL
LAST_NAME	VARCHAR(100)	COLUMN	Y	NULL	N	N	NULL	NULL	NULL
FIRST_NAME	VARCHAR(100)	COLUMN	Y	NULL	N	N	NULL	NULL	NULL
EMAIL	VARCHAR(100)	COLUMN	Y	NULL	N	N	NULL	NULL	NULL
COMPANY	VARCHAR(100)	COLUMN	Y	NULL	N	N	NULL	NULL	NULL
PHONE	VARCHAR(100)	COLUMN	Y	NULL	N	N	NULL	NULL	NULL
ADDRESS1	VARCHAR(16777216)	COLUMN	Y	NULL	N	N	NULL	NULL	NULL
ADDRESS2	VARCHAR(16777216)	COLUMN	Y	NULL	N	N	NULL	NULL	NULL
CITY	VARCHAR(100)	COLUMN	Y	NULL	N	N	NULL	NULL	NULL
STATE	VARCHAR(100)	COLUMN	Y	NULL	N	N	NULL	NULL	NULL
POSTAL_CO...	VARCHAR(15)	COLUMN	Y	NULL	N	N	NULL	NULL	NULL
COUNTRY	VARCHAR(50)	COLUMN	Y	NULL	N	N	NULL	NULL	NULL

Figure 2.13 – Output of the DESCRIBE statement after the changes in the table

Please note the data types. We shall discuss this in the *How it works…* section along with how REPLACE works and how it is a shorthand for a two-step process typically required for managing the life cycle of a table.

5. Let's now load this table with some data before we continue with the rest of the recipe. To do so, run the following command:

```
COPY INTO customers
FROM s3://snowflake-cookbook/Chapter02/r3/customer.csv
FILE_FORMAT = (TYPE = csv SKIP_HEADER = 1 FIELD_
OPTIONALLY_ENCLOSED_BY = '"');
```

This should complete with the following message:

file	status	rows_parsed	rows_loaded
s3://snowflake-...	LOADED	100	100

Figure 2.14 – Table loaded

6. Let's now look at scenarios where the creation of a table is based on an existing table. A common pattern in the table life cycle involves deriving a table from an existing table. This is called CTAS or CREATE TABLE ... AS SELECT. To explain the use of CTAS, we will have some records inserted into the CUSTOMERS table. The dataset has 100 rows, as shown in the following screenshot (showing the first six columns of the table):

ID	LAST_NAME	FIRST_NAME	EMAIL	COMPANY	PHONE	ADDRESS1	ADDRESS2	CITY	STATE
1	Mayo	Leslie	vitae.aliqua...	Hendrerit LLP	705-5969	496-5176 Ti...	NULL	Kupang	NT
2	Armstrong	Eleanor	Phasellus@p...	In Aliquet Co...	1-193-367-4...	602-5330 V...	NULL	Serang	Banten
3	Fleming	Kasper	non.justo.Pr...	Facilisi Sed ...	559-4754	698 Erat Road	NULL	Hengelo	Ov
4	Sellers	Sawyer	nibh.Donec ..	Nec Incorpo...	1-286-709-4 ..	9979 Nonum...	NULL	Rezzoaglio	LIG
5	Simon	Sarah	neque@adip...	Orci Foundat...	216-3047	409-2909 C...	NULL	Bath	ON
6	Wiggins	Brianna	nec@musPr...	Eu Corp.	1-737-230-2...	6112 Tellus A...	NULL	Robelmont	Luxemburg
7	Smail	Melodie	turpis.in@en...	Sociis Natoq...	659-8573	P.O. Box 373...	NULL	Bekasi	West Java

Figure 2.15 – Sample data shown for the customer table

7. The dataset will be copied into a new table that will have the same structure as the CUSTOMERS table. The statements to be executed are as follows:

```
CREATE OR REPLACE TABLE
customers_deep_copy
AS
SELECT *
FROM customers;
```

This should succeed with the following message:

status

Table CUSTOMERS_DEEP_COPY successfully created.

Figure 2.16 – Deep copy table created

What we now have created is a deep copy of the CUSTOMERS table and a new table, which has received all data from CUSTOMERS and is called CUSTOMERS_ DEEP_COPY. The deep copy means that the table structure and data has been copied, as opposed to a shallow copy, which would copy the table structure only. This copied table is now an independent copy that can have a life cycle of its own with no changes or side effects originating from any operations performed on the CUSTOMERS table. A SELECT QUERY statement on this new table would generate the same results as shown in the previous table.

8. Now let's look at another table copying method – *shallow* copy. In certain situations, a new table is required to be created with the same structure as an existing table, but the data is not to be copied, in which case a shallow copy is created. This is achieved by using the LIKE keyword as provided by Snowflake:

```
CREATE OR REPLACE TABLE
customers_shallow_copy
LIKE customers;
```

This should succeed with the following message:

status

Table CUSTOMERS_SHALLOW_COPY successfully created.

Figure 2.17 – Shallow copy table created

9. This should create a table that has the same structure as the CUSTOMERS table but with no data in it:

```
SELECT
COUNT(*)
FROM
customers_shallow_copy;
```

The result of the following count query is 0 rows, as shown:

COUNT(*)

0

Figure 2.18 – New empty table created

10. Until now, we have seen the creation of tables with permanent life – the table will exist and store data until explicitly dropped. This is the default behavior from a life cycle perspective. There are tables that handle transitory data and so they might be required only temporarily. For such scenarios, there are temporary and transient tables. Let's create these tables by running the following SQL statements:

```
CREATE TEMPORARY TABLE customers_temp AS SELECT * FROM
customers WHERE TRY_TO_NUMBER(postal_code) IS NOT NULL;
CREATE TRANSIENT TABLE customers_trans AS AS SELECT *
FROM customers WHERE TRY_TO_NUMBER(postal_code) IS NULL;
```

11. The preceding SQL script will allow you to create two tables, `customers_temp` and `customers_trans`. The two tables are not permanent, but the tables have limitations. If you end the web UI session at this point, then the `customers_temp` table will not be recoverable after a re-login. Transient tables are available after a session has been closed and will retain data in a subsequent session created by user login; however, they don't consume fail-safe storage. This is an important mechanism for retaining data across sessions and can have applications in scenarios that require state management or in ETL jobs.

How it works...

`REPLACE` is actually a shorthand for a two-step process that's required when a table has to be deleted (dropped) and then recreated. That would typically be done by executing the two statements in sequence as follows:

```
DROP TABLE IF EXISTS
CREATE TABLE customers …
```

The deep and shallow copies can be explained by the following query and the result generated by Snowflake:

```
show tables like 'customers%';
```

This shows a table with three rows, each showing a summary of the three tables that we have generated previously, explaining the differences and similarities. The following table shows that the deep copies of the dataset are exactly the same while the shallow copy has been deprived of data, though the metadata is the same:

created_on	name	database_name	schema_name	kind	comment	cluster_by	rows	bytes
2021-02-15 01:33:27.035 -0800	CUSTOMERS	SFUSER_DB	PUBLIC	TABLE			100	14336
2021-02-15 01:36:09.155 -0800	CUSTOMERS_DEEP_COPY	SFUSER_DB	PUBLIC	TABLE			100	14336
2021-02-15 01:36:36.915 -0800	CUSTOMERS_SHALLOW_C...	SFUSER_DB	PUBLIC	TABLE			0	0

Figure 2.19 – The show tables command output showing the copies of the table

A thing to note in the preceding table is the **kind** column. The column is showing that the tables created have the `kind` attribute set as **TABLE**, which is the default type of table – a permanent table structure to be populated with data rows. (Please note that a select set of columns is being shown here for the sake of clarity.)

A local temporary table (also known as a volatile table) persists for the duration of the user session in which it was created and is not visible to other users. A temporary table's definition and contents are dropped at the end of the user session.

Transient tables are non-permanent tables, but unlike temporary tables, transient tables exist until explicitly dropped and are visible to any user with the appropriate privileges. Transient tables have a lower level of data protection than permanent tables. Data in a transient table may be lost in the event of a system failure. Transient tables should only be used for data that can be recreated in the event that the data is lost.

A `show tables` command for the `customers_temp` and `customers_trans` tables will show a table similar to the following table (please note that a limited set of columns is shown here for the sake of clarity):

created_on	name ↓	database_name	schema_name	kind
2021-02-15 01:41:42.976 -0800	CUSTOMERS_TRANS	SFUSER_DB	PUBLIC	TRANSIENT
2021-02-15 01:40:58.116 -0800	CUSTOMERS_TEMP	SFUSER_DB	PUBLIC	TEMPORARY

Figure 2.20 – The show tables command output highlighting the temporary
and transient nature of tables

Please note the content for the `kind` column. It shows that the tables are not permanent.

There's more...

One aspect of `CREATE TABLE` statements, `CLONE`, has been left for discussion in *Chapter 8, Back to the Future with Time Travel*. Temporary tables, however, cannot be cloned. Only permanent tables are fail-safe. Fail-safes will be discussed further in later chapters.

Managing external tables and stages

An important aspect of ETL applications is managing the loading of data. This recipe introduces you to managing incoming data by creating a stage and querying that data for loading into native Snowflake tables. The process is very different from traditional data warehouses as it mixes concepts from modern big data systems. Details around ETL will not be covered here but are deferred till later chapters to explain how an ETL pipeline can be managed.

Getting ready

The following example requires SnowSQL to run the different steps. Apart from that, you will need to have access to an AWS S3 bucket where data can be placed and made available as files.

How to do it...

The following steps start with the creation of a stage, which is used to temporarily store data before it can be copied into Snowflake:

1. Let's first create a stage. A **stage** is a logical concept or an abstraction of a filesystem location that is external or internal to Snowflake. In this case, an external stage has been used. The location can be managed in one of the object stores supported by the underlying cloud storage. In the case of AWS, S3 is used for this purpose. This recipe uses S3. The following statement creates a stage named `sfuser_ext_stage`. The stage should be accessible to Snowflake:

```
CREATE OR REPLACE STAGE sfuser_ext_stage
URL='s3://snowflake-cookbook/Chapter02/r4/';
```

The response should say that a stage has been created successfully, as shown:

status ↓
Stage area SFUSER_EXT_STAGE successfully created.

Figure 2.21 – Stage area created

2. Let's now do a listing on the `SFUSER_EXT_STAGE` stage pointing to the `snowflake-cookbook` S3 bucket:

```
LIST@SFUSER_EXT_STAGE;
```

This statement should generate the following output in the web UI:

name ↓	size
s3://snowflake-cookbook/ch2/r4/parquet/userdata1.parquet	113629
s3://snowflake-cookbook/ch2/r4/csv/electronic-card-transactions-may-2020.csv	3071640
s3://snowflake-cookbook/ch2/r4/csv/electronic-card-transactions-may-2020-headless.csv	3071481

Figure 2.22 – Listing the stage to the S3 bucket

We can see that there are two types of files in the preceding listing: `csv` and `parquet`. In the case of `csv`, the `electronic-card-transactions-may-2020-headless.csv` file is a header-less version of the `electronic-card-transactions-may-2020.csv` file. There is a `parquet` format file as well called `userdata1.parquet`. We shall create external tables on both files. An external table is different from usual database tables because unlike tables that point to data inside a database, external tables provide a view on top of files stored in a stage.

These are read-only tables that maintain metadata that's helpful in interpreting the contents of a file, which could be formatted as `parquet`, `csv`, and so on.

3. Let's now look at how the `parquet` file can be loaded into an external table. We shall be creating an external table called `ext_tbl_userdata1`. The creation of the table would require a location from which data can be read into the table. It would also require a file format. In this case, the file type is `parquet`:

```
create or replace external table ext_tbl_userdata1
with location = @sfuser_ext_stage
file_format = (type = parquet);
```

4. Let's query the newly created external table. This would show each row of the result set as a JSON document. Within each row, you should be able to see different columns with their respective values as key-value pairs:

```
select * from ext_tbl_userdata1;
```

The following screenshot is only showing some of the key-value pairs due to size constraints:

Row	VALUE
1	{ "birthdate": "3/8/1971", "cc": "6759521864920116", "comments": "1E+02", "country": "Indonesia", "email": "ajordan0@com.com", "first_name": "Amanda", "gender": "Female", "id": 1...
2	{ "birthdate": "1/16/1968", "cc": "", "comments": "", "country": "Canada", "email": "afreeman1@is.gd", "first_name": "Albert", "gender": "Male", "id": 2, "ip_address": "218.111.175.34", "la...
3	{ "birthdate": "2/1/1960", "cc": "6767119071901597", "comments": "", "country": "Russia", "email": "emorgan2@altervista.org", "first_name": "Evelyn", "gender": "Female", "id": 3, "ip_a...
4	{ "birthdate": "4/8/1997", "cc": "3576031598965625", "comments": "", "country": "China", "email": "driley3@gmpg.org", "first_name": "Denise", "gender": "Female", "id": 4, "ip_addres...
5	{ "birthdate": "", "cc": "5602256255204850", "comments": "", "country": "South Africa", "email": "cburns4@miitbeian.gov.cn", "first_name": "Carlos", "gender": "", "id": 5, "ip_address...

Figure 2.23 – Output of the query showing key-value pairs

5. Similarly, by pointing to a different location, the CSV file can be loaded into another external table. An `ext_card_data` table is created that has the location pointing to the stage. In this case, the file is located in a `.../ch2/r4/csv` subfolder. This gets us to the folder where the file is located. `file_format`, in this case, is providing the information that the file is a CSV, and finally, a file filter is provided to constrain the search to CSVs with `headless` in their names:

```
create or replace external table ext_card_data
with location = @sfuser_ext_stage/csv
file_format = (type = csv)
pattern = '.*headless[.]csv';
```

6. Let's query the new external table:

```
select * from ext_card_data;
```

The following screenshot of the resulting records shows some of the rows generated by the query. Please note the difference here. There are no meaningful column names in this case, unlike the previous case of the Parquet file:

Row	VALUE
1	{ "c1": "ECTA.S19A1", "c10": "Actual", "c11": "RTS total industries", "c2": "2001.03", "c3": "2462.5", "c5": "F", "c6": "Dollars", "c7": "6", "c8": "Electronic Card Transactions (ANZSIC06) -...
2	{ "c1": "ECTA.S19A1", "c10": "Actual", "c11": "RTS total industries", "c2": "2002.03", "c3": "17177.2", "c5": "F", "c6": "Dollars", "c7": "6", "c8": "Electronic Card Transactions (ANZSIC06) ...
3	{ "c1": "ECTA.S19A1", "c10": "Actual", "c11": "RTS total industries", "c2": "2003.03", "c3": "22530.5", "c5": "F", "c6": "Dollars", "c7": "6", "c8": "Electronic Card Transactions (ANZSIC06...
4	{ "c1": "ECTA.S19A1", "c10": "Actual", "c11": "RTS total industries", "c2": "2004.03", "c3": "28005.1", "c5": "F", "c6": "Dollars", "c7": "6", "c8": "Electronic Card Transactions (ANZSIC06)...
5	{ "c1": "ECTA.S19A1", "c10": "Actual", "c11": "RTS total industries", "c2": "2005.03", "c3": "30629.6", "c5": "F", "c6": "Dollars", "c7": "6", "c8": "Electronic Card Transactions (ANZSIC06)...

Figure 2.24 – Output of the select statement

7. As we have observed, an external table always ends up having data in JSON format at the end of a copy process. This step shows how some meaningful names can be given to the dummy or automatically created columns in the JSON document and how it can be flattened to generate column-oriented rows. The following query shows how aliases can be created for the automatically created column names. Please note that the query only selects two columns, c3 and c2, and creates the card_sum and period aliases, respectively. Moreover, to use the columns effectively, casting has been carried out for each column value:

```
select top 5 value:c3::float as card_sum,
value:c2::string as period
from ext_card_data;
```

The result of the query is shown:

Row	CARD_SUM	PERIOD
1	2462.5	2001.03
2	17177.2	2002.03
3	22530.5	2003.03
4	28005.1	2004.03
5	30629.6	2005.03

Figure 2.25 – Output of the query selecting two columns

8. Now that we have loaded tables and we can see how this data can be used in queries, we can drop the tables. This would end the life of the external tables that had been created to run queries of raw data – a typical purge-on-load pattern is applicable:

```
drop table ext_card_data;
drop table ext_tbl_userdata1;
```

How it works...

The stage created in *step 1* can be thought of as a reference to a storage location. It is treated as a read-only location that can only be accessed using the appropriate access rights. The S3 bucket in *step 1* is a public bucket and does not need credentials to be accessed. In later chapters, when we look at staging in more detail, we shall start delving into securing the staging locations.

Step 2 is dereferencing the specified S3 bucket to list all the files that are available along with the last modified dates.

In *step 3*, when the Parquet file is loaded into the external table, the table rows have all the field names captured, as shown in *step 4*. But in *step 5*, when the CSV-formatted file is loaded into the external table, there are dummy column names created by Snowflake, as can be seen in *step 6*. This is because a Parquet file has metadata stored inside the file, while a CSV file does not have that metadata embedded in it. This is a major difference and would usually require additional steps as shown in *step 7* to generate meaningful column names, plus the casting of data types.

There's more...

In this recipe, we did not look at how data could be loaded into a stage. It is possible to load data into a stage from a local filesystem. This method will be discussed in the later chapters.

Looking at the metadata limitations for external tables, it can be argued that Avro files can be the best format for staging data as Avro files can specify field names and data types as well. We shall look into an example in a later chapter where we discuss ETL processing.

Please note that the last modified dates for each file in a stage can be a useful mechanism to trigger updating data in an external table and can be used for running the ETL process.

Managing views in Snowflake

This recipe will introduce you to different variations of views that are specific to Snowflake and in what scenario a variant of a view should be used. The recipe will cover simple views and materialized views and will provide guidance on when to use what type of view.

Getting ready

The following examples can be run either via the Snowflake web UI or the SnowSQL command-line client. Please make sure that you have access to the SNOWFLAKE_SAMPLE_DATA database in your Snowflake instance. The SNOWFLAKE_SAMPLE_DATA database is a database that is shared by Snowflake automatically and provides sample data for testing and benchmarking purposes.

How to do it...

Let's start with the creation of views in Snowflake. We shall look into the creation of simple views on tables and then talk about materialized views:

1. The SNOWFLAKE_SAMPLE_DATA database contains a number of schemas. We will be making use of the schema called TPCH_SF1000. Within this schema, there are multiple tables, and our view will make use of the STORE_SALES table to produce an output that shows the sales against order dates. Before we create our first view, let's create a database where we will create the views:

    ```
    CREATE DATABASE test_view_creation;
    ```

2. Create the view called date_wise_profit that, as the name suggests, shows the profit against the date:

    ```
    CREATE VIEW test_view_creation.public.date_wise_orders
    AS
    SELECT L_COMMITDATE AS ORDER_DATE,
    SUM(L_QUANTITY) AS TOT_QTY,
    SUM(L_EXTENDEDPRICE) AS TOT_PRICE
    FROM SNOWFLAKE_SAMPLE_DATA.TPCH_SF1000.LINEITEM
    GROUP BY L_COMMITDATE;
    ```

The view is successfully created with the following message:

```
status

View DATE_WISE_ORDERS successfully created.
```

Figure 2.26 – View created successfully

3. Let's select some data from this view:

```
SELECT * FROM test_view_creation.public.date_wise_orders;
```

The view will take some time (2-3 minutes) to execute as there is a large amount of data in the underlying tables. This latency in execution can be managed by opting for a larger warehouse. An extra-small warehouse has been used in this case. After some time, you should see the result set returned (as shown in the following screenshot), which will be approximately 2,500 rows:

Row	ORDER_DATE	TOT_QTY	TOT_PRICE
1	1994-03-30	63622799.00	95411212824.65
2	1995-03-03	63456797.00	95128548537.07
3	1993-02-28	63617322.00	95384743432.46

✔ Query ID SQL 2m30s 2,466 rows

Filter result... Copy Columns ▾

Figure 2.27 – Selecting data from the view

4. Selecting data from this view, as you will have noticed, took a reasonable amount of time to execute, and this time would increase if the amount of data in the table increased over time. To optimize performance, you can choose to create this view as a materialized view. Please note that you will require at least an Enterprise license of Snowflake in order to create materialized views:

```
CREATE MATERIALIZED VIEW test_view_creation.public.date_
wise_orders_fast
AS
SELECT L_COMMITDATE AS ORDER_DATE,
SUM(L_QUANTITY) AS TOT_QTY,
SUM(L_EXTENDEDPRICE) AS TOT_PRICE
FROM SNOWFLAKE_SAMPLE_DATA.TPCH_SF1000.LINEITEM
GROUP BY L_COMMITDATE;
```

The first thing that you will notice when creating the materialized view is that it will not be immediate:

Figure 2.28 – Creating a materialized view

It will take a fair bit of time to create the view as opposed to the immediate creation that we saw in *step 2*, mainly because materialized views store data, unlike normal views, which just store the DDL commands and fetch data on the fly when the view is referenced.

5. Let's now select from the materialized view:

```
SELECT * FROM test_view_creation.public.date_wise_orders_
fast;
```

The results are returned almost immediately as we are selecting from a materialized view, which performs much better than a simple view.

How it works...

A standard view in Snowflake is a way to treat the result of a query as if it were a table. The query itself is part of the view definition. When data is selected from a standard view, the query in the view definition is executed and the results are presented back as a table to the user. Since the view appears as a table, it can be joined with other tables as well and used in queries in most places where tables can be used. Views are a powerful method to abstract complex logic from the users of data; that is, a reusable query with complex logic can be created as a view. As such, this takes the burden off the end users to know the logic. Views can also be used to provide access control on data, so for various departments in an organization, different views can be created, each of which provides a subset of the data.

Since a standard view executes its definition at runtime, it can take some time to execute. If there is a complex query that is commonly used, it can be created as a materialized view. A materialized view looks similar to a standard view, but it doesn't run the query in its definition at runtime. Rather, when a materialized view is created, it runs the query right away and stores the results. The advantage is that when the materialized view is queried, it does not need to execute but can retrieve the stored results immediately, providing a performance boost. A materialized view will however incur additional maintenance and storage costs since every time the underlying table is changed, the view recalculates the results and updates the storage.

There's more...

In addition to standard views and materialized views, Snowflake also provides the concepts of secure views and recursive views. We will explore the application of secure views in *Chapter 5, Data Protection and Security in Snowflake.*

3
Loading and Extracting Data into and out of Snowflake

For any modern data warehouse system, getting data into the system and extracting data out of the system are key activities. This chapter provides a set of recipes that will guide you through the various nuances of loading data into Snowflake. The chapter talks about techniques for loading bulk data from on-premises systems and cloud storage and provides insights into the steps required to load streaming data into Snowflake by using Snowpipe.

The following recipes are included in this chapter:

- Configuring Snowflake access to private S3 buckets
- Loading delimited bulk data into Snowflake from cloud storage
- Loading delimited bulk data into Snowflake from your local machine
- Loading Parquet files into Snowflake

- Making sense of JSON semi-structured data and transforming to a relational view

- Processing Newline-Delimited JSON (or NDJSON) into a Snowflake table

- Processing near real-time data into a Snowflake table using Snowpipe

- Extracting data from Snowflake

Technical requirements

This chapter requires access to a modern internet browser (for instance, Chrome, Internet Explorer, or Firefox) and access to the internet to connect to your Snowflake instance in the cloud. Since we will be loading data from on-premises systems using internal stages, we will need to have the SnowSQL client installed.

The code for this chapter can be found at the following GitHub URL:

```
https://github.com/PacktPublishing/Snowflake-Cookbook/tree/
master/Chapter03
```

Configuring Snowflake access to private S3 buckets

This recipe walks you through configuring access to private or restricted S3 buckets. The access configuration is a necessary step before you can load data from cloud storage, specifically from cloud storage buckets that are not public.

Getting ready

By now, you must have already created an S3 bucket that you intend to use to load data from the cloud to Snowflake. You should also have the privileges required to create a new **Identity and Access Management (IAM)** user and configure security settings in AWS. This recipe does not cover AWS configurations as it is assumed that you are well versed in managing AWS accounts and S3 storage. You should also know which AWS region your Snowflake instance is located in. You will require access to the ACCOUNTADMIN role in Snowflake as well.

How to do it...

Let's go through the steps required to set up a private or restricted S3 bucket for use with Snowflake:

1. Log in to the AWS console and navigate to Identity & Access Management (IAM) under the Services dropdown. You will also be able to navigate to Identity & Access Management (IAM) using the following link: `https://console.aws.amazon.com/iam/home#/home`. When you're on the IAM page, click on Account Settings in the left pane.

2. Within Account Settings under Security Token Service (STS), locate the endpoint corresponding to the region where your Snowflake instance is located and ensure that the endpoint is activated. To find the region of your Snowflake instance, the simplest way is to look at the URL that you use to access the Snowflake web UI; so, if your URL is `http://oh11223.ap-southeast-2.snowflakecomputing.com`, then ap-southeast-2 is your Snowflake region.

3. Next, choose Policies from the left pane and create a new policy. We want to create a policy that enables at least read access. Pay special attention to the highlighted parts of the Policy document (shown in the code block that follows) in JSON format. These are for enabling write access. If you are configuring access for an S3 bucket that will be used to read files only, then remove the highlighted parts. Select the JSON tab on the Create policy page. In the JSON document, add the following and change the highlighted segment enclosed in pointed brackets (<>) within the following JSON to match with your bucket name:

```
{
    "Version": "2012-10-17",
    "Statement": [
        {
            "Effect": "Allow",
            "Action": [
                "s3:GetObject",
                "s3:GetObjectVersion",
                "s3:PutObject",
                "s3:DeleteObject",
                "s3:DeleteObjectVersion"
            ],
            "Resource": "arn:aws:s3:::<bucket>/*"
        },
```

```
                    {
                         "Effect": "Allow",
                         "Action": "s3:ListBucket",
                         "Resource": "arn:aws:s3:::<bucket>"
                    }
               ]
          }
```

4. Click on Review Policy and the resulting screen will show you that the policy allows list and read access on S3 buckets as shown in the following screenshot:

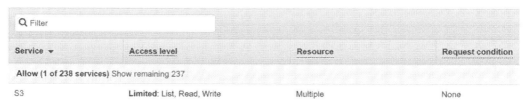

Figure 3.1 – Review policy page showing the allowed services

5. Give the policy a name, for example, ETL_Access, and save.

6. Now click on Roles in the left pane and select Create Role from the resulting screen. Select Another AWS account when prompted to select a type. For the Account ID parameter, enter your account ID temporarily. Please see the following help page on how to find your account ID: `https://docs.aws.amazon.com/IAM/latest/UserGuide/console_account-alias.html#FindingYourAWSId`. Under Require External ID, enter 00000. In the following steps, we will modify the trusted relationship and replace these values.

7. Click Next: Permissions and search for the policy that we created in the previous steps, that is, the policy called ETL_Access (or the name that you assigned in step 4). Check the checkbox against the policy and click Next:

Figure 3.2 – Checking a policy to grant permissions

8. Press Next on the following screen until you get to the review screen. Give the role a name such as Role_For_Snowflake and save:

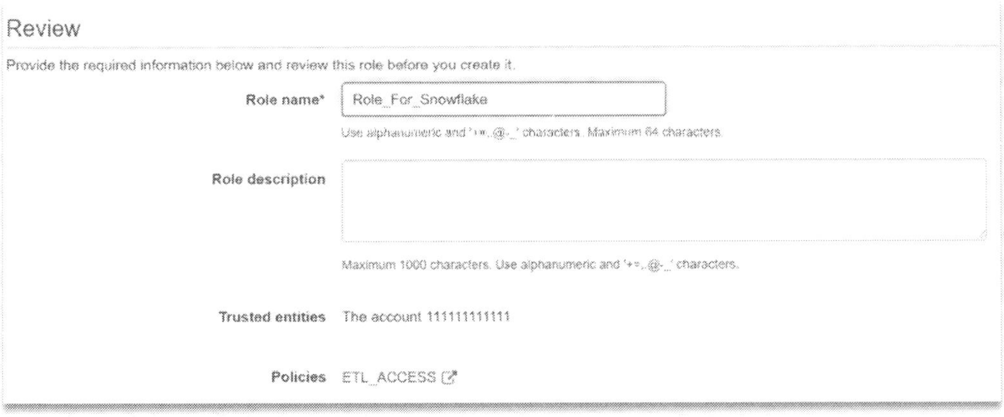

Figure 3.3 – Review page

9. Once the role is created, click on it and copy the value shown in Role ARN. We will be using the ARN to create the integration between Snowflake and the cloud storage:

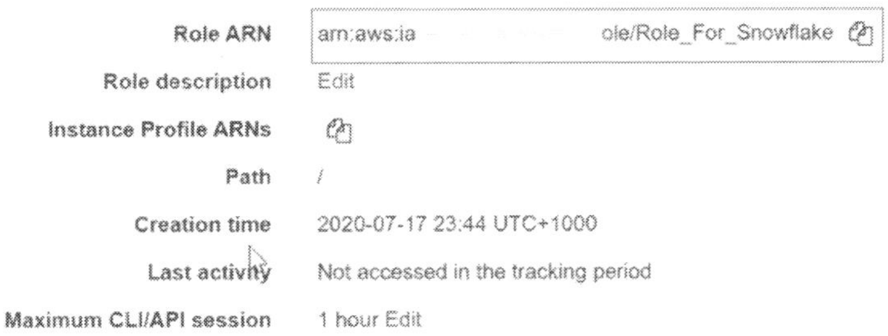

Figure 3.4 – Role page of a created role

10. Let's now log in to Snowflake, where we will create a cloud storage integration object as follows. Under STORAGE_AWS_ROLE_ARN, paste the ARN that you copied in the previous step; STORAGE_ALLOWED_LOCATIONS denotes the paths that you want to allow your Snowflake instance access to. Please note that your role must be ACCOUNTADMIN in order to create a storage integration object:

```
CREATE STORAGE INTEGRATION S3_INTEGRATION
  TYPE = EXTERNAL_STAGE
  STORAGE_PROVIDER = S3
  ENABLED = TRUE
  STORAGE_AWS_ROLE_ARN =
'<arn:aws:iam::123456789123:role/Role_For_Snowflake>'
  STORAGE_ALLOWED_LOCATIONS = ('s3://<bucket>');
```

Please note that `<bucket>` is to be replaced with your bucket's name.

11. Now run a describe statement on the storage integration object that we just created and note down the values for STORAGE_AWS_IAM_USER_ARN and STORAGE_AWS_EXTERNAL_ID:

```
DESC INTEGRATION S3_INTEGRATION;
```

12. The output for the describe statement is shown in the following screenshot. Important items have been marked by red rectangles:

Row	property	property_type	property_value	
1	ENABLED	Boolean	true	
2	STORAGE_PROVIDER	String	S3	
3	STORAGE_ALLOWED_LOCATIONS	List	s3://snowflake-cookbook-c3-r2	
4	STORAGE_BLOCKED_LOCATIONS	List		
5	STORAGE_AWS_IAM_USER_ARN	String	arn:aws:iam	user/aqnm-...
6	STORAGE_AWS_ROLE_ARN	String	arn:aws:iam	role/Role_Fo...
7	STORAGE_AWS_EXTERNAL_ID	String	OH95958_S	}+olPvw7lk...

Figure 3.5 – Output of the DESC statement

13. Now, return to the AWS console, select IAM, and click Roles from the left side menu. Select the role that we created earlier, that is, Role_For_Snowflake. Click the Trust relationships tab and click edit trust relationship:

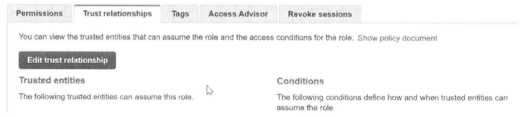

Figure 3.6 – Trust relationships tab

14. In the policy document, replace the text with the text shown in the code block that follows and replace the highlighted values with the values you copied in the previous step:

```
{
    "Version": "2012-10-17",
    "Statement": [
        {
```

```
        "Effect": "Allow",
        "Principal": {
          "AWS": "<STORAGE_AWS_IAM_USER_ARN>"
        },
        "Action": "sts:AssumeRole",
        "Condition": {
          "StringEquals": {
            "sts:ExternalId": "<STORAGE_AWS_EXTERNAL_ID>"
          }
        }
      }
    ]
}
```

Click **Update Trust Policy**.

15. We will now go back to Snowflake and grant the integration object to the SYSADMIN role so that the system admin can use the integration object in the definition of other external stages. This step must be run as ACCOUNTADMIN:

```
GRANT USAGE ON INTEGRATION S3_INTEGRATION TO ROLE
SYSADMIN;
```

16. Let's create an external stage that uses the storage integration object we created earlier. We will try and list the files in the stage, and if we do not get any issues, it means that the configuration is correctly set up. Please ensure that you put in your desired bucket name in the following code segment. Also, make sure that you select a database and a schema before running the following commands:

```
USE ROLE SYSADMIN;
CREATE STAGE S3_RESTRICTED_STAGE
   STORAGE_INTEGRATION = S3_INTEGRATION
   URL = 's3://<bucket>';
```

17. Let's try running LIST on the stage we just created:

```
LIST @S3_RESTRICTED_STAGE;
```

There should not be any authorization errors and the result should show any files that may be present in the bucket:

Row	name	size	md5
1	s3://snowflake-cookbook-...	0	d41d8cd98f00b204e

Figure 3.7 – Output of LIST

So, this is it: we have successfully performed the configuration needed so that we can access our S3 buckets via Snowflake with proper authorization.

How it works...

The secure access that we just established can be best understood using the diagram that follows. When you create an external stage over an AWS bucket and execute a load, behind the scenes an AWS user is used by Snowflake to access the S3 bucket and read the data.

If the S3 bucket is private (which most S3 buckets should be), it is required to perform configuration so that the AWS user used by Snowflake has read access to the S3 bucket. For this configuration, we created a role and attached it with a policy. The policy allows read access on the S3 bucket, therefore any user in the role gets read access to the S3 bucket:

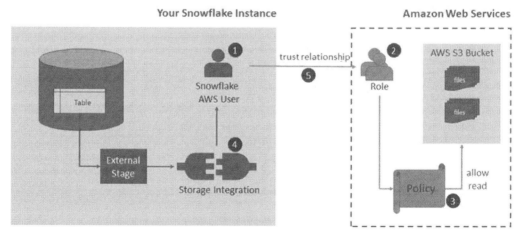

Figure 3.8 – Configuring Snowflake access to private S3 buckets

We create the storage integration that will help us in this configuration. The storage integration object exposes the AWS IAM user, which we then use in further configuration. We establish a trust relationship between the AWS IAM user and the role, which gives the AWS IAM user read access to the S3 bucket as well.

Loading delimited bulk data into Snowflake from cloud storage

This recipe demonstrates several important concepts related to loading data stored in cloud storage, for example, Amazon S3 bucket, Azure Blob Storage, and so on, into your Snowflake instance. To load data from cloud storage, we will make use of the external stage concept in Snowflake.

Getting ready

As we will be loading a file from cloud storage to Snowflake, you should have a cloud storage bucket created with files present in the bucket. To save time, you can download a previously created sample file from `https://github.com/PacktPublishing/Snowflake-Cookbook/blob/master/Chapter03/r2/cc_info.csv`.

Before proceeding with this recipe, follow the steps in the *Configuring Snowflake access to private S3 buckets* recipe to set up access when using a private or restricted bucket.

How to do it...

In order to load a file from cloud storage, we will create an external stage pointing to the cloud storage and use the COPY command to load the external file into Snowflake. The steps are as follows:

1. Let's first create a database where we will create our table and load it with some sample data:

    ```
    CREATE DATABASE C3_R2;
    ```

2. Execute the following statement to set the database to C3_R2:

    ```
    USE C3_R2;
    ```

3. Now that we have a database created, let's create a new table. The new table will be named CREDIT_CARDS. We will load the sample data into this table:

    ```
    CREATE TABLE CREDIT_CARDS
    (
        CUSTOMER_NAME STRING,
        CREDIT_CARD STRING,
        TYPE STRING,
        CCV INTEGER,
    ```

```
    EXP_DATE STRING
);
```

4. Define the format of the file that we want to load into the table. The file format describes a standard CSV file, therefore we will be expecting a comma-separated file. Since the first row in the file is a header row, we will skip the header in our definition and we will specify that the individual fields in the file may be enclosed by double quotes. We are also creating the file format as a named file format so that it can be reused multiple times:

```
CREATE FILE FORMAT GEN_CSV
TYPE = CSV
SKIP_HEADER = 1
FIELD_OPTIONALLY_ENCLOSED_BY = '"';
```

5. To make this recipe simpler, we have already uploaded the data to a public Amazon S3 bucket called snowflake-cookbook. Follow the steps in the *Configuring Snowflake access to private S3 buckets* recipe to set up access when using a private or restricted bucket. For the time being, we will create an external stage over this public bucket, from which we will then load the data into Snowflake:

```
CREATE OR REPLACE STAGE C3_R2_STAGE
url='s3://snowflake-cookbook/Chapter03/r2'
FILE_FORMAT = GEN_CSV;
```

> **Note**
> Note that keeping your data in public buckets is a security risk and is being done in this recipe only for simplification.

Note that we have specified a complete path in the create stage statement; that is, /Chapter03/r2 is included in the create stage statement. We can also create the stage using only 's3://snowflake-cookbook' and then provide the rest of the path when loading the files through the COPY command.

6. Let's try and list the files in the stage so that we can be sure that we are able to access the data in the S3 bucket:

```
LIST @C3_R2_STAGE;
```

You should see the list of files in the bucket, which indicates that Snowflake is able to access the data:

Row	name	size	md5
1	s3://snowflake-cookbook/ch3/r2/cc_info.csv	65974	5eec1827b8d77f62a5ccaedea04880d6

Figure 3.9 – List of files in the bucket

7. Now that the data is accessible via a Snowflake external stage, we can simply run the COPY command and load the data into the transactions table:

```
COPY INTO CREDIT_CARDS
FROM @C3_R2_STAGE;
```

You should see a success message and an indication of how many rows have been loaded. If all goes well and you are using the files supplied with this book, 1,000 rows will have been loaded into the table.

8. Verify that the table has data by selecting from the customer table and that there are indeed 1,000 rows in the table:

```
USE C3_R2;
SELECT COUNT(*) FROM CREDIT_CARDS;
```

How it works...

There are two methods that you can use to load data from cloud storage. The recommended method is to use the **external stage** method. An external stage can be thought of as a virtual stage existing inside Snowflake referencing the data in a public cloud storage bucket. The referencing part is important as the external stage itself does not contain any data; rather, it shows everything that is present in the cloud storage.

The alternate method of loading from cloud storage is directly referencing the cloud storage in your COPY commands. In this recipe, we have focused on the external stage method, which is also highlighted in the following diagram:

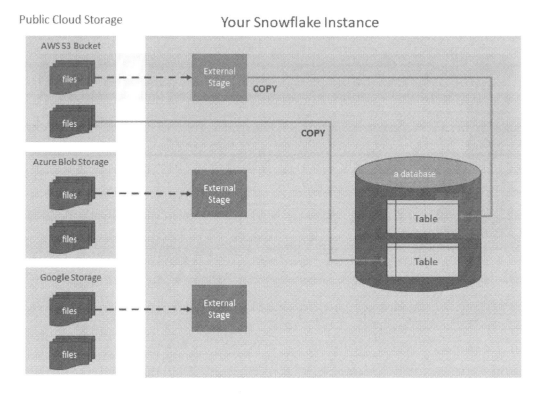

Figure 3.10 – Loading from cloud storage via external stages

To load files from public cloud storage, we start by creating a *file format* that specifies that we are loading data that is in CSV format and has a header that we want to skip.

Next, we have created a stage that points to s3://location. Since the stage is pointing to public cloud storage, it acts as an external stage. Before loading, we try to list the files present in the external stage. If the operation is successful, it means that Snowflake can access our cloud storage data via the external stage. Now that everything is set up, it is a matter of executing the standard COPY command to copy the data from the external stage to the target table.

Loading delimited bulk data into Snowflake from your local machine

This recipe demonstrates several important concepts related to loading data from an on-premises system to your Snowflake instance. We will make use of the internal stages in Snowflake to load the data from an on-premises system. This system could be a host machine running on your network or your laptop with files to be loaded stored in its storage.

Getting ready

Since we will be loading a file from your local system into Snowflake, we will need to first get such a file ready on the local system. To save time you can download a previously created sample file from `https://github.com/PacktPublishing/Snowflake-Cookbook/blob/master/Chapter03/r3/customers.csv`.

Now, since we will be loading data from your local system, we will need to use `snowsql` to upload the file to Snowflake. Please make sure that SnowSQL is installed on your system and you can successfully connect to your Snowflake instance.

How to do it...

The following steps start with creating a database and a table to store the data. Then, a format is created that will be used to align the table with the file being loaded:

1. Let's first create a database where we will create our table and load it with some sample data:

    ```
    CREATE DATABASE C4_LD_EX;
    ```

2. Create a new table called CUSTOMER. We will load the sample data into this table:

    ```
    CREATE TABLE CUSTOMER
    (
      FName STRING,
      LName STRING,
      Email STRING,
      Date_Of_Birth DATE,
      City STRING,
      Country STRING
    );
    ```

3. Define the format of the file that we want to load into the table. Here we are creating a named file format so that it can be reused multiple times. The file format describes a delimited file in which columns are delimited by the pipe (|) character. It also describes that when a file is loaded using this file format, the header of the file is to be skipped:

```
CREATE FILE FORMAT PIPE_DELIM
TYPE = CSV
FIELD_DELIMITER = '|'
FIELD_OPTIONALLY_ENCLOSED_BY = '"'
SKIP_HEADER = 1
DATE_FORMAT = 'YYYY-MM-DD';
```

4. Let's create a new internal stage that we will use to load the data into the table. We will associate the stage with the file format we just created. If we hadn't created a named file format, we could have specified the file format directly in the CREATE STAGE statement:

```
CREATE STAGE CUSTOMER_STAGE
FILE_FORMAT = PIPE_DELIM;
```

5. Upload the file into the stage that we just created. This step must be run through SnowSQL from the machine where the file is located. Notice that we have supplied file://customers.csv as the file path, as we were running SnowSQL from the directory where the file was. You may need to provide a full path if your files are in a different directory:

```
PUT file://customers.csv @CUSTOMER_STAGE;
```

6. Verify that only the customers.csv file is present in the stage by listing the stage. The following LIST command should generate the output:

```
LIST @CUSTOMER_STAGE;
```

7. Now that the data is in a Snowflake internal stage, we can simply run the COPY command and load the data into the customer table. Please note that now that the data has been moved from on-premises to the Snowflake internal stage, we can run the following commands from the Snowflake web UI as well:

```
COPY INTO CUSTOMER
FROM @CUSTOMER_STAGE;
```

You should see a success message and an indication of how many rows have been loaded, if all goes well. If you are using the files supplied with this book, 200 rows will have loaded into the table.

8. Verify that the table has data and that there are indeed 200 rows in the table by selecting from the customer table. The output from the table will be followed by a message from the database that 200 rows have been processed:

```
USE C4_LD_EX;
SELECT * FROM CUSTOMER;
```

9. Once the data is loaded into the target table, it is generally not required to keep the data in the internal stage. It is a good idea to clear the internal stage as data stored in an internal stage will also contribute toward the costs:

```
REMOVE @CUSTOMER_STAGE;
```

How it works...

There are three types of staging that you can use for loading files from an on-premises system into a Snowflake instance. The three stages are **Internal Named Stage**, **User Stage**, and **Table Stage**. In this recipe, we used the internal named stage method, which is highlighted in the following diagram:

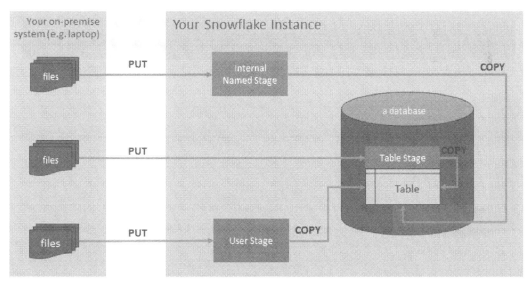

Figure 3.11 – Loading from on-premises systems to Snowflake via an internal named stage

Before we create an internal stage, it is useful to identify the format and file structure of the files that will be landing in this stage. For that purpose, we created a *file format* that specifies that we are loading data that is in CSV format and has a header that we want to skip. Additionally, we specified the format of the date field in this file by specifying YYYY-MM-DD as the date format. Next, while creating the *internal named stage*, we associated the file format with the stage. Creating a named file format has several advantages as it can be re-used in several stages and can be centrally managed.

Once we had the stage created, the next steps were to push the file into the stage. When loading from an on-premises system, we must use a tool that has access to the on-premises filesystem, which means that using the Snowflake web UI to manage the movement of the file from on-premises to the internal stage is not possible. We have, therefore, used the SnowSQL command-line client, which can access the local files and connect to your Snowflake instance. Using SnowSQL, we have performed a PUT query (or a transfer) on the file to the stage.

Note that the file is automatically compressed when it is moved to the internal stage and it is automatically encrypted as well. Now that the file is in the internal stage, it is a matter of executing a standard COPY command to copy the data from the internal stage to the target table. Once the table is successfully loaded, it is useful to clear the stage so that you do not incur any storage costs related to the files that are present in the internal stage.

Loading Parquet files into Snowflake

This recipe demonstrates how to load Parquet-format data from files present on cloud storage. We will make use of an external stage created on top of an AWS S3 bucket and will load the Parquet-format data into a new table.

Getting ready

Since we will be loading a file from our local system into Snowflake, we will need to first get such a file ready on the local system. To save time, you can download a previously created sample file from https://github.com/PacktPublishing/Snowflake-Cookbook/blob/master/Chapter03/r4.

How to do it...

We shall start by creating a database, followed by creating a table that will contain the Parquet file. We need will then create a file format for the Parquet file. The steps are as follows:

1. Let's first create a database where we will create our table and load it with some sample data:

    ```
    CREATE DATABASE C3_R4;
    ```

2. Create a new table called TRANSACTIONS. We will load the sample data into this table:

    ```
    CREATE TABLE TRANSACTIONS
    (
            TRANSACTION_DATE DATE,
            CUSTOMER_ID NUMBER(38,0),
            TRANSACTION_ID NUMBER(38,0),
            AMOUNT NUMBER(38,0)
    );
    ```

3. Define the format of the file that we want to load into the table. Here we are creating a named file format so that it can be reused multiple times. The file format describes a Parquet-format file, with automatic detection of compression, and also defines string values that should be converted to NULL; that is, if the value MISSING is found in any of the loaded data, it will be converted to NULL:

    ```
    CREATE FILE FORMAT GEN_PARQ
    TYPE = PARQUET
    COMPRESSION = AUTO
    NULL_IF = ('MISSING','');
    ```

4. To make this recipe simpler, we have already uploaded the file to a public Amazon S3 bucket called snowflake-cookbook. Later in this recipe, we will walk you through the steps involved in loading data from an S3 bucket that is not public and requires authorization in order to be accessed. For the time being, we will create an external stage over this public bucket, from which we will then load the data into Snowflake (note that keeping your data in public buckets is a security risk and is being done in this recipe only for simplification):

```
CREATE OR REPLACE STAGE C3_R4_STAGE
url='s3://snowflake-cookbook/Chapter03/r4'
FILE_FORMAT = GEN_PARQ;
```

Note that we have specified a complete path in the create stage statement; that is, /Chapter03/r4 is included in the create stage statement. We can also create the stage using only 's3://snowflake-cookbook' and then provide the rest of the path when loading the files through the COPY command.

5. Let's try and list the files in the stage so that we can be sure that we are able to access the data in the S3 bucket:

```
LIST @C3_R4_STAGE;
```

You should see the list of files in the bucket, which indicates that Snowflake is able to access the data:

Row	name	size	md5 ↓
1	s3://snowflake-cookbook/ch3/r4/transactions.parquet	3929	aac8101db9d3de72231fb9f2d...

Figure 3.12 – List of files in the bucket

6. Now that the data is accessible via a Snowflake external stage, we will select from the stage and preview the data:

```
SELECT $1 FROM @C3_R4_STAGE;
```

You will see output similar to what is shown in the following screenshot. This is essentially Parquet data shown in JSON format:

Row	$1
1	{ "_COL_0": "2018-12-18", "_COL_1": 1649050999199, "_COL_2": 192224, "_COL_3": 97 }
2	{ "_COL_0": "2019-09-21", "_COL_1": 1648122211299, "_COL_2": 192248, "_COL_3": 59 }
3	{ "_COL_0": "2020-08-07", "_COL_1": 1672030807799, "_COL_2": 192272, "_COL_3": 86 }

Figure 3.13 – Previewing the data in the stage

7. We can now access the individual fields in the JSON through the syntax shown and load them into the table. The syntax used is $1:<fieldname>::<datatype_to_cast_to>:

```
INSERT INTO TRANSACTIONS
SELECT
$1:_COL_0::Date,
$1:_COL_1::NUMBER,
$1:_COL_2::NUMBER,
$1:_COL_3::NUMBER

FROM @C3_R4_STAGE;
```

You should see a success message and an indication of how many rows have been loaded. If all goes well and you are using the files supplied with this book, 200 rows will have been loaded into the table.

8. Verify that the table has data by selecting from the customer table and that there are indeed 200 rows in the table:

```
USE C3_R4;
SELECT * FROM TRANSACTIONS;
```

How it works...

We have defined a new format, GEN_PARQ, by using the CREATE FILE FORMAT statement. Within that statement, a few keywords have been used that define some specific operations that the file format object will do when it encounters data in the file to be loaded. The first specification item, TYPE, tells the system that the file to be loaded is PARQUET format. The second specification, COMPRESSION, tells the system that no specific compression has been applied and the PARQUET-formatted file will have the default compression. The third specification item, NULL_IF, tells the system that the resulting table (created in *step 2*) will have a NULL value inserted when the system encounters a 'MISSING' string or an empty string: ' '. The order in which these substitutions will be made is the order in which these strings have been specified.

When loading Parquet data, the data is loaded as JSON by Snowflake and is loaded as a VARIANT data type. Therefore, we use the same syntax that is reserved for processing JSON data to extract information out of the Parquet-format data. Since the data is loaded into a single variant column, we can access the column using the $1 syntax. To access individual fields, the syntax is $1:fieldname and we can then cast the data into the desired data types by adding ::<desired_data_type> at the end.

Once we have extracted the columns and converted them into the appropriate data types, we can simply insert into the target table.

Making sense of JSON semi-structured data and transforming to a relational view

This recipe walks you through the process of loading JSON data into a Snowflake table and transforming it into a relational form that can then be further processed.

Getting ready

Since our objective is to demonstrate the processing of data in JSON format, we will not describe the process of creating stages and external data from cloud storage as that has been covered in previous recipes. For simplicity, we have made available a sample JSON file in a public cloud bucket that we will read and process. The JSON sample data is shown in the screenshot that follows. The data consists of two fields called `data_set` and `extract_date` and an array of objects called `credit_cards`. We are going to convert this data into columns and rows so that it can be processed in a relational manner:

```
{
    "data_set":"credit_cards",
    "extract_date":"2019-10-26",
    "credit_cards": [
        {
            "CreditCardNo": "527147 8139869068",
            "CreditCardHolder": "Alfreda Y. Meyers",
            "CardPin": "1634",
            "CardCVV": "929",
            "CardExpiry": "03/20"
        },
        {
            "CreditCardNo": "577056658951575987",
            "CreditCardHolder": "Libby I. Delaney",
            "CardPin": "7235",
            "CardCVV": "596",
            "CardExpiry": "03/20"
        },
        {
            "CreditCardNo": "6473 9323 3107 7122",
            "CreditCardHolder": "Libby T. Ray",
```

Figure 3.14 – Sample JSON data

The JSON sample file can be found at `https://github.com/PacktPublishing/Snowflake-Cookbook/blob/master/Chapter03/r5/json_sample.json`.

Please download and familiarize yourself with the JSON structure. Also, if you like, you can download it and use it in your own cloud storage buckets for testing purposes.

How to do it...

We will load the JSON data into a VARIANT column and then perform further processing on the loaded data to convert it into relational format. The steps are as follows:

1. Let's first create a database where we will create our table and load it with some sample data:

    ```
    CREATE DATABASE JSON_EX;
    ```

2. To make this recipe simpler, we have already uploaded the data to a public Amazon S3 bucket called snowflake-cookbook. Follow the steps in the Configuring Snowflake access to private S3 buckets recipe to set up access when using a private or restricted bucket. For the time being, we will create an external stage over this public bucket, from which we will then load the data into Snowflake (note that keeping your data in public buckets is a security risk and is being done in this recipe only for simplification):

    ```
    CREATE OR REPLACE STAGE JSON_STG url='s3://snowflake-
    cookbook/Chapter03/r5'
    FILE_FORMAT = (TYPE = JSON);
    ```

3. Let's try and list the files in the stage so that we can be sure that we are able to access the data in the S3 bucket:

    ```
    LIST @JSON_STG;
    ```

    You should see the list of files in the bucket, which indicates that Snowflake is able to access the data:

Row	name	size	md5
1	s3://snowflake-cookbook/ch3/r9/json_sample.json	33395	2b050d44a704

Figure 3.15 – List of files in the bucket

4. Now that the data is accessible via a Snowflake external stage, let's try and parse the JSON data so that we can validate that everything is working well:

```
SELECT  PARSE_JSON($1)
FROM @JSON_STG;
```

There shouldn't be any errors and you should see a single line that has all of the JSON data:

Row	PARSE_JSON($1)
1	{ "credit_cards": [{ "CardCVV": "929", "CardExpiry": "03/20", "CardPin": "1634", "CreditCardHolder": "Alfreda Y. Meyer

Figure 3.16 – Parsing and validating the JSON data

5. Let's create a new table and load the JSON data into that table. Please note that the table has only one field called MY_JSON_DATA and the data type for that is VARIANT. Next, we run the COPY command and load the JSON data into this table:

```
CREATE TABLE CREDIT_CARD_TEMP
(
    MY_JSON_DATA VARIANT
);
COPY INTO CREDIT_CARD_TEMP
FROM @JSON_STG;
```

6. Let's try and access the fields called data_set and extract_date:

```
SELECT MY_JSON_DATA:data_set,MY_JSON_DATA:extract_date
FROM CREDIT_CARD_TEMP;
```

7. The process of querying the credit_cards array and the information within it is a little bit more involved. You can access the credit_cards array in the same manner as in the preceding step; however, it will return a single line of JSON, which is not very useful for further processing:

```
SELECT MY_JSON_DATA:credit_cards FROM
CREDIT_CARD_TEMP;
```

8. We can also select the values in the credit_cards array by explicitly hardcoding the array location and the fields that we want to access; however, that will return only the first row in the JSON dataset:

```
SELECT
MY_JSON_DATA:credit_cards[0].CreditCardNo,MY_JSON_DATA
:credit_cards[0].CreditCardHolder FROM
CREDIT_CARD_TEMP;
```

9. The easiest method to convert that array into a relation view is to use the flatten function. We have given the credit_cards array as an input to the flatten function, which then transposes the JSON array data into rows. As you can see we have selected 200 rows, with each segment of data in the credit_cards array being converted into a row. We have also selected extract_date, which was outside of the credit_cards array, and have joined it with the rest of the data such that it appears on each row:

```
SELECT
    MY_JSON_DATA:extract_date,
    value:CreditCardNo::String,
    value:CreditCardHolder::String,
    value:CardPin::Integer,
    value:CardCVV::String,
    value:CardExpiry::String
FROM
    CREDIT_CARD_TEMP
    , lateral flatten( input =>
MY_JSON_DATA:credit_cards );
```

The output is as follows:

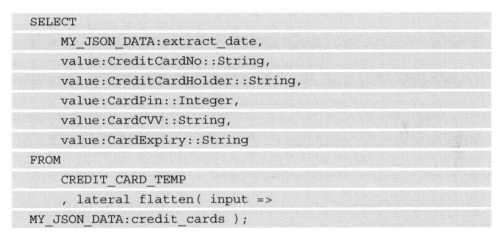

Figure 3.17 – Relation view using the flatten function

The data is now converted to a relational format and can be used for further processing just like an ordinary table.

How it works...

When we created the external stage for loading this JSON data, we set the file type to be JSON, which instructed Snowflake to expect JSON data. Next, we created a table with a single column that had the data type of `VARIANT`, which is a universal data type and can store data of any type. The data from the external stage was loaded into this single column.

Once the data is loaded into the table, we simply use `MY_JSON_DATA:<field_name>` to access the required fields; however, because the `credit_cards` data is an array containing further values, this syntax is not the most efficient way of processing array data. To convert the array into relational format, we use the `flatten` function, which is used to explode compound values into rows. The use of the `flatten` function simplifies the conversion from the JSON array to a relational view, producing 200 rows as an output, which is equal to the number of entries in the JSON array.

Processing newline-delimited JSON (or NDJSON) into a Snowflake table

This recipe walks you through the process of loading NDJSON data and transforming it into a relational form to then be loaded into a table. NDJSON is a JSON format in which each row is valid JSON in itself and therefore can be processed independently of the complete document. For more details about NDJSON, please see `http://ndjson.org/`.

Getting ready

Since our objective is to demonstrate the processing of NDJSON, we will not describe the process of creating stages and external data from cloud storage as it has already been covered in other recipes. For simplicity, we have made available a sample NDJSON file in a public cloud bucket that we will read and process. The NDJSON sample file can be found at `https://github.com/PacktPublishing/Snowflake-Cookbook/blob/master/Chapter03/r6/ndjson_sample.json.json` if you would like to download it and use it in your own cloud storage buckets.

How to do it...

To demonstrate the JSON parsing capabilities, we will load a NDJSON-format file that we have previously uploaded to an S3 bucket. We will create a stage pointing to that bucket and then parse the JSON file contained in that bucket. The steps are as follows:

1. Let's first create a database where we will create our table and load it with some sample data:

```
CREATE DATABASE NDJSON_EX;
```

2. To make this recipe simpler, we have already uploaded the data to a public Amazon S3 bucket called snowflake-cookbook. Follow the steps in the Configuring Snowflake access to private S3 buckets recipe to set up access when using a private or restricted bucket. For the time being, we will create an external stage over this public bucket, from which we will then load the data into Snowflake (note that keeping your data in public buckets is a security risk and is being done in this recipe only for simplification):

```
CREATE OR REPLACE STAGE NDJSON_STG
url='s3://snowflake-cookbook/Chapter03/r6'
FILE_FORMAT = (TYPE = JSON, STRIP_OUTER_ARRAY = TRUE);
```

3. Let's try and list the files in the stage so that we can be sure that we are able to access the data in the S3 bucket:

```
LIST @NDJSON_STG;
```

You should see the list of files in the bucket, which indicates that Snowflake is able to access the data:

Row	name	size	md5
1	s3://snowflake-cookbook/ch3/r6/ndjson_sample.json	14834	b681bffd8a60752d9446d6ea02d172c8

Figure 3.18 – List of files in the bucket

4. Now that the data is accessible via a Snowflake external stage, let's try and parse the JSON data so that we can verify that everything is working well:

```
SELECT  PARSE_JSON($1)
FROM @NDJSON_STG;
```

There shouldn't be any errors and you should see the JSON data appearing line by line:

Row	PARSE_JSON($1) ↓
1	{ "CardCVV": "979", "CardExpiry": "10/2020", "CardPin": "6609", "CreditCardHolder": "Price M. Cochran", "CreditCardNo": "36526505572729" }
2	{ "CardCVV": "197", "CardExpiry": "09/2019", "CardPin": "6954", "CreditCardHolder": "Daquan I. Sullivan", "CreditCardNo": "646 22682 40124 108" }
3	{ "CardCVV": "647", "CardExpiry": "11/2020", "CardPin": "8186", "CreditCardHolder": "Violet Y. Perkins", "CreditCardNo": "36118819196153" }
4	{ "CardCVV": "316", "CardExpiry": "09/2019", "CardPin": "8710", "CreditCardHolder": "Kerry L. Sandoval", "CreditCardNo": "512 62701 88375 080" }

Figure 3.19 – Parsing and validating the JSON data

5. Let's now parse and convert the fields into relational format so that they can then be loaded into a table. We will also apply data types to the fields so that the data is ready to be inserted into a table or be used in another query:

```
SELECT   PARSE_JSON($1):CreditCardNo::String AS
CreditCardNo
         ,PARSE_JSON($1):CreditCardHolder::String AS
CreditCardHolder
         ,PARSE_JSON($1):CardPin::Integer AS CardPin
         ,PARSE_JSON($1):CardExpiry::String AS
CardExpiry
         ,PARSE_JSON($1):CardCVV::String AS CardCVV
FROM @NDJSON_STG;
```

The output is as follows:

Row	CREDITCARDNO	CREDITCARDHOLDER	CARDPIN	CARDEXPIRY	CARDCVV
1	36526505572729	Price M. Cochran	6609	10/2020	979
2	646 22682 40124 108	Daquan I. Sullivan	6954	09/2019	197
3	36118819196153	Violet Y. Perkins	8186	11/2020	647
4	512 62701 88375 080	Kerry L. Sandoval	8710	09/2019	316

Figure 3.20 – Converting the fields into relational format

6. We have successfully loaded and parsed NDJSON data. At this point, you can re-use the preceding query to load the data into a table or use the query as it is and perform further transformations on the data:

```
CREATE TABLE CREDIT_CARD_DATA AS
SELECT   PARSE_JSON($1):CreditCardNo::String AS
CreditCardNo
```

```
          ,PARSE_JSON($1):CreditCardHolder::String AS
CreditCardHolder
          ,PARSE_JSON($1):CardPin::Integer AS CardPin
          ,PARSE_JSON($1):CardExpiry::String AS
CardExpiry
          ,PARSE_JSON($1):CardCVV::String AS CardCVV
FROM @NDJSON_STG;
SELECT * FROM CREDIT_CARD_DATA;
```

How it works...

NDJSON is a variant of JSON where each line in the file is valid JSON. See the example file at `https://github.com/PacktPublishing/Snowflake-Cookbook/blob/master/Chapter03/r6/ndjson_sample.json`. The full JSON document may be contained inside square brackets as well. When we created the external stage for loading this NDJSON data, we set the file type to be JSON and also instructed Snowflake to strip the outer square brackets as well. Next, we used the `PARSE_JSON` function, which takes an input string, parses it into JSON, and outputs with a variant data type that we can then further manipulate.

Notice that we used `PARSE_JSON($1)` to parse the file. $ notation is a way to reference columns from a staged file and in this case, we are basically instructing Snowflake to parse the first column in the file. It is worth noting that because we are loading JSON data, there is only a single column available anyway. We then parse the JSON and split out the JSON into multiple columns using the `PARSE_JSON($1):<FieldName>::<DataType>` syntax.

Processing near real-time data into a Snowflake table using Snowpipe

This recipe guides you through the process of setting up a Snowpipe and enabling the streaming of data from a cloud storage bucket.

Getting ready

Since we will be performing configuration with AWS to configure events on the S3 bucket, you should have the required privileges on the bucket. If you do not have access, you will need to ask your AWS administrator to configure the S3 bucket for you. The sample files, if you would like to download them for this recipe, can be found at `https://github.com/PacktPublishing/Snowflake-Cookbook/tree/master/Chapter03/r7`.

How to do it...

The steps for this recipe are as follows:

1. Let's first create a database where we will create our target table, Snowpipe, and the stage objects:

    ```
    CREATE DATABASE SP_EX;
    ```

2. Create the target table where we will load the data through Snowpipe:

    ```
    CREATE TABLE TRANSACTIONS
    (
        Transaction_Date DATE,
        Customer_ID NUMBER,
        Transaction_ID NUMBER,
        Amount NUMBER
    );
    ```

3. Create an external stage pointing to your desired S3 bucket. Please replace <bucket> with your intended S3 bucket and ensure that you have followed the steps in the Configuring Snowflake access to private S3 buckets recipe and have enabled read and write access for Snowflake to your bucket. We will use the storage integration object created in that recipe to establish write access for our S3 bucket:

    ```
    CREATE OR REPLACE STAGE SP_TRX_STAGE
    url='s3://<bucket>'
    STORAGE_INTEGRATION = S3_INTEGRATION;
    ```

4. Run LIST on the stage to ensure that you can successfully read the associated S3 bucket. The LIST command should not result in any errors:

```
LIST @SP_TRX_STAGE;
```

5. Let's now create a Snowpipe to enable the streaming of data. The CREATE PIPE command makes use of the same COPY command as we have previously used in several recipes in this chapter. Notice that we have set AUTO_INGEST to true while creating the Snowpipe. Once we configure the events on AWS, the Snowpipe will automatically load files as they arrive in the bucket:

```
CREATE OR REPLACE PIPE TX_LD_PIPE
AUTO_INGEST = true
AS COPY INTO TRANSACTIONS FROM @SP_TRX_STAGE
FILE_FORMAT = (TYPE = CSV SKIP_HEADER = 1);
```

6. It is worth noting that although the Snowpipe is created, it will not load any data unless it is triggered manually through a REST API endpoint or the cloud platform generates an event that can trigger the Snowpipe. Before we proceed to the AWS console, we need to perform one step. Run the SHOW PIPES command and copy the ARN value that is shown in the notification_channel field (as shown in the screenshot that follows). We will use that ARN value to configure event notification in AWS:

```
SHOW PIPES LIKE '%TX_LD_PIPE%';
```

The output for this command is as follows:

name	database_name	schema_name	definition	owner	notification_channel
TX_LD_PIPE	SP_EX	PUBLIC	COPY INTO ...	SYSADMIN	arn:aws:sqs:ap-southeast-2:708014598823:sf-...

Figure 3.21 – Output of the SHOW PIPES command

Make sure that you copy the full value shown in the `notification_channel` column.

7. Let's now proceed to the AWS console where we will set up an event notification for the S3 bucket so that the Snowpipe gets triggered automatically upon the creation of a new file in the bucket. Click on your S3 bucket and select the Properties tab, then within the tab, click on Events. Click Add Notification on the Events screen:

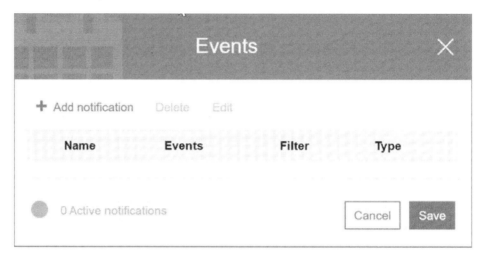

Figure 3.22 – Events screen

8. In the screen for adding new events, put in a name for the event, such as Trigger Snowpipe or similar. In the Events section, select All object create events, which basically means that the event will be triggered every time a new object is created. In the Send to section, select SQS Queue, select Add SQS queue ARN, and paste the ARN that you copied in step 6 into the SQS queue ARN field:

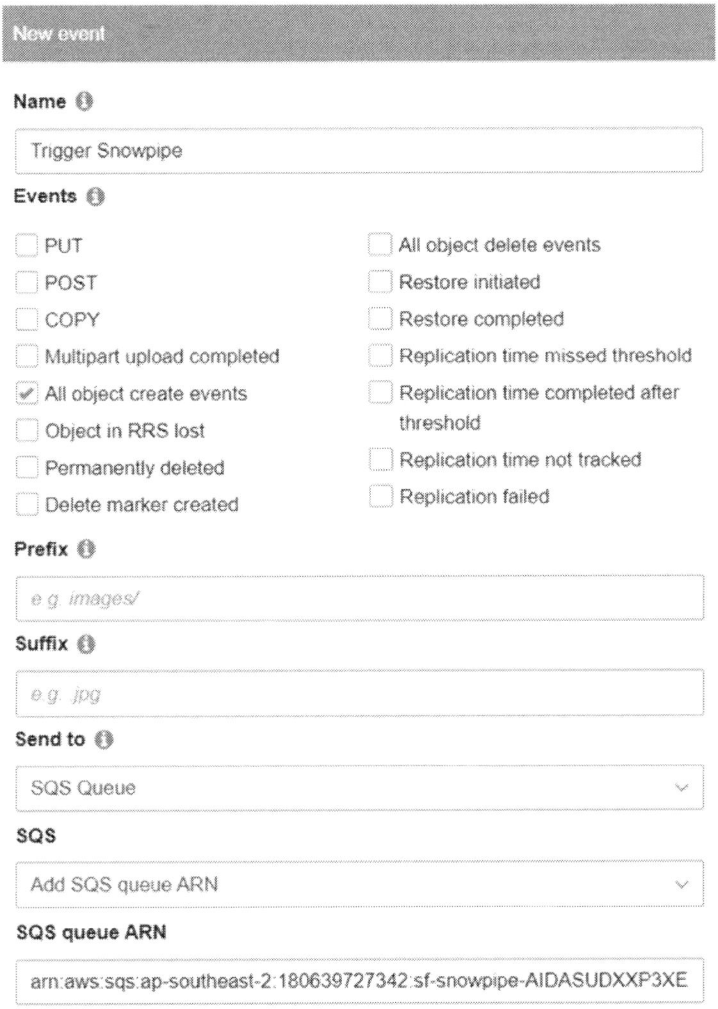

Figure 3.23 – New event window

9. Save the event and proceed to add a data file to the S3 bucket.

10. Wait for some time, and in the Snowflake web UI, execute a COUNT(*) query on the table. You will see new data loaded in the table:

```
SELECT COUNT(*) FROM TRANSACTIONS;
```

How it works...

Snowpipe makes use of the COPY statement, which makes it quite straightforward to set up a Snowpipe. Most of the commands and syntax that work with the COPY command also work with Snowpipe. However, additional configuration is required to invoke a Snowpipe.

There are two ways to trigger the Snowpipe and thus load the data present in the S3 bucket. You can either invoke the Snowpipe through a REST API call or you can rely on the notification sent by the cloud storage platforms to configure automatic triggering of the Snowpipe. We can configure an event to be generated every time a new file is created in the cloud storage bucket.

The two methods are shown in the following diagram:

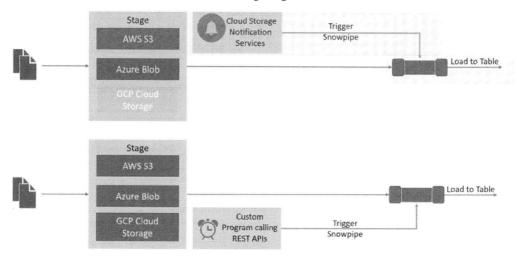

Figure 3.24 – The two methods to trigger Snowpipe

In this recipe, we created a notification event on the S3 bucket, which gets triggered upon new file creation. This in turn triggers the Snowpipe that we associated with the S3 bucket.

Extracting data from Snowflake

This recipe walks you through extracting data from a Snowflake table. We will extract the data into an internal stage and later demonstrate how to do the same via an external stage, which will result in data being written to an S3 bucket.

Getting ready

You should have a table already created and populated, from which we will extract data. This table can be any table that you have previously loaded as part of this chapter or any other table available in your environment.

Ensure that you have followed the steps in the *Configuring Snowflake access to private S3 buckets* recipe and have enabled **read and write access for Snowflake** to your bucket. If write access is not present, Snowflake will not be able to write the extract into your bucket.

We will use SnowSQL to get the file from the internal stage to the local directory, so make sure that SnowSQL is installed on your system and you can successfully connect to your Snowflake instance. We don't need to run all of the following steps using SnowSQL and will point out when a specific step should be run through SnowSQL.

How to do it...

The steps for this recipe are as follows:

1. Let's first create a database where we will create our internal stage object:

    ```
    CREATE DATABASE EXPORT_EX;
    ```

2. Create an internal stage and set the file format in which you would like to export your files. We have selected CSV for simplicity and have kept the compression to GZIP:

    ```
    CREATE OR REPLACE STAGE EXPORT_INTERNAL_STG
    FILE_FORMAT = (TYPE = CSV COMPRESSION=GZIP);
    ```

3. Extracting data from a table into a stage is as simple as running the COPY command, but the order of the copy is reversed; that is, we are now copying into the stage from the table. To demonstrate the extraction, we have used a table in one of the sample databases provided with Snowflake. You can replace the table name with your table name:

    ```
    COPY INTO @EXPORT_INTERNAL_STG/customer.csv.gz
    FROM SNOWFLAKE_SAMPLE_DATA.TPCH_SF1.CUSTOMER;
    ```

4. Let's list the files in the stage to verify that the data has indeed been unloaded into the stage:

    ```
    LIST @EXPORT_INTERNAL_STG;
    ```

You should see a number of files that have been extracted; Snowflake automatically splits large data into multiple files:

Row	name	size
1	export_internal_stg/customer.csv.gz_0_0_0.csv	4847904
2	export_internal_stg/customer.csv.gz_0_1_0.csv	9733520
3	export_internal_stg/customer.csv.gz_0_2_0.csv	4866096
4	export_internal_stg/customer.csv.gz_0_3_0.csv	4846704

Figure 3.25 – Listing files in the stage and checking the data

5. Use SnowSQL to download the files to a local directory on your computer. Please replace C:/Downloads/ with a directory of your choice:

```
GET @EXPORT_INTERNAL_STG 'file://C:/Downloads/';
```

6. Now that we have successfully extracted to an internal stage, let's extract the same table out to an external stage. Please replace <bucket> with your intended S3 bucket and ensure that you have followed the steps in the *Configuring Snowflake access to private S3 buckets* recipe and have enabled read and write access for Snowflake to your bucket. We will use the storage integration object created in that recipe to establish write access for our S3 bucket:

```
CREATE OR REPLACE STAGE EXPORT_EXTERNAL_STG
url='s3://<bucket>'
STORAGE_INTEGRATION = S3_INTEGRATION
FILE_FORMAT = (TYPE = PARQUET COMPRESSION=AUTO);
```

7. Extracting data from a table into an external stage is again quite simple. To demonstrate the extraction, we have used a table in one of the sample databases provided with Snowflake. You can replace the table name with your table name. Additionally, we are now extracting data that is the result of a query rather than the complete table and have changed the file format to parquet as in the preceding step:

```
COPY INTO @EXPORT_EXTERNAL_STG/customer.parquet
FROM (SELECT * FROM
SNOWFLAKE_SAMPLE_DATA.TPCH_SF1.CUSTOMER SAMPLE (10));
```

If you now navigate to your S3 bucket, you will see the data unloaded into your S3 bucket as shown in the following screenshot:

	Name ▼
☐	🗋 customer.parquet_0_0_0.snappy.parquet
☐	🗋 customer.parquet_0_1_0.snappy.parquet
☐	🗋 customer.parquet_0_3_0.snappy.parquet

Figure 3.26 – Data unloaded into your S3 bucket

How it works...

Extracting data from Snowflake is a similar operation to loading data into Snowflake. The same COPY command that is used to load data is also used to extract data. When extracting, data is copied into the stage from a table using the COPY INTO command. The extraction can be performed into an internal stage or an external stage that in turn points to cloud storage. If you have extracted data to an internal stage and are aiming to download the data to your local machine, you must use the GET command through SnowSQL to download that data.

It is also worth noting that you can extract data from a table or a view, or you can extract the results of a SELECT query.

4
Building Data Pipelines in Snowflake

Snowflake, like other data platforms, offers tools and abstractions to developers/users to build data pipelines to enable data processing and analytics. But being a cloud database, it has different ways of handling data pipelines. In a typical data pipeline, there are ways to execute a piece of code, sequence pieces of code to execute one after the other, and create dependencies within the pipeline and on the environment. Snowflake structures pipelines using the notions of *tasks* and *streams*. A pipeline allows developers to create a sequence of data processes that are represented by tasks. A task represents a data process that can be logically atomic. The other concept of a stream allows data processing applications to be intelligent, triggering data processing based on a change happening in the data landscape.

This chapter deals with setting up pipelines using tasks and streams and applying different techniques for transforming data within tasks and failure management. By the end of this chapter, you will know how to create tasks and streams and how to use them together to handle complex data processing scenarios.

The following recipes will be covered in this chapter:

- Creating and scheduling a task
- Conjugating pipelines through a task tree
- Querying and viewing the task history
- Exploring the concept of streams to capture table-level changes
- Combining the concept of streams and tasks to build pipelines that process changed data on a schedule
- Converting data types and Snowflake's failure management
- Managing context using different utility functions

Technical requirements

This chapter assumes that you have a Snowflake account already set up. The code for this chapter can be found at the following GitHub URL:

```
https://github.com/PacktPublishing/Snowflake-Cookbook/tree/
master/Chapter04
```

Creating and scheduling a task

In this recipe, we will create a new task that runs a set of steps for processing data and configures the task to execute on a set schedule.

Getting ready

Note that the steps for this recipe can be run either in the Snowflake web UI or the SnowSQL command-line client.

How to do it...

To demonstrate the concept of a *task*, we will first create an aggregation query that we assume is being used in a report. We are assuming that the query takes a long time to run, therefore we are going to save the results of the query to a physical table and then refresh it periodically through a scheduled task. Let's see how to run tasks:

1. To simplify the process for you, we have used the sample data provided by Snowflake and created an aggregation query on top of that. (Please note that sample data is included with your Snowflake instance and can be found under the SNOWFLAKE_SAMPLE_DATA database.) We will be using a fictitious query on the sample data, as follows:

```
SELECT C.C_NAME,SUM(L_EXTENDEDPRICE),SUM(L_TAX)

FROM SNOWFLAKE_SAMPLE_DATA.TPCH_SF1.CUSTOMER C

INNER JOIN SNOWFLAKE_SAMPLE_DATA.TPCH_SF1.ORDERS O
ON O.O_CUSTKEY = C.C_CUSTKEY

INNER JOIN SNOWFLAKE_SAMPLE_DATA.TPCH_SF1.LINEITEM LI
ON LI.L_ORDERKEY = O.O_ORDERKEY

GROUP BY C.C_NAME;
```

A sample of the output of the preceding query looks as follows:

Row	C_NAME	SUM(L_EXTENDEDPRICE)	SUM(L_TAX)
1	Customer#000052858	2593511.11	2.55
2	Customer#000090793	2525706.08	2.57
3	Customer#000132863	1643014.32	1.78

Figure 4.1 – Sample output

2. We will now create a target table where we will save the results of this query. Note that in addition to the columns produced by the preceding query, we have added a Reporting_Time column as well. We will insert the current timestamp into this column every time we insert data:

```
CREATE DATABASE task_demo;
USE DATABASE task_demo;
```

```
CREATE TABLE ordering_customers
(
    Reporting_Time TIMESTAMP,
    Customer_Name STRING,
    Revenue NUMBER(16,2),
    Tax NUMBER(16,2)
);
```

3. We will now create a task using the preceding SQL statement to insert data into the `ordering_customers` table. To start with, we will configure the task to run every 30 minutes:

```
CREATE TASK refresh_ordering_customers
    WAREHOUSE = COMPUTE_WH
    SCHEDULE = '30 MINUTE'
    COMMENT = 'Update Ordering_Customers Table with latest
      data'
AS
    INSERT INTO ordering_customers
    SELECT CURRENT_TIMESTAMP, C.C_NAME,
          SUM(L_EXTENDEDPRICE), SUM(L_TAX)
    FROM SNOWFLAKE_SAMPLE_DATA.TPCH_SF1.CUSTOMER C
    INNER JOIN SNOWFLAKE_SAMPLE_DATA.TPCH_SF1.ORDERS O
    ON O.O_CUSTKEY = C.C_CUSTKEY
    INNER JOIN SNOWFLAKE_SAMPLE_DATA.TPCH_SF1.LINEITEM LI
    ON LI.L_ORDERKEY = O.O_ORDERKEY
    GROUP BY CURRENT_TIMESTAMP, C.C_NAME;
```

4. Let's validate that the task has been created correctly by running the DESC command:

```
DESC TASK refresh_ordering_customers;
```

The output from the preceding code is shown as follows and has been split onto multiple lines for visibility. Note that by default, a new task is created in a suspended state, as shown in the output:

created_on	name	id	databas... ↓	schema_name	owner
2021-02-15 02:15:0...	REFRESH_ORDERING_CUSTOME...	019a4e07-5...	TASK_DEMO	PUBLIC	SYSADMIN

comment	warehouse	schedule	predecessors	state	definition ↓	condition
Update Ordering_...	COMPUTE_...	30 MINUTE	NULL	suspended	INSERT INTO ordering_custome...	NULL

Figure 4.2 – DESC command output

5.   If you are running your code through a role other than ACCOUNTADMIN, you must grant that role the privilege to execute the task, as follows:

```
USE ROLE ACCOUNTADMIN;
GRANT EXECUTE TASK ON ACCOUNT TO ROLE SYSADMIN;
```

6.   We must now set the task status to Resumed so that it can start executing on schedule. We will do that by running a describe command again to ensure the task has successfully been moved from the suspended state to the started state. Note that the following step must be run as ACCOUNTADMIN or alternatively, you can grant the required rights to another role as done in the previous step:

```
ALTER TASK refresh_ordering_customers RESUME;
DESC TASK refresh_ordering_customers;
```

Here is the output of the preceding code:

comment	warehouse	schedule	predecessors	state	definition	condition
Update Orde...	COMPUTE_...	30 MINUTE	NULL	started	INSERT INT...	NULL

Figure 4.3 – Output of the describe command

Note that now, the state of the task is set to started, which means the task is now scheduled and should execute in the next 30 minutes.

7.   We will now keep an eye on the task execution to validate that it runs successfully. To do that, we need to query task_history, as follows:

```
SELECT name, state,
       completed_time, scheduled_time,
       error_code, error_message

FROM TABLE(information_schema.task_history())
WHERE name = 'REFRESH_ORDERING_CUSTOMERS';
```

The output from the query is as follows:

NAME	STATE	COMPLETED_TIME	SCHEDULED_TIME	ERROR_CODE	ERROR_MESSAGE
REFRESH_ORDERING_CUSTOMERS	SCHEDULED	NULL	2021-02-15 02:48:3...	NULL	NULL

Figure 4.4 – Output of task_history

As evident from the output, the task has not been executed yet and the scheduled time when the task will execute is shown. Let's check the status in another 30 minutes and this task should have executed.

8. After waiting 30 minutes, re-run the preceding query. As expected, the task executed successfully, as shown in the following output, and the next instance is scheduled for execution:

NAME	STATE	COMPLETED_TIME	SCHEDULED_TIME	ERROR_CODE	ERROR_MESSAGE
REFRESH_ORDERING_CU...	SCHEDULED	NULL	2021-02-15 03:18:36.406 -0800	NULL	NULL
REFRESH_ORDERING_CU...	SUCCEEDED	2021-02-15 02:48:53.693 -0800	2021-02-15 02:48:36.406 -0800	NULL	NULL

Figure 4.5 – New task scheduled

9. Let's validate that the task has indeed executed successfully by selecting from the `ordering_customers` table:

```
SELECT * FROM ordering_customers;
```

As shown in the following screenshot, the query returned around 100,000 records, which indicates that the task executed successfully:

✔ Query ID SQL   867ms   99,996 rows

Filter result...   ⬇ Copy   Columns ▾ ↗

Row	REPORTING_TIME	CUSTOMER_NAME	REVENUE	TAX
1	2021-02-15 02:48:50.740	Customer#000009883	1501315.56	1.73
2	2021-02-15 02:48:50.740	Customer#000061001	966905.86	1.34
3	2021-02-15 02:48:50.740	Customer#000073957	1577889.21	1.22
4	2021-02-15 02:48:50.740	Customer#000036964	1988282.69	2.26

Figure 4.6 – Validating the task

How it works...

Tasks in Snowflake enable the scheduled execution of SQL statements and can be used to process regular workloads such as converting a base table into an aggregate, transforming data for a report, or even processing staged data. When creating a task, you must provide a virtual warehouse name, as that is used during the scheduled execution of the task. Currently, a task cannot be kicked off manually; a schedule must be added that can be configured based on every x minute interval or a more complex CRON-based schedule.

Now, tasks are created in a suspended state by default, so we are required to resume the task in order for that task to start executing on a schedule. Setting a task to resume can only be performed by an ACCOUNTADMIN role or another role that has been configured specifically and has been granted the EXECUTE TASK privilege. Once the task is resumed, it is kicked off on schedule by Snowflake and the history of the execution can be viewed via the task_history table function.

Conjugating pipelines through a task tree

In this recipe, we will connect multiple tasks together in a tree to produce a data pipeline that performs multiple functions as it executes.

Getting ready

The following steps describe the various ways to create and schedule a task. Note that these steps can be run either in the Snowflake web UI or the SnowSQL command-line client.

How to do it...

To demonstrate the concept of a **task tree**, we will first create an aggregation query that we assume is being used in a report. We are assuming that the query takes a long time to run, therefore we are going to save the results of the query to a physical table and then refresh it periodically through a scheduled task. The steps are as follows:

1. To simplify the process for you, we have used the sample data provided by Snowflake and created an aggregation query on top of that. (Please note that sample data is included with your Snowflake instance and can be found under the SNOWFLAKE_SAMPLE_DATA database.) We will be using a fictitious query on the sample data, as shown:

```
SELECT C.C_NAME,SUM(L_EXTENDEDPRICE),SUM(L_TAX)

FROM SNOWFLAKE_SAMPLE_DATA.TPCH_SF1.CUSTOMER C

INNER JOIN SNOWFLAKE_SAMPLE_DATA.TPCH_SF1.ORDERS O
ON O.O_CUSTKEY = C.C_CUSTKEY

INNER JOIN SNOWFLAKE_SAMPLE_DATA.TPCH_SF1.LINEITEM LI
ON LI.L_ORDERKEY = O.O_ORDERKEY

GROUP BY C.C_NAME;
```

A sample of the output of the preceding query is as follows:

Row	C_NAME	SUM(L_EXTENDEDPRICE)	SUM(L_TAX)
1	Customer#000052858	2593511.11	2.55
2	Customer#000090793	2525706.08	2.57
3	Customer#000132863	1643014.32	1.78

Figure 4.7 – Sample data provided by Snowflake

2. We will now create a target table where we will save the results of this query:

```
CREATE DATABASE task_demo;
USE DATABASE task_demo;
CREATE TABLE ordering_customers
(
   Customer_Name STRING,
```

```
    Revenue NUMBER(16,2),
    Tax NUMBER(16,2)
);
```

3. We will create an initialization task to clean up the table before we insert new data into the table:

```
USE DATABASE task_demo;
CREATE TASK clear_ordering_customers
  WAREHOUSE = COMPUTE_WH
  COMMENT = 'Delete from Ordering_Customers'
AS
  DELETE FROM task_demo.public.ordering_customers;
```

4. We will now create a task using the SQL statement in *step 1* to insert data into the `ordering_customers` table:

```
CREATE TASK insert_ordering_customers
  WAREHOUSE = COMPUTE_WH
  COMMENT = 'Insert into Ordering_Customers the latest
data'
AS
  INSERT INTO ordering_customers
  SELECT C.C_NAME, SUM(L_EXTENDEDPRICE), SUM(L_TAX)
  FROM SNOWFLAKE_SAMPLE_DATA.TPCH_SF1.CUSTOMER C
  INNER JOIN SNOWFLAKE_SAMPLE_DATA.TPCH_SF1.ORDERS O
  ON O.O_CUSTKEY = C.C_CUSTKEY
  INNER JOIN SNOWFLAKE_SAMPLE_DATA.TPCH_SF1.LINEITEM LI
  ON LI.L_ORDERKEY = O.O_ORDERKEY
  GROUP BY C.C_NAME;
```

5. So far, we have created two tasks, one to delete the data and one to insert the data. Now, we will connect the two together to create a small pipeline. We will make the insert task run after the clear task:

```
ALTER TASK insert_ordering_customers
ADD AFTER clear_ordering_customers;
```

6. Let's run a describe command on the task to validate that the tasks have been connected:

```
DESC TASK insert_ordering_customers;
```

The output shows that the `clear_ordering_customers` task has been set as a predecessor to the `INSERT` task:

schedule	predecessors	state	definition	condition
NULL	TASK_DEMO.PUBLIC.CLEAR_ORDERING_CUSTOMERS	suspended	INSERT INT...	NULL

Figure 4.8 – Output of the describe command

7. Let's now schedule our `clear_ordering_customers` task to execute on a schedule. We will set it to run for 10 minutes for demonstration purposes:

```
ALTER TASK clear_ordering_customers
SET SCHEDULE = '10 MINUTE';
```

The statement should run successfully.

8. If you are running your code through a role other than `ACCOUNTADMIN`, you must grant that role the privilege to execute the task:

```
GRANT EXECUTE TASK ON ACCOUNT TO ROLE SYSADMIN;
```

9. Let's now set the tasks to `Resume` since tasks are created as suspended by default and would not work unless we set them this way. The following step must be run as `ACCOUNTADMIN` or alternatively, you can grant the required rights to another role as done in the previous step.

Note that the child tasks must be resumed first before resuming the parent tasks:

```
ALTER TASK insert_ordering_customers RESUME;
ALTER TASK clear_ordering_customers RESUME;
```

Both statements should complete successfully.

10. We will now keep an eye on the task execution to validate that it runs successfully. To do that, we need to query `task_history`, as follows:

```
SELECT name, state,
       completed_time, scheduled_time,
       error_code, error_message
FROM TABLE(information_schema.task_history())
WHERE name IN
```

```
('CLEAR_ORDERING_CUSTOMERS','INSERT_ORDERING_CUSTOMERS
');
```

Immediately after the creation of the task, the output from the preceding command will show only the root task (that is, the task we scheduled):

NAME	STATE	COMPLETED_TIME	SCHEDULED_TIME	ERROR_CODE	ERROR_MESSAGE
CLEAR_ORDERING_CUSTOMERS	SCHEDULED	NULL	2021-02-15 03:13:41.555 -0800	NULL	NULL

Figure 4.9 – Output showing the root task

As evident from the output, the task has not been executed yet and the scheduled time when the task will execute is shown. Let's check the status in another 10 minutes and this task and its child tasks should have executed.

11. After 10 minutes, re-run the preceding query. As expected, the tasks are executed successfully, as shown in the output, and the next instance is scheduled for execution. Notice that only the root task appears in the scheduled state; however, when the execution occurs, all child tasks get executed as well:

Row	NAME	STATE	COMPLETED_TIME	SCHEDULED_TIME	ERROR_CODE	ERROR_MESSAGE
1	CLEAR_ORDERING_CUSTOMERS	SCHEDULED	NULL	2021-02-15 03:47:53.14...	NULL	NULL
2	INSERT_ORDERING_CUSTOMERS	SUCCEEDED	2021-02-15 03:38:19.6...	2021-02-15 03:38:09.9...	NULL	NULL
3	CLEAR_ORDERING_CUSTOMERS	SUCCEEDED	2021-02-15 03:38:09.9...	2021-02-15 03:37:53.14...	NULL	NULL

Figure 4.10 – Output showing the new root task

12. Let's validate that the tasks have indeed executed successfully by selecting from the `ordering_customers` table:

```
SELECT * FROM ordering_customers;
```

As shown by the result, the query returned around 100,000 records, which indicates that the task executed successfully:

Figure 4.11 – Validating the tasks

How it works...

Snowflake provides functionality to connect multiple tasks together in a parent-child relationship. This feature allows the building of pipelines that consist of multiple steps of execution:

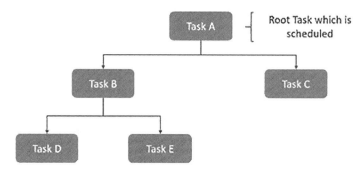

Figure 4.12 – Task tree in Snowflake

For a given task, a predecessor can be set up by specifying the AFTER configuration for the task. The task specified in the AFTER configuration becomes the parent of the task. Through this, a hierarchy of tasks is maintained. The predecessor task must complete before the child tasks can execute.

Querying and viewing the task history

In this recipe, we will explore techniques that can be used to view the history of task execution, using the TASK_HISTORY table function.

Getting ready

The following steps describe the various ways to view and analyze the history of the execution of a single task as well as a series of tasks. Note that these steps can be run either in the Snowflake web UI or the SnowSQL command-line client.

To proceed with this recipe, ensure that you have already created and executed a few tasks; otherwise, no results will be returned.

How to do it...

To perform this recipe, let's try out the following steps:

1. We will use the `task_history` table function, which can be used to query the history of task execution. The function takes several parameters but all of them are optional, so to start with, we will run a query without any parameters. This will return the execution history of all the tasks:

```
SELECT * FROM TABLE(information_schema.task_history())
ORDER BY SCHEDULED_TIME;
```

A sample of the output of the preceding query is shown as follows. Please note the output is split over two rows due to lack of space:

Row	QUERY_ID	NAME	DATABASE_NAN	SCHEMA_NAME	QUERY_TEXT	CONDITION_TE	STATE
1	019a4e28-0...	REFRESH_ORDERING_CUSTOMERS	TASK_DEMO	PUBLIC	INSERT INTO orde...	NULL	SUCCEEDED
2	019a4e41-0...	CLEAR_ORDERING_CUSTOMERS	TASK_DEMO	PUBLIC	DELETE FROM tas...	NULL	SUCCEEDED
3	019a4e42-0...	INSERT_ORDERING_CUSTOMERS	TASK_DEMO	PUBLIC	INSERT INTO orde...	NULL	FAILED

ERROR_CODE	ERROR_MESSAG	SCHEDULED_TII	QUERY_START_	NEXT_SCHEDUL	COMPLETED_TII	ROOT_TASK_ID	GRAPH_VERSIO	RUN_ID	RETURN_VALUE
NULL	NULL	2021-02-15 ...	2021-02-15 ...	2021-02-15 ...	2021-02-15 ...	019a4e07-5...	1	1613386116...	NULL
NULL	NULL	2021-02-15 ...	2021-02-15 ...	2021-02-15 ...	2021-02-15 ...	019a4e35-f7...	1	1613387621...	NULL
002020	SQL compila...	2021-02-15 ...	2021-02-15 ...	NULL	2021-02-15 ...	019a4e35-f7...	1	1613387621...	NULL

Figure 4.13 – Sample output of the preceding query

2. We will now query the view to return the task history between two timestamps. In this case, the query is for a 10-minute interval. Please change the timestamp according to your requirements before running this query:

```
SELECT * FROM
TABLE(information_schema.task_history(
    scheduled_time_range_start=>to_timestamp_ltz
    ('2020-08-13 14:00:00.000 -0700'),
    scheduled_time_range_end=>to_timestamp_ltz('2020-
08-13 14:10:00.000 -0700')
))
ORDER BY SCHEDULED_TIME;
```

The output is shown as follows, and has the task executions only from the given 10-minute interval between the two timestamps:

QUERY_ID	NAME	DATABASE_NAM	SCHEMA_NAME	QUERY_TEXT	CONDITION_TE)	STATE	ERROR_CODE
019a4e5a-0...	CLEAR_ORDERING_CUSTOMERS	TASK_DEMO	PUBLIC	DELETE FRO...	NULL	SUCCEEDED	NULL
019a4e5a-0...	INSERT_ORDERING_CUSTOMERS	TASK_DEMO	PUBLIC	INSERT INT...	NULL	SUCCEEDED	NULL

Figure 4.14 – Querying the view to return the task history between two timestamps

3. The third way to query and limit data from this view is to use the RESULT_LIMIT parameter. We will run a query without providing any other parameters but will supply the RESULT_LIMIT parameter to reduce the number of rows returned. In this instance, we will limit the results to 5:

```
SELECT * FROM
TABLE(information_schema.task_history(
        result_limit => 5
))
ORDER BY SCHEDULED_TIME;
```

The output is shown as follows and as expected, shows the last five steps executed. It is worth noting that if the result set before applying the limit is more than 5, the result set is executed by the latest execution and then the limit of 5 is applied, so you always see the latest information first after the application of the result limit:

QUERY_ID	NAME	DATABASE_NAM	SCHEMA_NAME	QUERY_TEXT	CONDITION_TE)	STATE
019a4e5a-0...	CLEAR_ORDERING_CUSTOMERS	TASK_DEMO	PUBLIC	DELETE FRO...	NULL	SUCCEEDED
019a4e5a-0...	INSERT_ORDERING_CUSTOMERS	TASK_DEMO	PUBLIC	INSERT INT...	NULL	SUCCEEDED
019a4e64-0...	CLEAR_ORDERING_CUSTOMERS	TASK_DEMO	PUBLIC	DELETE FRO...	NULL	SUCCEEDED
019a4e64-0...	INSERT_ORDERING_CUSTOMERS	TASK_DEMO	PUBLIC	INSERT INT...	NULL	SUCCEEDED
NULL	CLEAR_ORDERING_CUSTOMERS	TASK_DEMO	PUBLIC	DELETE FRO...	NULL	SCHEDULED

Figure 4.15 – Querying and limiting the data from the view

4. Now, we will query the TASK_HISTORY view based on the task name itself. This can be performed by using the TASK_NAME parameter. Let's see how that is done:

```
SELECT * FROM
TABLE(information_schema.task_history(
        task_name => 'CLEAR_ORDERING_CUSTOMERS'
))
ORDER BY SCHEDULED_TIME;
```

Several results are returned; however, note that the results are filtered on the provided name and only history related to the task used in the filter is showing:

Row	QUERY_ID	NAME	DATABASE_NAM	SCHEMA_NAME	QUERY_TEXT	CONDITION_TE)	STATE
1	019a4e41-0...	CLEAR_ORDERING_CUSTOMERS	TASK_DEMO	PUBLIC	DELETE FRO...	NULL	SUCCEEDED
2	NULL	CLEAR_ORDERING_CUSTOMERS	TASK_DEMO	PUBLIC	DELETE FRO...	NULL	FAILED
3	019a4e50-0...	CLEAR_ORDERING_CUSTOMERS	TASK_DEMO	PUBLIC	DELETE FRO...	NULL	SUCCEEDED
4	019a4e5a-0...	CLEAR_ORDERING_CUSTOMERS	TASK_DEMO	PUBLIC	DELETE FRO...	NULL	SUCCEEDED
5	019a4e64-0...	CLEAR_ORDERING_CUSTOMERS	TASK_DEMO	PUBLIC	DELETE FRO...	NULL	SUCCEEDED
6	NULL	CLEAR_ORDERING_CUSTOMERS	TASK_DEMO	PUBLIC	DELETE FRO...	NULL	SCHEDULED

Figure 4.16 – Querying the TASK_HISTORY view based on the task name

5. Finally, all the parameters that we have used can be combined into a single query as well to narrow down our results:

```
SELECT * FROM
TABLE(information_schema.task_history(
      task_name => 'CLEAR_ORDERING_CUSTOMERS',
      result_limit => 2
))
ORDER BY SCHEDULED_TIME;
```

The output is shown only for the provided task, and only the last two rows are shown:

Row	QUERY_ID	NAME	DATABASE_NAM	SCHEMA_NAME	QUERY_TEXT	CONDIT...	STATE
1	019a4e64-0...	CLEAR_ORD...	TASK_DEMO	PUBLIC	DELETE FRO...	NULL	SUCCEEDED
2	NULL	CLEAR_ORD...	TASK_DEMO	PUBLIC	DELETE FRO...	NULL	SCHEDULED

Figure 4.17 – Combining all parameters into a single query

How it works...

TASK_HISTORY is a table function that can be used to query the history of scheduled and executed tasks. The function returns the last 7 days of the history of task execution. The function has several parameters through which users can query for the task history between two specific timestamps or filter on a specific task name, as well as use a combination of various filters.

Exploring the concept of streams to capture table-level changes

In this recipe, we will explore the concept of streams, configure a stream on a table, and capture the changes that occur at the table level. Streams are Snowflake's way of performing change data capture on Snowflake tables and can be useful in data pipeline implementation.

Getting ready

The steps for this recipe can be run either in the Snowflake web UI or the SnowSQL command-line client.

How to do it...

The steps for this recipe are as follows:

1. Let's start by creating a database and a staging table on which we will create our stream object. We create a staging table to simulate data arriving from outside Snowflake and being processed further through a stream object:

    ```
    CREATE DATABASE stream_demo;
    USE DATABASE stream_demo;
    CREATE TABLE customer_staging
    (
      ID INTEGER,
      Name STRING,
      State STRING,
      Country STRING
    );
    ```

2. The process of creating a stream is quite straightforward with a simple command such as the following:

    ```
    CREATE STREAM customer_changes ON TABLE customer_staging;
    ```

3. Let's describe the stream to see what has been created:

    ```
    DESC STREAM customer_changes;
    ```

Notice the mode of the stream is set to DEFAULT, which indicates it will track inserts, updates, and deletes that are performed on the table:

created_on	name	database_name ↓	schema_name	owner	comment	table_name	type	stale	mode
2021-02-15 ...	CUSTOMER_CHANGES	STREAM_DEMO	PUBLIC	ACCOUNTA...		STREAM_DE...	DELTA	false	DEFAULT

Figure 4.18 – The created stream

4. Let's insert some data into the staging table to simulate data arriving into Snowflake:

```
INSERT INTO customer_staging VALUES (1,'Jane
Doe','NSW','AU');
INSERT INTO customer_staging VALUES
(2,'Alpha','VIC','AU');
```

5. Validate that the data is indeed inserted into the staging table by selecting it from the table:

```
SELECT * FROM customer_staging;
```

As expected, two rows are present in the staging table:

Row	ID	NAME	STATE	COUNTRY
1	1	Jane Doe	NSW	AU
2	2	Alpha	VIC	AU

Figure 4.19 – Validating whether the data is inserted into the table

6. Now, let's view how the changing data has been captured through the stream. We can view the data by simply selecting from the stream object itself, which is shown as follows:

```
SELECT * FROM customer_changes;
```

The following output shows the data that has been recorded by the stream. Notice both rows have been recorded with an action code of INSERT:

Row	ID	NAME	STATE	COUNTRY	METADATA$ACT	METADATA$ISUP	METADATA$ROW
1	1	Jane Doe	NSW	AU	INSERT	FALSE	546c1da8c5e...
2	2	Alpha	VIC	AU	INSERT	FALSE	562a8a2d053...

Figure 4.20 – Viewing the changing data

7. Now that we have our stream set up successfully, we can process the data from the stream into another table. You would usually do this as part of a data pipeline. Create a table first in which we will insert the recorded data:

```
CREATE TABLE customer
(
    ID INTEGER,
    Name STRING,
    State STRING,
    Country STRING
);
```

8. Retrieving data from a stream and inserting it into another table is as simple as performing a query on the stream itself. As shown ahead, the query selects the required columns from the stream and inserts them into the customer table. Do note that we have used a WHERE clause on metadata$action equal to INSERT. This is to ensure that we only process new data:

```
INSERT INTO customer
SELECT ID,Name,State,Country
FROM customer_changes
WHERE metadata$action = 'INSERT';
```

9. Let's select the data from the customer table to validate that the correct data appears there:

```
SELECT * FROM customer;
```

As expected, the two rows that were originally inserted into the staging table appear here:

Row	ID	NAME	STATE	COUNTRY
1	1	Jane Doe	NSW	AU
2	2	Alpha	VIC	AU

Figure 4.21 – Validating the data from the customer table

10. Let's find out what happens to the stream after data has been processed from it. If we perform SELECT now, there will be zero rows returned since that data has already been processed:

```
SELECT * FROM customer_changes;
```

The output shows zero rows returned:

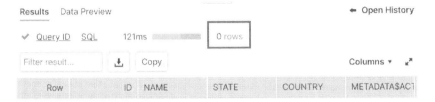

Figure 4.22 – Zero rows returned

11. Let's update a row in the staging table. We are then going to see in the stream how that update appears:

```
UPDATE customer_staging SET name = 'John Smith' WHERE
ID = 1;
```

This operation will show the following output:

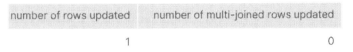

number of rows updated	number of multi-joined rows updated
1	0

Figure 4.23 – Updated row in the staging table

12. Select the data from the stream:

```
SELECT * FROM customer_changes;
```

You will see two records appear in the result set, as shown:

ID	NAME	STATE	COUNTRY	METADATA$ACTION	METADATA$ISU	METADATA$RO
1	John Smith	NSW	AU	INSERT	TRUE	546c1da8c5...
1	Jane Doe	NSW	AU	DELETE	TRUE	546c1da8c5...

Figure 4.24 – Selecting the data from the stream

An update operation is essentially captured as DELETE followed by INSERT. Therefore, you will see both INSERT and UPDATE appear in the result. If you are processing the stream for deletes as well, you will need additional logic in the consuming code to process DELETE correctly.

How it works...

This recipe demonstrates the functioning of streams, which is a mechanism in Snowflake to capture changed data. A stream is created for a table and monitors any changes performed on that table. This includes all the inserts, updates, and deletes performed on the table. Streams can be queried just like a table, allowing the user to select and transform the data recorded in a stream. Once the changes recorded in a stream have been processed, they are removed so that the next processing of stream doesn't encounter records that are already processed.

Combining the concept of streams and tasks to build pipelines that process changed data on a schedule

In this recipe, we will combine the concept of streams and tasks and set up a scheduled Snowflake data pipeline that processes only changed data into a target table.

How to do it...

The following steps describe how to set up a stream to track and process changes that occur on table data. The steps are as follows:

1. Let's start by creating a database and a staging table on which we will create our stream object. We will be creating a staging table to simulate data arriving from outside Snowflake and being processed further through a stream object:

```
CREATE DATABASE stream_demo;
USE DATABASE stream_demo;
CREATE TABLE customer_staging
(
    ID INTEGER,
    Name STRING,
    State STRING,
    Country STRING
);
```

2. Next, create a stream on the table that captures only the inserts. The insert-only mode is achieved by setting APPEND_ONLY to TRUE:

```
CREATE STREAM customer_changes ON TABLE
customer_staging APPEND_ONLY = TRUE;
```

3. Let's describe the stream to see what has been created:

```
DESC STREAM customer_changes;
```

As shown in the following output, notice that the mode of the stream is set to APPEND_ONLY, which indicates it will only track inserts:

name	database_name	schema_name	owner	comment	table_name	type	stale	mode
CUSTOMER_...	STREAM_DE...	PUBLIC	SYSADMIN		STREAM_DE...	DELTA	false	APPEND_ONLY

Figure 4.25 – The created stream

4. So, we have created a staging table and a stream on top of it. Now, we are going to create the actual table into which all the new customer data will be processed:

```
CREATE TABLE customer
(
    ID INTEGER,
    Name STRING,
    State STRING,
    Country STRING
);
```

5. Let's now create a task that we will use to insert any new data that appears in the stream:

```
CREATE TASK process_new_customers
    WAREHOUSE = COMPUTE_WH
    COMMENT = 'Process new data into customer'
AS
    INSERT INTO customer
SELECT ID,Name,State,Country
FROM customer_changes
WHERE metadata$action = 'INSERT';
```

6. Let's schedule this task to run every 5 minutes. We are assuming that new customer data is getting inserted into the staging table all the time and we need to process it every 5 minutes. Please note that to resume a task, you will need to run the command as `ACCOUTNADMIN` or another role with the appropriate privileges:

```
ALTER TASK process_new_customers
SET SCHEDULE = '10 MINUTE';
ALTER TASK process_new_customers RESUME;
```

7. Let's check that the target table, that is, `customer`, is empty:

```
SELECT * FROM customer;
```

As expected, no rows are present in the `customer` table:

Figure 4.26 – Customer table is empty

8. We will now insert some data into the staging table (effectively simulating data that has arrived into Snowflake from an external source):

```
INSERT INTO customer_staging VALUES (1,'Jane
Doe','NSW','AU');
INSERT INTO customer_staging VALUES
(2,'Alpha','VIC','AU');
```

9. Now, let's view how the changing data has been captured through the stream. We can view the data by adding `SELECT` from the stream object itself:

```
SELECT * FROM customer_changes;
```

The following output shows the data that has been recorded by the stream. Notice both rows have been recorded with an action code of `INSERT`:

ID	NAME	STATE	COUNTRY	METADATA$ACTI	METADATA$ISUP	METADATA$ROW
2	Alpha	VIC	AU	INSERT	FALSE	c9801d993af...
1	Jane Doe	NSW	AU	INSERT	FALSE	49e84564a18...

Figure 4.27 – Viewing the changing data

10. Retrieving data from a stream and inserting it into another table is as simple as performing a query on the stream itself. As shown ahead, the query selects the required columns from the stream and inserts them into the `customer` table. Do note that we have used a `WHERE` clause on `metadata$action` set to `INSERT`. This is to ensure that we only process new data:

```
INSERT INTO customer
SELECT ID,Name,State,Country
FROM customer_changes
WHERE metadata$action = 'INSERT';
```

11. Let's select the data from the `customer` table to validate that the correct data appears there:

```
SELECT * FROM customer;
```

As expected, the two rows that were originally inserted into the staging table appear here:

ID	NAME	STATE	COUNTRY
2	Alpha	VIC	AU
1	Jane Doe	NSW	AU

Figure 4.28 – Two rows inserted into the staging table

12. We will now insert some more data into the staging table and let it be processed by the scheduled task:

```
INSERT INTO customer_staging VALUES
(3,'Mike','ACT','AU');
INSERT INTO customer_staging VALUES
(4,'Tango','NT','AU');
```

13. Now, we wait for our scheduled task to run, which will process this staging data into the target table. You can also keep an eye on the execution and the next scheduled time by running the following query. Once the scheduled task has executed, the results will look like what is shown as follows:

```
SELECT * FROM
TABLE(information_schema.task_history(
      task_name => 'PROCESS_NEW_CUSTOMERS'
```

```
))
ORDER BY SCHEDULED_TIME DESC;
```

Once the task has been successfully executed, you will see output similar to the following screenshot. The task that has been run successfully will have a `QUERY_ID` value assigned and a `STATE` value of `SUCCEEDED`:

QUERY_ID	NAME	DATABASE_NAN	SCHEMA_NAME	QUERY_TEXT	CONDITION_TE)	STATE	ERROR_CODE	ERROR_MESSAC	SCHEDULED_TIME
NULL	PROCESS_N...	STREAM_DE...	PUBLIC	INSERT INT...	NULL	SCHEDULED	NULL	NULL	2021-02-15 04...
019a4e7d-0...	PROCESS_N...	STREAM_DE...	PUBLIC	INSERT INT...	NULL	SUCCEEDED	NULL	NULL	2021-02-15 04...

Figure 4.29 – Processing the staging data into the target table

14. Once the task has been successfully executed, select the data from the target table to validate that the rows in the staging table have been inserted into the target table:

```
SELECT * FROM customer;
```

You will see two additional records appear in the result set, indicating that the data from the staging table was processed through a combination of tasks and streams and inserted into the target table:

ID	NAME	STATE ↓	COUNTRY
4	Tango	NT	AU
2	Alpha	VIC	AU
1	Jane Doe	NSW	AU
3	Mike	ACT	AU

Figure 4.30 – Validating the rows in the staging table

How it works...

This recipe demonstrates combining change data capture through streams and the concept of tasks to automate the processing when changes are detected. We started by setting up a stream that captures only inserts into a staging table. The intent is that in a real-world scenario, data from external sources or data via Snowpipe may be inserted into a similar staging table. We next created a stream on top of the staging table that keeps track of the rows that are being inserted into the table. Since this is just a staging table, we would like to take data from here and insert it into an actual table, which we have referred to as the target table. A task is created that uses SQL to read new data from the stream and insert it into the target table. The task is then scheduled to run every 10 minutes. Any new rows that are recorded in the stream are processed and inserted into the target table.

Converting data types and Snowflake's failure management

SQL queries frequently need to convert between data types. This recipe provides us with examples of conversion. Something that comes with conversion is failure – data type mismatches, for example. Snowflake provides a novel as well as a very structured way of handling such failure scenarios, and recovery methods. This allows the Snowflake user to build high-quality data processing pipelines that avoid failures and if they occur, know how to handle them, how to recover, and how to leave the system stable. Let's now look into Snowflake's unique approach to avoid errors during query execution by using TRY_ versions of different conversion functions.

How to do it...

The following steps walk you through various data type conversion scenarios:

1. Let's start with the common scenario of converting a number stored as a string into a numeric value. We will explore the example of converting to a NUMBER type. The TO_NUMBER function takes the input string as a required parameter and can optionally also take in the precision and scale. If the scale is not specified, it will be assumed to be zero. The following query demonstrates the use of the conversion:

```
SELECT '100.2' AS input,
       TO_NUMBER(input),
       TO_NUMBER(input, 12, 2);
```

As shown in the following output, in the first conversion, we did not specify any scale, therefore 100.2 was converted to 100; the decimal part was dropped. In the second case, the scale was 2, therefore the result is 100.20:

INPUT	TO_NUMBER(INPUT)	TO_NUMBER(INPUT, 12, 2)
100.2	100	100.20

Figure 4.31 – Converting data from a string to a numeric value

2. The TO_NUMBER function works great until it encounters a non-numeric value. If it encounters a non-numeric input, the data type conversion will fail (and the query will fail as well):

```
SELECT 'not a number' AS input,
       TO_NUMBER(input);
```

As shown in the following output, the query failed with a not recognized error:

Numeric value 'not a number' is not recognized

Figure 4.32 – Failed query message

3. In order to ensure that any data type conversion errors are handled gracefully, Snowflake has type conversion functions that have a `TRY_` clause at the start. Let's use one of these functions on a non-numeric input:

```
SELECT 'not a number' AS input,
       TRY_TO_NUMBER(input);
```

As the output shows, the type conversion does not fail any more but rather returns with a `NULL` value. This will ensure that your query doesn't fail due to type conversion:

Row	INPUT	TRY_TO_NUMBER(INPUT)
1	not a number	NULL

Figure 4.33 – Data type conversion with no fails

The `TRY_` type of functions perform the type conversion as normal when a proper numeric input is provided:

```
SELECT '100.2' AS input,
       TRY_TO_NUMBER(input);
```

As shown, the output of `TRY_TO_NUMBER` is similar to `TO_NUMBER`; the only difference is the `TRY_` type of functions will not fail on invalid input:

INPUT	TRY_TO_NUMBER(INPUT)
100.2	100

Figure 4.34 – Type conversion with no fails on invalid input

4. Let's explore another common scenario, which is the conversion of string values into a Boolean data type. Snowflake supports a variety of string values as a data type. As shown in the following query, the True, true, tRue, T, yes, on, and 1 string values are considered to be Boolean value TRUE:

```
SELECT   TO_BOOLEAN('True'),
         TO_BOOLEAN('true'),
         TO_BOOLEAN('tRuE'),
         TO_BOOLEAN('T'),
         TO_BOOLEAN('yes'),
         TO_BOOLEAN('on'),
         TO_BOOLEAN('1');
```

As shown in the following output, all of these values converted successfully to TRUE:

TO_BOOLEAN('TRUE')	TO_BOOLEAN('TRUE')	TO_BOOLEAN('TRUE')	TO_BOOLEAN('T')	TO_BOOLEAN('YES')	TO_BOOLEAN('ON')	TO_BOOLEAN('1')
TRUE	TRUE	TRUE	TRUE	TRUE	TRUE	TRUE

Figure 4.35 – Converting string values to the Boolean type

5. Conversely, the False, false, FalsE, f, no, off, and 0 string values all convert into FALSE:

```
SELECT   TO_BOOLEAN('False'),
         TO_BOOLEAN('false'),
         TO_BOOLEAN('FalsE'),
         TO_BOOLEAN('f'),
         TO_BOOLEAN('no'),
         TO_BOOLEAN('off'),
         TO_BOOLEAN('0');
```

The following is the output showing the conversion results. All values are converted into a Boolean FALSE value:

TO_BOOLEAN('FALSE')	TO_BOOLEAN('FALSE')	TO_BOOLEAN('FALSE')	TO_BOOLEAN('F')	TO_BOOLEAN('NO')	TO_BOOLEAN('OFF')	TO_BOOLEAN('0')
FALSE	FALSE	FALSE	FALSE	FALSE	FALSE	FALSE

Figure 4.36 – Converting string values to the Boolean type

6. Let's now convert a string value that contains a date. The TO_DATE function requires a string parameter that contains the date value. Optionally, you can specify a format as well and if the format is not supplied, the system defaults are picked up:

```
SELECT TO_DATE('2020-08-15'),
       DATE('2020-08-15'),
       TO_DATE('15/08/2020','DD/MM/YYYY');
```

The preceding conversion produces the following result:

TO_DATE('2020-08-15')	DATE('2020-08-15')	TO_DATE('15/08/2020','DD/MM/YYYY')
2020-08-15	2020-08-15	2020-08-15

Figure 4.37 – Converting string values that contain a date

7. Finally, let's try and convert to a timestamp. We will use the TO_TIME_STAMP_NTZ function, which is used for conversion to a timestamp with no time zones. Notice that we have tried to convert a simple date string to a timestamp as well as the conversion of a proper timestamp:

```
SELECT TO_TIMESTAMP_NTZ ('2020-08-15'),
       TO_TIMESTAMP_NTZ ('2020-08-15 14:30:50');
```

As shown in the output, if only the date is provided to this function, the timestamp component defaults to 00:00:0.000:

TO_TIMESTAMP_NTZ ('2020-08-15')	TO_TIMESTAMP_NTZ ('2020-08-15 14:30:50')
2020-08-15 00:00:00.000	2020-08-15 14:30:50.000

Figure 4.38 – Converting to the timestamp type

How it works...

Snowflake provides a variety of data type conversion functions. In addition to the standard conversion function, it also provides a TRY_ variant of the functions. The TRY_ type of functions do not fail if the input data doesn't convert successfully.

There's more...

At the time of writing, Snowflake supports the following data type conversion functions. Please note that the TRY_ variants of these functions have not been listed for brevity:

List of data type functions in Snowflake (excluding the TRY_ variant of these functions)			
TO_CHAR	TO_VARCHAR		
TO_BINARY	TO_VARIANT		
TO_DECIMAL	TO_NUMBER	TO_NUMERIC	TO_DOUBLE
TO_BOOLEAN			
TO_DATE	DATE	TO_TIME	TIME
TO_TIME	TO_ TIME	TO_TIMESTAMP	TO_TIMESTAMP_*
TO_GEOGRAPHY	ST_GEOGFROMGEOHASH	ST_GEOGRAPHYFROMWKB	ST_GEOGRAPHYFROMWKT

Table 4.39 – Some of the data type conversion functions in Snowflake

Managing context using different utility functions

This recipe provides you with examples of context management by the use of different Snowflake functions. These functions enable the contextual data processing commonly required in ETL.

Getting ready

The following steps explore the various contextual functions available, their intent, and how they may be used in broader processing.

How to do it...

Perform the following steps to try this recipe:

1. This step elaborates on some of the most frequently used information in contextual processing, which is the current date. Snowflake provides the CURRENT_DATE function, which, as the name suggests, returns the current date in the default date format:

```
SELECT CURRENT_DATE();
```

A result set showing the output of CURRENT_DATE looks as follows:

CURRENT_DATE()

2020-08-15

Figure 4.40 – Output of CURRENT_DATE

2. We can also combine the output of CURRENT_DATE with other processing logic. As an example, the following statement extracts the day name from the current date to determine whether we are processing during weekend timings or normal timings:

```
SELECT IFF ( DAYNAME( CURRENT_DATE() ) IN ( 'Sat',
'Sun'), TRUE, FALSE) as week_end_processing_flag;
```

3. Similar to the current date, Snowflake provides the CURRENT_TIMESTAMP function, which in addition to the date also provides the time component:

```
SELECT CURRENT_TIMESTAMP();
```

4. You can also detect the client that a query is running from, using the CURRENT_CLIENT context function. Depending on what method you are connecting via, the output of this function will vary:

```
SELECT CURRENT_CLIENT();
```

5. You can also find out the region of your Snowflake instance. This will be the region that you selected when you created your Snowflake instance:

```
SELECT CURRENT_REGION();
```

The output shows the current region as Asia Pacific South East 2. Also note that the cloud provider is added to the region as a prefix, which in this case is AWS, and AP represents the Asia Pacific region:

CURRENT_REGION()

AWS_AP_SOUTHEAST_2

Figure 4.41 – Output showing the current region

6. Snowflake also provides security-specific contextual functions, for example, the current role function:

```
SELECT CURRENT_ROLE();
```

The output showing that the query is being run under the SYSADMIN role looks as follows:

CURRENT_ROLE()

SYSADMIN

Figure 4.42 – Output showing that the query is run under the SYSADMIN role

You can combine CURRENT_ROLE() in your view definitions to provide specific security processing, for example, creating views that limit the number of rows based on which role is being used to query.

7. Similar to CURRENT_ROLE() is the CURRENT_USER() function, which, as the name describes, returns the current user:

```
SELECT CURRENT_USER();
```

8. Finding out which database you are currently in is one of the most common actions. Snowflake provides the CURRENT_BATABASE function, which returns the database selected for the session. If there is no database selected, the function returns NULL:

```
USE DATABASE SNOWFLAKE_SAMPLE_DATA;
SELECT CURRENT_DATABASE();
```

9. Finding out which schema you are currently in is again one of the most common actions. Snowflake provides the CURRENT_SCHEMA function, which returns the schema selected for the session. If there is no schema selected, the function returns NULL:

```
USE DATABASE SNOWFLAKE_SAMPLE_DATA;
USE SCHEMA INFORMATION_SCHEMA;
SELECT CURRENT_SCHEMA();
```

10. You can also find out the current warehouse that has been selected to run the query by using the CURRENT_WAREHOUSE function:

```
SELECT CURRENT_WAREHOUSE();
```

How it works...

The context functions provide information about various elements, such as session, account, users, and so on, in the context of the executing query. You may want to perform slightly different processing based on the output of the context function. For example, say on the weekend, you would like to add a specific flag to your table. You can do that via the CURRENT_DATE context function. The results of the context functions change depending on when, where, and how they are being executed.

There's more...

At the time of writing, the following contextual functions are available in Snowflake:

General Context	Session Context	Session Context Object
CURRENT_CLIENT	CURRENT_ACCOUNT	CURRENT_DATABASE
CURRENT_DATE	CURRENT_ROLE	CURRENT_SCHEMA
CURRENT_REGION	CURRENT_SESSION	CURRENT_SCHEMAS
CURRENT_TIME	CURRENT_STATEMENT	CURRENT_WAREHOUSE
CURRENT_TIMESTAMP	CURRENT_TRANSACTION	INVOKER_ROLE
CURRENT_VERSION	CURRENT_USER	INVOKER_SHARE
LOCALTIME	LAST_QUERY_ID	IS_GRANTED_TO_INVOKER_ROLE
LOCALTIMESTAMP	LAST_TRANSACTION	IS_ROLE_IN_SESSION
SYSDATE		

Table 4.43 – Contextual functions available in Snowflake

5
Data Protection and Security in Snowflake

For any data analytics solution, securing access to data is of paramount importance. There are two components to this security: authentication (that is, letting a user connect) and authorization (that is, what objects a connected user has access to). Snowflake provides discretionary access control and role-based access control through out-of-the-box and custom roles. This chapter will explore techniques for setting up role hierarchies, adding custom roles, and setting default roles for users.

The following recipes will be covered in this chapter:

- Setting up custom roles and completing the role hierarchy
- Configuring and assigning a default role to a user
- Delineating user management from security and role management
- Configuring custom roles for managing access to highly secure data
- Setting up development, testing, pre-production, and production database hierarchies and roles
- Safeguarding the ACCOUNTADMIN role and users in the ACCOUNTADMIN role

Technical requirements

The chapter assumes that you have a Snowflake account already set up.

The code for this chapter can be found at `https://github.com/PacktPublishing/Snowflake-Cookbook/tree/master/Chapter05`.

Setting up custom roles and completing the role hierarchy

In this recipe, we will introduce new custom roles and learn how and why to complete the role hierarchy. We will also understand how the role hierarchy works in Snowflake.

Getting ready

Before proceeding with this recipe, please ensure that the user you will use has access to the `SECURITYADMIN` role. Note that this recipe's steps can be run either in the Snowflake web UI or the SnowSQL command-line client.

How to do it...

To create a new custom role, we need to have access to the `SECURITYADMIN` role, using which we will create a new custom role:

1. We will start by creating a database called `DEV`:

    ```
    USE ROLE SYSADMIN;
    CREATE DATABASE DEV;
    ```

    The database should be created successfully.

2. Next, we will create a table called `CUSTOMER`, which we will use to grant privileges on:

    ```
    USE DATABASE DEV;
    CREATE TABLE CUSTOMER
    ( ID STRING,
    NAME STRING);
    ```

    The table should be created successfully.

3. Now, change your role to SECURITYADMIN so that you have the required privileges to create a new user and a new role:

```
USE ROLE SECURITYADMIN;
```

The USE ROLE statement should return with a success message (provided the user you are using has been granted permission to use the SECURITYADMIN role).

4. We will now create a new user, which we will use to demonstrate the role privileges:

```
CREATE USER dev_dba_user1 PASSWORD='password123' MUST_
CHANGE_PASSWORD = TRUE;
```

The new user is successfully created.

5. Log in as dev_dba_user1 and try to run a SELECT query on the CUSTOMER table:

```
USE DATABASE DEV;
SELECT * FROM CUSTOMER;
```

The query will fail as this user does not have the required rights yet:

Results   Data Preview

✖ Query ID   SQL   20ms

SQL compilation error: Object does not exist, or operation cannot be performed.

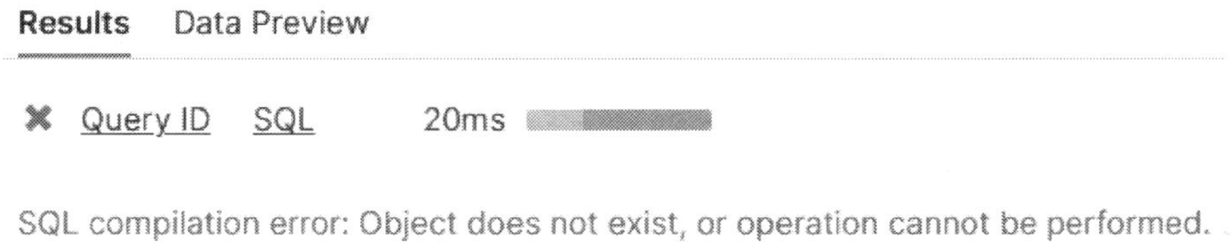

Figure 5.1 – Query failed as the user does not have the required rights yet

6. Log out of dev_dba_user1 and log back in as the user used in *step 3*, who has access to the SECURITYADMIN role. We will now create a new role to manage access to the DEV database, hence the name DEV_DBA. The creation of a new role is straightforward, as shown in the following code:

```
USE ROLE SECURITYADMIN;
CREATE ROLE DEV_DBA;
```

The new role is successfully created:

status

Role DEV_DBA successfully created.

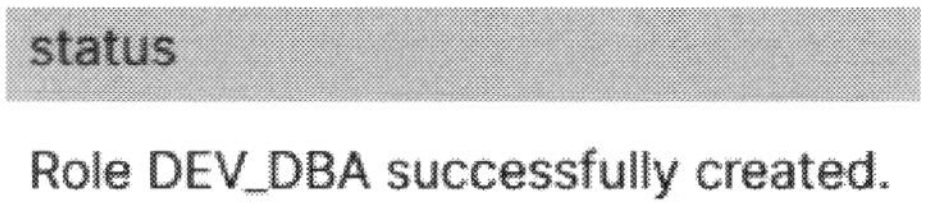

Figure 5.2 – New role created

7. However, a new role has no default privileges after creation, which we can validate with the following SQL:

```
SHOW GRANTS TO ROLE DEV_DBA;
```

Zero grants are returned, signifying that the DEV_DBA role has no privileges yet:

Figure 5.3 – DEV_DBA has no privileges yet

8. Let's now provide the new role with some privileges on the DEV database. We will grant ALL privileges to the DEV database and the DEV database schemas, and explicit permission to the DEV.PUBLIC.CUSTOMER table:

```
GRANT ALL ON DATABASE DEV TO ROLE DEV_DBA;
GRANT ALL ON ALL SCHEMAS IN DATABASE DEV TO ROLE DEV_DBA;
GRANT ALL ON TABLE DEV.PUBLIC.CUSTOMER TO ROLE DEV_DBA;
SHOW GRANTS TO ROLE DEV_DBA;
```

The grant statements should execute successfully, and the output to the SHOW GRANTS statement will now look like what is shown in the following screenshot:

created_on	privilege	granted_on	name	granted_to	grantee_name	grant_option	granted_by
2021-02-07 02:43:0...	CREATE SCHEMA	DATABASE	DEV	ROLE	DEV_DBA	false	SYSADMIN
2021-02-07 02:43:0...	MODIFY	DATABASE	DEV	ROLE	DEV_DBA	false	SYSADMIN
2021-02-07 02:43:0...	MONITOR	DATABASE	DEV	ROLE	DEV_DBA	false	SYSADMIN
2021-02-07 02:43:0...	REFERENCE_USAGE	DATABASE	DEV	ROLE	DEV_DBA	false	SYSADMIN
2021-02-07 02:43:0...	USAGE	DATABASE	DEV	ROLE	DEV_DBA	false	SYSADMIN
2021-02-07 02:43:0...	ADD SEARCH OPTI...	SCHEMA	DEV.PUBLIC	ROLE	DEV_DBA	false	SYSADMIN

Figure 5.4 – Output of the SHOW GRANTS statement

9. Let's now grant the DEV_DBA role to dev_dba_user1:

```
USE ROLE SECURITYADMIN;
GRANT ROLE DEV_DBA TO USER dev_dba_user1;
```

10. Log in as `dev_dba_user1` and try to select from the CUSTOMER table:

```
USE ROLE DEV_DBA;
USE DATABASE DEV;
SELECT * FROM CUSTOMER;
```

The SELECT query will now work since dev_dba_user1 has access to the DEV_
DBA role, and the DEV_DBA role has rights on the DEV database.

We have created a custom role for use by development **database administrators** (**DBAs**).
Similarly, you can set up additional roles according to the requirements.

How it works...

In Snowflake, privileges cannot be directly granted to a user. Privileges are granted to
a **role**, and the role is then granted to one or more users.

There's more...

When creating a new custom role, it is recommended to complete the role hierarchy.
Completing the role hierarchy refers to ensuring that the roles are set up so that all custom
roles are granted to the **SYSTEM ADMIN** role. The concept is depicted in the following
diagram:

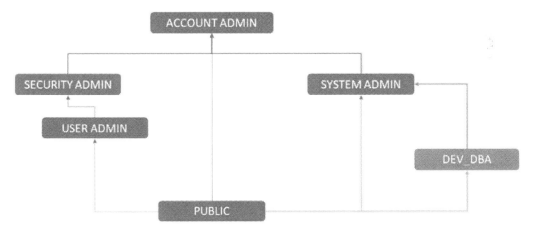

Figure 5.5 – Role hierarchy

Configuring and assigning a default role to a user

In this recipe, we will assign a default role to a user and understand the sequence in which the default role is determined for a session.

Getting ready

Before proceeding with this recipe, please ensure that the user you will use has access to the SECURITYADMIN role. Note that this recipe's steps can be run in either the Snowflake web UI or the SnowSQL command-line client.

How to do it...

To create a new user and grant a default role, we need to log in as a user who has access to the SECURITYADMIN role, using which we will create a new user:

1. Create a new user, which we will call marketing_user1. Notice that no role has been granted to the user, and no default role has been specified:

    ```
    USE ROLE SECURITYADMIN;
    CREATE USER marketing_user1 PASSWORD='password123' MUST_
    CHANGE_PASSWORD = TRUE;
    ```

    The user will be created successfully

2. Now, log in as marketing_user1 and run the following query to view what the default role for the user is:

    ```
    SELECT CURRENT_ROLE();
    ```

    The output will show PUBLIC as the current role.

3. You can also validate the default role for marketing_user1 by logging in to the Snowflake web UI and viewing the available role in the top-right corner under the username. You will see that the PUBLIC role has been selected by default:

Figure 5.6 – Viewing the available role in the UI

If you try and switch roles, you will see that only the PUBLIC role is available to you:

Figure 5.7 – Switching roles in the Snowflake web UI

4. We will now log in as the user with access to the SECURITYADMIN role and assign a new role to marketing_user1:

```
USE ROLE SECURITYADMIN;
CREATE ROLE MKT_USER;
GRANT ROLE MKT_USER TO USER marketing_user1;
```

The role will be created and granted to the marketing user with a success message.

5. Note that the role has been granted only. It has not been set as the default role. Granting a role and making it the default role are two different actions. Granting a role does not make it the default role for a user and vice versa; making a role the default role for a user does not automatically grant it. Let's now make the role the default role for the user:

```
USE ROLE SECURITYADMIN;
ALTER USER marketing_user1 SET DEFAULT_ROLE = '
  MKT_USER';
```

The default role for the user is updated with a success message.

6. Now, re-log in as marketing_user1 and run the following query to view the user's default role. Make sure to open a new worksheet if you are attempting this through the Snowflake web UI:

```
SELECT CURRENT_ROLE();
```

The output will show `MKT_USER` as the current role:

Figure 5.8 – Viewing the current role

7. You can also validate the default role for `marketing_user1` by logging in to the Snowflake web UI and viewing the available role in the rightmost corner under the username. You will see that the `MKT_USER` role has been selected by default:

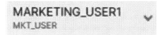

Figure 5.9 – Viewing the role from the UI

If you try and switch roles, you will see that you have the `MKT_ROLE` and `PUBLIC` roles available to you. `MKT_ROLE` is set as the default:

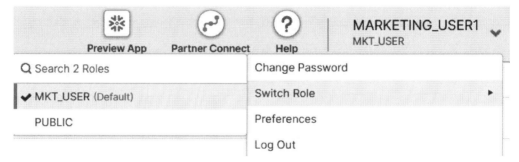

Figure 5.10 – Switching roles

A user may be granted several roles; however, if there is a specific role they will primarily be using, it is useful to set that as the user's default role to improve their experience.

How it works...

Setting a default role ensures that a user's current role is set to the default role every time they log in. This improves the user experience as the user does not have to change the role upon every login. Granting a role and setting a default role are related but slightly different. For a default role to work correctly, you must grant the role separately. Merely assigning a default role does not automatically grant the role to the user.

There's more...

It is useful to understand how the current role for a session is determined. This can be easily understood through the following diagram:

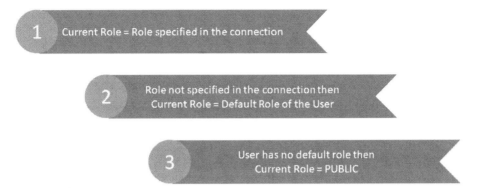

1 Current Role = Role specified in the connection

2 Role not specified in the connection then
   Current Role = Default Role of the User

3 User has no default role then
   Current Role = PUBLIC

Figure 5.11 – Diagram showing how to check the role in a session

The preceding steps are explained in detail as follows:

- If the role is specified as part of the connection and the user has been granted the role, the role becomes the session's current role.

- If no role was specified as part of the connection and the user has a default role, the default role becomes the session's current role.

- If no role has been specified as part of the connection and the user does not have a default role, the current role is set to PUBLIC.

You can specify the current role in the connection string for ETL/ELT jobs and avoid using the USE ROLE statement in every script, helping you to simplify your code.

Delineating user management from security and role management

In this recipe, we will be using Snowflake's built-in roles to isolate access for operational teams that create users and roles and security teams that manage and control the access rights. The USERADMIN Snowflake role provides privileges for creating and managing users without requiring a higher privilege as with SECURITYADMIN. Therefore, the USERADMIN role can be granted to the operations team responsible for onboarding and offboarding users to your Snowflake instance.

Getting ready

Before proceeding with this recipe, please ensure that the user you will modify can use the SECURITYADMIN role. Note that this recipe's steps can be run in either the Snowflake web UI or the SnowSQL command-line client.

How to do it...

We will create a new user to whom we will grant the USERADMIN role:

1. Create a new database that will be used to demonstrate privilege management:

```
USE ROLE SYSADMIN;
CREATE DATABASE test_database;
```

The statement should run successfully.

2. Create a new user, which we will call user_operations1:

```
USE ROLE SECURITYADMIN;
CREATE USER user_operations1 PASSWORD='password123'
MUST_CHANGE_PASSWORD = TRUE;
```

The user should be created successfully.

3. We will now grant the USERADMIN role to this user and make it their default role:

```
USE ROLE SECURITYADMIN;
GRANT ROLE USERADMIN TO USER user_operations1;
ALTER USER user_operations1 SET DEFAULT_ROLE = USERADMIN;
```

4. Let's now log in as the user_operations1 user and validate the default role for the user:

```
SELECT CURRENT_ROLE();
```

As expected, the current role for the user is set to USERADMIN:

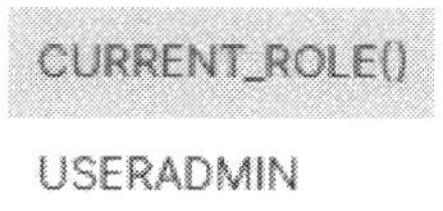

CURRENT_ROLE()

USERADMIN

Figure 5.12 – Validating the default role

5. Let's now try to create a new user using the user_operations1 user:

```
CREATE USER new_analyst1 PASSWORD='password123' MUST_
CHANGE_PASSWORD = TRUE;
```

The user is successfully created.

6. Let's now create a new role using the user_operations1 user:

```
CREATE ROLE BA_ROLE;
```

The role should be created successfully.

7. We will now grant BA_ROLE to the new_analyst1 user created previously and will also set it as the default role for new_analyst1:

```
GRANT ROLE BA_ROLE TO USER new_analyst1;
ALTER USER new_analyst1 SET DEFAULT_ROLE = BA_ROLE;
```

The role is granted, and the default role is set up with a success message.

8. Let's now try and grant BA_ROLE some privileges. Since we are performing this action as USERADMIN, the command should fail as USERADMIN is not allowed to manage privileges:

```
GRANT USAGE ON DATABASE test_database TO ROLE BA_ROLE;
```

The action fails with the following message:

```
SQL compilation error: Database 'TEST_DATABASE' does not exist or not authorized.
```

Figure 5.13 – Error message as the user is not authorized

9. Let's try the same action while logged in as a user who has access to the SECURITYADMIN role:

```
USE ROLE SECURITYADMIN;
GRANT USAGE ON DATABASE test_database TO ROLE BA_ROLE;
```

The grant should be provided with a success message.

How it works...

The built-in USERADMIN role is introduced explicitly in Snowflake to segregate user management from the rest of the security management. The USERADMIN role provides the capability to create and manage users. It can also be used to create and grant roles to users. However, it does not have the privilege to grant privileges on objects such as databases, tables, views, and so on. Therefore, the USERADMIN role can easily be assigned to your operations team responsible for user provisioning. The USERADMIN role provides them with the required permissions without giving them the extra capability to assign privileges to objects. The following diagram shows the hierarchy:

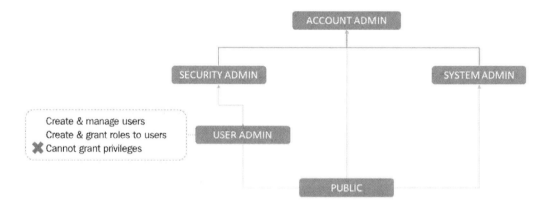

Figure 5.14 – Hierarchy diagram of user roles

As depicted in the preceding diagram, the **USER ADMIN** role is inherited by **SECURITY ADMIN**. Therefore, the **SECURITY ADMIN** role can do everything that **USER ADMIN** does, and it can also grant privileges on other objects.

Configuring custom roles for managing access to highly secure data

In this recipe, we will explore securing access to highly confidential data through a custom role. We will also explore how we can deny access to specific datasets to even the administrative users.

Getting ready

Before proceeding with this recipe, please ensure that the user you will use can use the SECURITYADMIN role. Note that this recipe's steps can be run in either the Snowflake web UI or the SnowSQL command-line client.

How to do it...

We will create a new custom role and demonstrate how it can be configured to control access to sensitive data:

1. Let's start by creating the database that will hold the sensitive data. In this database, we will also create a table that contains salary information:

```
USE ROLE SYSADMIN;
CREATE DATABASE sensitive_data;
CREATE TABLE SALARY
(
   EMP_ID INTEGER,
   SALARY NUMBER
);
```

You should see the database and the table created successfully.

2. Next, we will create a role that will have access to this data:

```
USE ROLE SECURITYADMIN;
CREATE ROLE HR_ROLE;
```

You should see the role created successfully.

3. Let's now grant the necessary privileges to this role. We will transfer the ownership of the database and the table that we previously created to this role:

```
GRANT OWNERSHIP ON TABLE sensitive_data.PUBLIC.SALARY TO
ROLE HR_ROLE;
GRANT OWNERSHIP ON SCHEMA sensitive_data.PUBLIC TO ROLE
HR_ROLE;
GRANT OWNERSHIP ON DATABASE sensitive_data TO ROLE HR_
ROLE;
```

You should see the statements execute successfully.

At this point, we have effectively given HR_ROLE access to the sensitive_data database and have locked down access to all other roles.

4. Let's validate that no other role can access the data. As the SYSADMIN role, try to access the data in this table:

```
USE ROLE SYSADMIN;
SELECT * FROM sensitive_data.PUBLIC.SALARY;
```

You should see the following error:

SQL compilation error: Database 'SENSITIVE_DATA' does not exist or not authorized.

Figure 5.15 – Testing SYSADMIN's access to sensitive data

5. Let's check whether the ACCOUNTADMIN role can access the data:

```
USE ROLE ACCOUNTADMIN;
SELECT * FROM sensitive_data.PUBLIC.SALARY;
```

You should again get an error indicating that even ACCOUNTADMIN is unable to access the data:

SQL access control error: Insufficient privileges to operate on table 'SALARY'

Figure 5.16 – Testing ACCOUNTADMIN's access to sensitive data

6. The only way to access this data now is through the HR_ROLE role. We will now create a new user and add that user to the HR_ROLE role:

```
USE ROLE SECURITYADMIN;
CREATE USER hr_user1 PASSWORD='password123' MUST_CHANGE_
PASSWORD = TRUE;
GRANT ROLE HR_ROLE to USER hr_user1;
```

The preceding query should complete successfully, with a new user created and the HR_ROLE role granted to the new user.

7. Let's now log in as hr_user1 and see whether we can access the SALARY data:

```
USE ROLE HR_ROLE;
SELECT * FROM sensitive_data.PUBLIC.SALARY;
```

The SELECT query will successfully execute; however, zero rows are returned as we did not load any data in the table.

By not completing the role hierarchy, we have successfully limited access to sensitive data to one role and have even blocked off administrative roles from accessing this data.

How it works...

Snowflake recommends that you complete the role hierarchy when creating a new custom role. Completing the role hierarchy means that you grant the newly created role to the **SYSTEM ADMIN** role. This completes the role hierarchy and automatically inherits the role privileges to **SYSTEM ADMIN** and the **ACCOUNT ADMIN** role. This is shown in the following diagram:

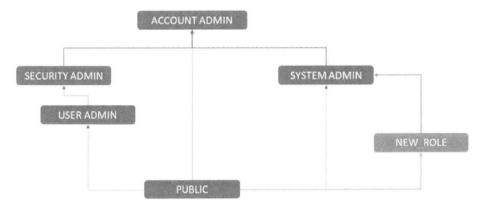

Figure 5.17 – Role hierarchy granting a newly created role to SYSTEM ADMIN

However, if there is sensitive data that you would not like even the administrators to see, you can break the role hierarchy and not grant the new role to **SYSTEM ADMIN**, as shown in the following diagram:

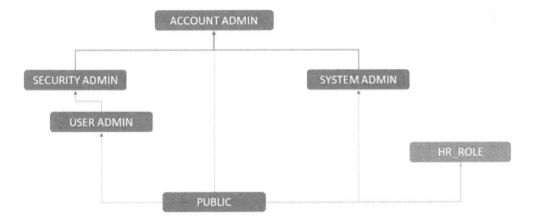

Figure 5.18 – Role hierarchy disabling the HR_ROLE role for administrators

HR_ROLE is not granted to the **SYSTEM ADMIN** role; therefore, **HR_ROLE** privileges given to **HR_ROLE** are not automatically inherited, effectively disabling access for the administrators.

Setting up development, testing, pre-production, and production database hierarchies and roles

This recipe will walk you through the setup of different environments, such as development, testing, pre-production and production databases, and schemas, and configuring custom roles for managing access.

Getting ready

Before proceeding with this recipe, please ensure that the user you will use can use the SECURITYADMIN role. Note that this recipe's steps can be run in either the Snowflake web UI or the SnowSQL command-line client.

How to do it...

We will demonstrate the creation of development and production databases, roles, and users. The same concept can be extended if other environments are needed:

1. Let's start by creating a new user who will act as a DBA for the development environment:

    ```
    USE ROLE SECURITYADMIN;

    CREATE USER dev_dba_1
    PASSWORD = 'password123'
    DEFAULT_ROLE = DEV_DBA_ROLE
    MUST_CHANGE_PASSWORD = TRUE;
    ```

    The user is created with a success message.

2. Next, we will create a role for the development DBA and grant it to the development user:

    ```
    CREATE ROLE DEV_DBA_ROLE;
    GRANT ROLE DEV_DBA_ROLE TO USER dev_dba_1;
    ```

The role is created and granted with a success message.

3. Next, we switch to the `SYSADMIN` role and create the development database:

```
USE ROLE SYSADMIN;
CREATE DATABASE DEV_DB;
```

The database is created with a success message.

4. With the database now created, it is time to grant full access to the `DEV_DBA_ROLE` role:

```
GRANT ALL ON DATABASE DEV_DB TO ROLE DEV_DBA_ROLE;
```

The specified privilege is granted to the role with a success message.

At this point, the `dev_dba_1` user has full rights to the `DEV_DB` database and can create objects and grant further permissions.

5. Let's now create the production database, roles, and user using the same approach:

```
USE ROLE SECURITYADMIN;

CREATE USER prod_dba_1
PASSWORD = 'password123'
DEFAULT_ROLE = PROD_DBA_ROLE
MUST_CHANGE_PASSWORD = TRUE;
```

The user should be created successfully.

6. Next, we will create a role for the production DBA and grant it to the production user:

```
CREATE ROLE PROD_DBA_ROLE;
GRANT ROLE PROD_DBA_ROLE TO USER prod_dba_1;
```

This should complete with a success message.

7. Next, we switch to the `SYSADMIN` role and create the production database:

```
USE ROLE SYSADMIN;
CREATE DATABASE PROD_DB;
```

The production database is created successfully.

8. With the database now created, it is time to grant full access to the `PROD_DBA_ROLE` role:

```
GRANT ALL ON DATABASE PROD_DB TO ROLE PROD_DBA_ROLE;
```

This should complete with a success message.

At this point, the `prod_dba_1` user has full rights to the `PROD_DB` database and can create objects and grant further permissions.

We have successfully created production and development databases. The two databases are segregated, and only DBA users with the correct privileges can access their respective databases.

How it works...

Snowflake's role-based access control security model allows security administrators to configure object security at a role level. Using role-based security, we have set up a development database and production database segregated from each other in terms of access. The DBA user setup for the development database has full access to the development database but has no access to the production database. Since we have given full privileges to the DBA user, they can create additional schemas and other objects under the development database. Through this segregation and role assignment, you can free up your `SYSADMIN` users from development environment maintenance and delegate that function to specific users designated as DBAs for development environments.

Using the same principle, you can set up several different environments, such as test, system integration testing, pre-production, and so on, and manage them independently through different roles and privileges.

Safeguarding the ACCOUNTADMIN role and users in the ACCOUNTADMIN role

This recipe will walk you through techniques to safeguard the `ACCOUNTADMIN` role from unauthorized access and introduce redundancy in the role membership. The recipe will then walk you through the process of securing users in the `ACCOUNTADMIN` role through **multi-factor authentication** (**MFA**).

Getting ready

Before proceeding with this recipe, please ensure that you have access to the ACCOUNTADMIN user. Note that the steps in this recipe should be run through the Snowflake web UI.

How to do it...

To introduce redundancy in the ACCOUNTADMIN role, we will create a new user and grant that user the ACCOUNTADMIN role. Next, we will enable MFA for the newly created user:

1. Create a new user that we will give the ACCOUTNADMIN role using the syntax that follows. Make sure that you provide a *valid email address* for the user. The email address will be used in the next steps to set up MFA:

   ```
   USE ROLE SECURITYADMIN;


   CREATE USER second_account_admin
   PASSWORD = 'password123'
   EMAIL = 'john@doe.com'
   MUST_CHANGE_PASSWORD = TRUE;
   ```

   The new user is created successfully.

2. Grant the ACCOUNTADMIN role to the newly created user:

   ```
   GRANT ROLE ACCOUNTADMIN TO USER second_account_admin;
   ```

   The role is successfully granted to the new user.

3. We are now going to configure the default role for the newly created user. We will set the default role of the new user to be SECURITYADMIN rather than ACCOUNTADMIN to ensure that there is no inadvertent use of the ACCOUNTADMIN role:

   ```
   ALTER USER second_account_admin
   SET DEFAULT_ROLE = SECURITYADMIN;
   ```

   The statement should execute successfully.

4.   Now that the user is created, log in with that user to the Snowflake web UI. Once logged in, you should see that SECURITYADMIN is the default role selected in the top-right corner of the Snowflake web UI, as shown in the following screenshot:

Figure 5.19 – Viewing the default role of the new user

5.   You should also be able to see the ACCOUNTADMIN role under the **Switch Role** menu item, which indicates that the new user has the capability to be ACCOUNTADMIN:

Figure 5.20 – Switch Role options

6.   Now we are going to set up MFA for the new user. To do that, click on **Preferences**, as shown in the following screenshot. You should already be logged in as the new user:

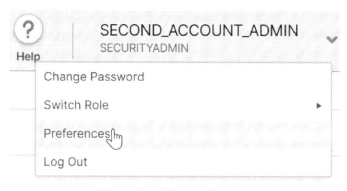

Figure 5.21 – User preferences

7. Click on **Enroll in MFA** under **Multi-factor Authentication**:

Multi-factor Authentication

Enroll in MFA, edit the phone number associated with your MFA account.

Status   Not Enrolled <u>Enroll in MFA</u>

Phone   -

Figure 5.22 – Enrolling in MFA

8. You will be shown an initial setup screen like the following:

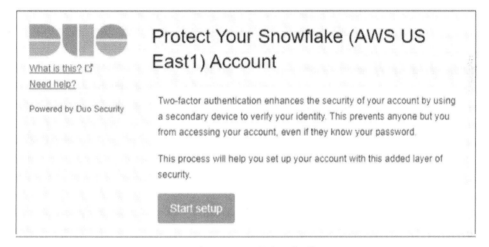

Figure 5.23 – Setting up MFA – the first screen

Click **Start setup** to continue.

9. Choose the type of device you will be using on the following screen:

Figure 5.24 – Device selection

You can choose any of the provided options; however, this recipe uses the **Mobile phone** process, which is the recommended option. Therefore, choose **Mobile phone** and click **Continue**.

10. Provide your phone number on the resulting screen. Snowflake requires a phone number to send SMS token codes used for MFA:

Figure 5.25 – Providing a phone number for MFA

After providing a phone number, press **Continue**.

11. On the following screen, you will be asked to provide information on what type of phone is associated with the phone number you provided on the previous screen. Select the appropriate type and click **Continue**:

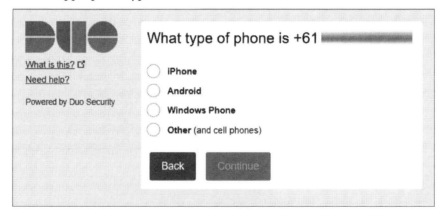

Figure 5.26 – Specifying the type of phone

> **Note**
> The rest of this recipe's instructions are tested and validated for an Android phone, but expect similar steps for other smartphones.

12. You will need to verify that the phone belongs to you. To do so, you can choose to receive a call or a six-digit code through SMS. Select **Text me** to receive a six-digit code as a text message on your phone. Once you receive the six-digit code, type the code in the text box, click **Verify**, and then click **Continue** once it becomes enabled:

Figure 5.27 – Verifying the phone number

13. On the following screen, you will be requested to install the **Duo Mobile** application, as shown:

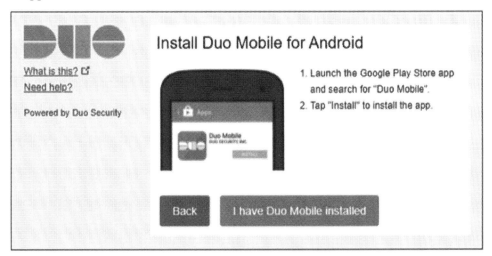

Figure 5.28 – Prompt to install Duo Mobile

Depending on the mobile platform you are using, go to the application store or the marketplace and install the **Duo Mobile** application. Once installed, click **I have Duo Mobile installed**.

14. You will be shown a barcode on the following screen and will be requested to scan it through the Duo Mobile app on your phone. Follow the instructions shown on the screen to do so:

Figure 5.29 – Request to scan barcode

15. Once you have scanned the barcode in Duo Mobile, the **Continue** button will become active, as shown:

Figure 5.30 – The Continue button becomes active after the barcode is scanned

Press the **Continue** button to navigate to the next step in the process.

16. The **Continue** button will take you to the settings screen, as shown:

Figure 5.31 – MFA settings

17. The screen shows your device and the available authentication methods. Select **Ask me to choose an authentication method** from the dropdown and click **Continue to Login**. You will see the enrollment success message shown in the following screenshot:

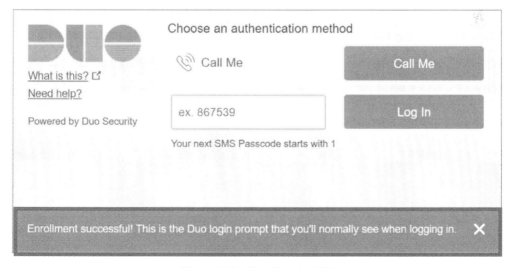

Figure 5.32 – Enrolling in MFA

18. You should see a message stating that a login request has been pushed to your device, as shown:

Figure 5.33 – Enrolling in MFA

Check the Duo Mobile app on your mobile phone and approve the request. Once approved, you will be returned to the **User Preferences** screen, where you can see that the user is now enrolled in MFA, as shown:

Multi-factor Authentication

Enroll in MFA, edit the phone number associated with your MFA account.

Status   Enrolled

Phone   +6

Figure 5.34 – User enrolled in MFA

19. Now, log out and try to log back in. Since MFA is now enabled, you will not be logged in immediately but instead will see the following message on the screen:

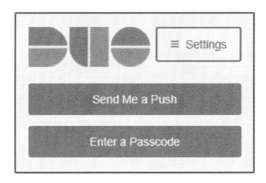

Figure 5.35 – Duo message on the login screen

Choose **Send Me a Push**, which will result in an authentication request being sent to your device. Open Duo Mobile and approve the request, and you will be logged in successfully.

We created a new user with the ACCOUNTADMIN role and enabled MFA for the new user in the preceding steps. You should ideally enable MFA for the existing ACCOUNTADMIN user as well.

How it works...

When you sign up for a new Snowflake instance, the first user created automatically gets the ACCOUNTADMIN role. Since that is the only user with account administration privileges, the recommended practice is to create an additional user with account administration privileges. This is done to ensure that if one account administrator cannot log in for any reason, there is always an alternative.

Once a new account admin user is created, it is crucial to enable MFA for the user. MFA ensures that if the password is compromised, there is an additional security layer that stops any unauthorized access:

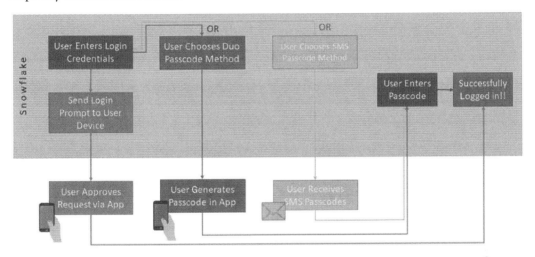

Figure 5.36 – Typical MFA flow in Snowflake

The preceding diagram shows the typical MFA authentication flow in Snowflake. A user can complete MFA through a variety of methods, which include the following:

- Approve a request via the Duo Mobile app.
- Use the passcode generated in the Duo Mobile app.
- Use passcodes sent over SMS.

As depicted, there are multiple ways to provide the second factor of authentication, and you can choose from any of them to complete the authentication flow.

6
Performance and Cost Optimization

Snowflake has built-in capabilities to optimize queries and performance through various out-of-the-box features, such as caching, auto-scaling, and automatically clustering tables. However, there is always an opportunity to positively influence performance by tweaking table structures, introducing physicalization techniques, and optimizing your compute to the maximum. In this chapter, we will explore some of the techniques that can be used to make a Snowflake-based data warehouse run more efficiently and, therefore, at a lower cost. The chapter also explores optimization strategies for reducing unnecessary storage costs.

The following recipes are included in this chapter:

- Examining table schemas and deriving an optimal structure for a table
- Identifying query plans and bottlenecks
- Weeding out inefficient queries through analysis
- Identifying and reducing unnecessary Fail-safe and Time Travel storage usage
- Projections in Snowflake for performance
- Reviewing query plans to modify table clustering
- Optimizing virtual warehouse scale

Technical requirements

This chapter requires access to a modern internet browser (Chrome, Edge, Firefox, and so on) and access to the internet to connect to your Snowflake instance in the cloud.

The code for this chapter can be found at `https://github.com/PacktPublishing/Snowflake-Cookbook/tree/master/Chapter06`.

Examining table schemas and deriving an optimal structure for a table

This recipe walks you through analyzing a table's structure in conjunction with the data it contains and provides suggestions on optimizing the table structure.

Getting ready

This recipe uses a public S3 bucket for a sample file that is loaded into an example table to demonstrate the concepts. You will need to be connected to your Snowflake instance via the web UI or the SnowSQL client to execute this recipe successfully.

How to do it...

We will create a new table with a not-so-optimal structure and load it with sample data. Later, we will optimize the table and load it with the same data and analyze the two tables' storage differences. The steps for this recipe are as follows:

1. We will start by creating a new database and a table that will hold the sample data:

```
CREATE DATABASE C6_R1;
CREATE TABLE CUSTOMER
(
  CustomerID VARCHAR(100),
  FName VARCHAR(1024),
  LName VARCHAR(1024),
  Email VARCHAR(1024),
  Date_Of_Birth VARCHAR(1024),
  City VARCHAR(1024),
  Country VARCHAR(1024)
);
```

The table will be created successfully.

2. We will now create a new file format that defines the CSV format:

```
CREATE FILE FORMAT CSV_FORMAT
     TYPE = CSV
     FIELD_DELIMITER = ','
     FIELD_OPTIONALLY_ENCLOSED_BY = '"'
     SKIP_HEADER = 1
     DATE_FORMAT = 'YYYY-MM-DD';
```

You should see the file format successfully created.

3. Create a new stage that will point to the public S3 bucket. The bucket contains the sample file, which we will load into the table:

```
CREATE OR REPLACE STAGE C6_R1_STAGE url='s3://snowflake-cookbook/Chapter06/r1'
FILE_FORMAT = CSV_FORMAT;
```

The stage is created successfully.

4. List the files in the stage to ensure that you can connect to the S3 bucket:

```
LIST @C6_R1_STAGE;
```

You should see a single file with the name customers.csv listed as shown:

name
s3://snowflake-cookbook/ch6/r1/customers.csv

Figure 6.1 – Listing the files in the stage

5. We will now load the sample data into the customer table:

```
COPY INTO CUSTOMER
FROM @C6_R1_STAGE;
```

You will see 200 rows being loaded, as shown:

status	rows_parsed	rows_loaded
LOADED	200	200

Figure 6.2 – Sample data loaded

6. Let's now see how much space this table is consuming by using the following command:

```
SHOW TABLES;
```

The result will be a list of tables along with the size in bytes that the table is taking up:

name	database_name	schema_name	kind	rows	bytes
CUSTOMER	C6_R6	PUBLIC	TABLE	200	12288

Figure 6.3 – List of tables with the size

7. We will now create a new customer table that has an optimized structure. The new table uses the DATE data type for the Date_Of_Birth field and the NUMERIC data type for the CustomerID field. We have also reduced the size of the other string fields to match the data contained in the table, as is best practice; however, this usually does not affect the table size:

```
CREATE TABLE CUSTOMER_OPT
(
    CustomerID DECIMAL(10,0),
    FName VARCHAR(50),
    LName VARCHAR(50),
    Email VARCHAR(50),
    Date_Of_Birth DATE,
    City VARCHAR(50),
    Country VARCHAR(50)
);
```

The table is created successfully.

8. Load the data into the new, optimized table:

```
COPY INTO CUSTOMER_OPT
FROM @C6_R1_STAGE;
```

You will see 200 rows being loaded, as shown:

status	rows_parsed	rows_loaded
LOADED	200	200

Figure 6.4 – Data loaded into the new, optimized table

9. Let's analyze the difference between the storage of the two tables:

```
SHOW TABLES;
```

As the results show, the optimized table is consuming 10% less storage than the original table. While for a small table the actual bytes difference is not significant, if you consider a table that is 1 TB in size, 10% less storage would equate to 100 GB:

name	database_name	schema_name	kind	comment	cluster_by	rows	bytes
CUSTOMER	C6_R1	PUBLIC	TABLE			200	13312
CUSTOMER_OPT	C6_R1	PUBLIC	TABLE			200	12288

Figure 6.5 – Difference between the storage of the two tables

How it works...

Assigning proper data types to your columns can help ensure that the table is structured and stored optimally. Storing numeric and date values in character data types takes up more storage and is less efficient during query processing. It is advisable to type your date and numeric columns correctly. The resultant storage savings can be quite significant for large tables.

Identifying query plans and bottlenecks

Through this recipe, you will understand Snowflake's query plans and learn how to identify bottlenecks and inefficiencies by reading through the query plans.

Getting ready

You will need to be connected to your Snowflake instance via the web UI or the SnowSQL client to execute this recipe.

How to do it...

We will be running a sample query using the TPCH sample dataset that is provided with Snowflake. The intent is to run an inefficient query, review its query plan, and identify which steps are using the most compute and contributing most to the overall query execution. The steps are as follows:

1. We will start by executing a sample query on the TPCH dataset. Now, I am running this query on the X-Small virtual warehouse, so it may take around 15–20 minutes for this query to complete. It will likely complete faster if you are using a larger virtual warehouse. Note that the sample data is present in the SNOWFLAKE_ SAMPLE_DATA database, which has several schemas under it, so we will select a schema first before the query is executed:

```
USE SCHEMA SNOWFLAKE_SAMPLE_DATA.TPCDS_SF10TCL;


SELECT *
FROM store_returns,date_dim
WHERE sr_returned_date_sk = d_date_sk;
```

2. You will see that the query has started executing. If you click on **Query ID**, you will be shown the unique query ID for your query. Clicking on the query ID value will take you to the query profile page:

Figure 6.6 – Finding the query ID

3. On the query profile page, which looks as in the following screenshot, click the **Profile** button so that you can view the query profile:

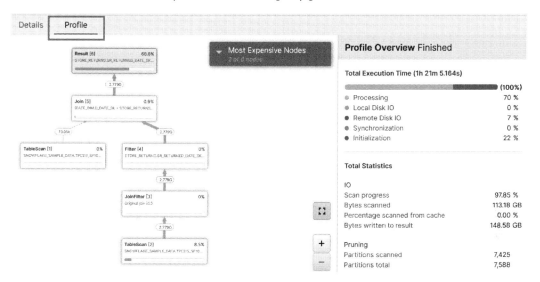

Figure 6.7 – Query profile page

The query profile page shows the execution plan of the query. It also shows information about the most expensive steps in the execution plan, which you can then review to identify bottlenecks and issues.

4. We will start by analyzing the very first step, which is the **TableScan** step. The **TableScan** step occurs when the data is read from the table or, in other words, from storage. Read from storage is usually an expensive operation, and so any improvements that you can perform here will result in an overall query improvement. So, go ahead and click the **TableScan** step to see more details about it. The results are shown in the screenshot that follows. Note that the query scanned 113 GB of data, and it scanned almost all the partitions of the table, which is far from ideal. Also, you will notice the query profile shows 21 columns being accessed, which is a result of SELECT * being used in the query:

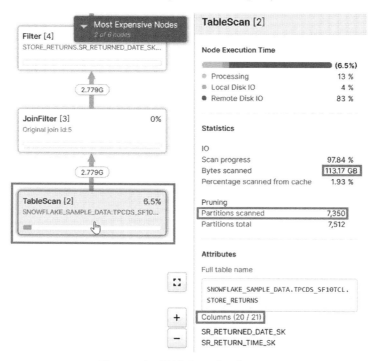

Figure 6.8 – TableScan details page

To optimize the query performance, we need to reduce the number of columns to just the columns that we actually need and, if possible, add a filter on the base table, which reduces the number of rows returned to only the ones we need.

5. Let's first reduce the number of columns that we are selecting. So, we replace SELECT * with just the four columns that we need:

```
USE SCHEMA SNOWFLAKE_SAMPLE_DATA.TPCDS_SF10TCL;


SELECT
```

```
d_year
,sr_customer_sk as ctr_customer_sk
,sr_store_sk as ctr_store_sk
,SR_RETURN_AMT_INC_TAX

FROM store_returns,date_dim
WHERE sr_returned_date_sk = d_date_sk;
```

6. This new query's query profile will show results like what we see in the screenshot that follows. The first noticeable thing is that the time taken to execute the query has come down to 13 minutes from 1 hour 21 minutes. The other thing that stands out is that the total bytes scanned have come down to 19.65 GB from 113 GB. This optimization is a direct result of not performing SELECT * but rather limiting it to just the columns that we need:

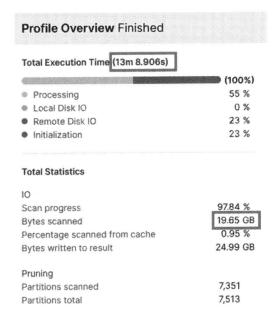

Figure 6.9 – Query profile improvements after replacing SELECT *

7. Next, we will add a WHERE clause to the query to ensure we scan a limited number of partitions:

```
USE SCHEMA SNOWFLAKE_SAMPLE_DATA.TPCDS_SF10TCL;


SELECT
```

```
d_year,sr_customer_sk as ctr_customer_sk,sr_store_sk as
ctr_store_sk,SR_RETURN_AMT_INC_TAX

FROM store_returns,date_dim

WHERE sr_returned_date_sk = d_date_sk
AND d_year = 1999;
```

8. Looking at the query profile of this new query will show the time taken to execute the query has come down further to 4 minutes, and the number of bytes scanned has come down to 3.82 GB due to partition elimination introduced by the additional WHERE clause we added:

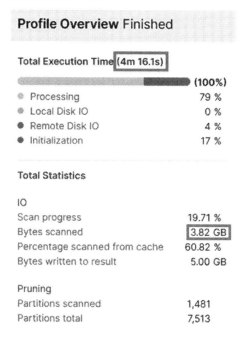

Figure 6.10 – Query profile improvements after we introduced the WHERE clause

How it works...

This recipe demonstrates how to make use of query profiles to identify costly steps in your query execution. Although this recipe demonstrates how to improve table scan performance, you can identify other steps in your query execution and improve them using a similar approach.

Specific to the example shown in this recipe, initially, we were selecting all columns in our queries, which required all the data to be scanned by Snowflake. It is recommended to select only the columns that you will use in the query as it will improve not only the initial table scan but also subsequent steps in the query due to reduced data volumes. Similarly, it is recommended that you introduce any predicates, that is, WHERE conditions, as early in the query as possible to reduce the amount of data. In this recipe, we added the clause to the year 1999, which resulted in much fewer partitions being scanned.

Weeding out inefficient queries through analysis

We will learn about techniques to identify possible inefficient queries through this recipe. The identified inefficient queries can then be re-designed to be more efficient.

Getting ready

You will need to be connected to your Snowflake instance via the web UI or the SnowSQL client to execute this recipe.

How to do it...

We will be querying the QUERY_HISTORY **Materialized View (MV)** under the SNOWFLAKE database and ACCOUNT_USAGE schema to identify queries that have taken a long time or scanned a lot of data. Based on that result set, we can identify which queries are potentially inefficient. The steps for this recipe are as follows:

1. We will start by simply selecting all rows from the QUERY_HISTORY view and order them by the time taken to execute:

```
USE ROLE ACCOUNTADMIN;
USE SNOWFLAKE;
SELECT QUERY_ID, QUERY_TEXT, EXECUTION_TIME,USER_NAME
FROM SNOWFLAKE.ACCOUNT_USAGE.query_history
ORDER BY EXECUTION_TIME DESC;
```

You should see a result like what is shown in the following screenshot. The results will vary based on what queries have been executed in your Snowflake instance in the past 7 days:

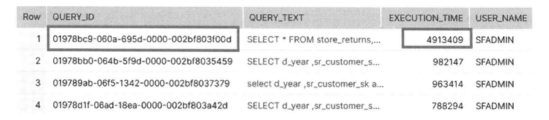

Row	QUERY_ID	QUERY_TEXT	EXECUTION_TIME	USER_NAME
1	01978bc9-060a-695d-0000-002bf803f00d	SELECT * FROM store_returns,...	4913409	SFADMIN
2	01978bb0-064b-5f9d-0000-002bf8035459	SELECT d_year ,sr_customer_s...	982147	SFADMIN
3	019789ab-06f5-1342-0000-002bf8037379	select d_year ,sr_customer_sk a...	963414	SFADMIN
4	01978d1f-06ad-18ea-0000-002bf803a42d	SELECT d_year ,sr_customer_s...	788294	SFADMIN

Figure 6.11 – List of queries with the time taken to execute

You will need to focus on the EXECUTION_TIME column and analyze queries that have taken too long to execute. In our case, we will focus on the first query in the list and try and analyze the profile for that query. To do so, copy the query ID of the query.

2. Next, change your role in the top-right corner of the screen and click on the **History** button:

Figure 6.12 – Screenshot of the top menu

The **History** button will take you to the query history page, as shown in the following screenshot. Change the filter to **Query ID** and paste the query ID that you copied in the previous step. This should bring up the single query in the result set:

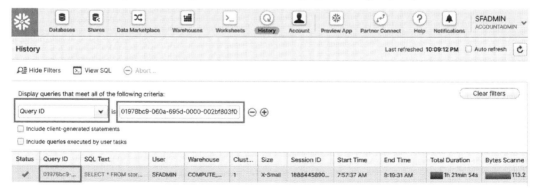

Figure 6.13 – Query history page

3. Click **Query ID** on the result set, which will result in the query profile being displayed, as shown. Here, you can analyze the query for inefficiencies:

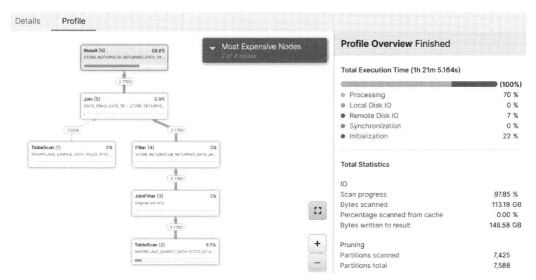

Figure 6.14 – Query profile page

4. Note that in previous steps, we focused on queries that have a long execution time. When improving performance, it is also beneficial to improve queries that execute too frequently, even if they do not take that much time for a single execution. Any small improvements on such queries will result in a much more significant performance gain since the query runs frequently. To identify such queries, we need to group the queries and find the aggregated time. We will remove QUERY_ID from our query for grouping purposes since it is unique and would stop the result set from aggregating. However, removing the query ID removes the ability to look at the query profile; therefore, we generate a hash of the query text and use that as a pseudo query ID:

```
USE ROLE ACCOUNTADMIN;
USE SNOWFLAKE;
SELECT QUERY_TEXT, USER_NAME, HASH(QUERY_TEXT) AS PSEUDO_QUERY_ID ,
COUNT(*) AS NUM_OF_QUERIES, SUM(EXECUTION_TIME) AS AGG_EXECUTION_TIME

FROM SNOWFLAKE.ACCOUNT_USAGE.query_history
GROUP BY QUERY_TEXT, USER_NAME
ORDER BY AGG_EXECUTION_TIME DESC;
```

You should see a result like what is shown in the screenshot that follows. Notice the PSEUDO_QUERY_ID and NUM_OF_QUERIES columns. What we would like to do is analyze the query in row **2**. For that, we first need to find the actual query ID. To achieve that, copy the PSEUDO_QUERY_ID column and follow the next step:

Row	QUERY_TEXT	USER_NAME	PUESDO_QUERY_ID	NUM_OF_QUERIES	AGG_EXECUTION_TIME
1	SELECT * FROM store_ret...	SFADMIN	-7240879760976611795	1	4913409
2	SELECT d_year ,sr_custom...	SFADMIN	-1127835272904793187	6	982147
3	select d_year ,sr_customer...	SFADMIN	-3538599904687560836	1	963414

Figure 6.15 – Grouped queries with aggregated execution times

5. We will take the PSEUDO_QUERY_ID column copied from the previous step and use it in this next query, where we find out the actual query ID:

```
USE ROLE ACCOUNTADMIN;
USE SNOWFLAKE;
SELECT QUERY_ID, QUERY_TEXT, USER_NAME, HASH(QUERY_TEXT)
   AS PSEUDO_QUERY_ID

FROM SNOWFLAKE.ACCOUNT_USAGE.query_history
WHERE PSEUDO_QUERY_ID = replace_with_pseudo_squery_id;
```

The result will look similar to as shown in the following screenshot. You will get one or many rows for the same query text. Copy any of the query IDs and follow *steps 3* and *4* to analyze these queries:

Row	QUERY_ID	QUERY_TEXT	USER_NAME	PUESDO_QUERY_ID
1	01978bad-0667-ff81-0000-002bf...	SELECT d_year ,sr_customer_sk as...	SFADMIN	-1127835272904793187
2	01978bad-066d-354f-0000-002b...	SELECT d_year ,sr_customer_sk as...	SFADMIN	-1127835272904793187
3	01978bb0-064b-5f9d-0000-002b...	SELECT d_year ,sr_customer_sk as...	SFADMIN	-1127835272904793187
4	01978bae-06e6-4669-0000-002...	SELECT d_year ,sr_customer_sk as...	SFADMIN	-1127835272904793187

Figure 6.16 – Finding the actual query ID

How it works...

You can use the QUERY_HISTORY view to identify badly performing queries based on various criteria, including execution time, bytes scanned, and so on. Once you find the query ID of a bad query, use the **History** tab to bring up the query profile of that query and analyze and improve the query.

Identifying and reducing unnecessary Fail-safe and Time Travel storage usage

Through this recipe, we will learn how to identify tables that may be used for ETL-like workloads and therefore do not need Fail-safe and Time Travel storage capabilities. Such tables can be altered to remove Fail-safe and Time Travel storage, resulting in lower overall storage costs.

Getting ready

You will need to be connected to your Snowflake instance via the web UI or the SnowSQL client to execute this recipe.

How to do it...

We will simulate a fictitious ETL process in which we use a temporary table for holding some data. Data from the interim table is then processed and aggregated into a target table. Once the target table is loaded, the ETL process deletes the data from the temporary table. The purpose of this is to explain what the best table type for interim ETL tables is. The steps for this recipe are as follows:

1. We will start by creating a new database and a table that will load through fictitious ETL processes. The table that we will create is based on a sample table in the TPCH benchmark sample data provided by Snowflake. Note that this table is created for interim processing as the intent is to simulate a table that is used to store data by an ETL process temporarily:

```
CREATE DATABASE C6_R4;
CREATE TABLE lineitem_interim_processing (
    L_ORDERKEY NUMBER(38,0),
    L_PARTKEY NUMBER(38,0),
    L_SUPPKEY NUMBER(38,0),
    L_LINENUMBER NUMBER(38,0),
    L_QUANTITY NUMBER(12,2),
    L_EXTENDEDPRICE NUMBER(12,2),
    L_DISCOUNT NUMBER(12,2),
    L_TAX NUMBER(12,2),
    L_RETURNFLAG VARCHAR(1),
    L_LINESTATUS VARCHAR(1),
```

```
    L_SHIPDATE DATE,
    L_COMMITDATE DATE,
    L_RECEIPTDATE DATE,
    L_SHIPINSTRUCT VARCHAR(25),
    L_SHIPMODE VARCHAR(10),
    L_COMMENT VARCHAR(44)
);
```

The table should be created successfully.

2. Now we will create another table, to simulate a table used by reporting tools. This table will contain aggregated information:

```
CREATE TABLE order_reporting (
    Order_Ship_Date DATE,
    Quantity NUMBER(38,2),
    Price NUMBER(38,2),
    Discount NUMBER(38,2)
);
```

The table should be created successfully.

3. Next, we will insert data into the temporary table. Before inserting, we will delete all existing data from this interim table as the intent is to simulate a step in the ETL processing:

```
DELETE FROM lineitem_interim_processing;


INSERT INTO lineitem_interim_processing
SELECT * FROM
snowflake_sample_data.tpch_sf1.lineitem
WHERE l_shipdate BETWEEN dateadd(day, -365,
    to_date('1998-12-31')) AND to_date('1998-12-31');
```

You should see a large number of rows inserted into the temporary table, as shown in the following output:

number of rows inserted

689291

Figure 6.17 – Data inserted into the temporary table

4. Next, we will aggregate data into our reporting table, but we will delete the last 7 days' worth of data from the table before doing so (again, we are just doing this to simulate a real-world process):

```
DELETE FROM order_reporting WHERE Order_Ship_Date >
    dateadd(day, -7, to_date('1998-12-01'));
```

5. On the first run, you will see no rows being deleted as there is no data in the order_reporting table; but after the first run, the DELETE command will result in some rows being removed:

```
INSERT INTO order_reporting
SELECT
    L_SHIPDATE AS Order_Ship_Date,
    SUM(L_QUANTITY) AS Quantity,
    SUM(L_EXTENDEDPRICE) AS Price,
    SUM(L_EXTENDEDPRICE) AS Discount
FROM lineitem_interim_processing
WHERE Order_Ship_Date NOT IN (SELECT Order_Ship_Date
    FROM order_reporting)
GROUP BY Order_Ship_Date;
```

This should result in a small number of rows being inserted into the order_reporting table. However, in subsequent runs, the number of rows will reduce to 7 as we are only deleting and re-inserting the last 7 days' worth of data.

6. As we do not need the data in the temporary table anymore, we will now delete all the data from it:

```
DELETE FROM lineitem_interim_processing;
```

This will result in all rows being deleted from the temporary table.

7. Now, to simulate an ETL process, run *steps 3* to *6* a couple of times. Once done, we will query Snowflake metadata to uncover some facts about this ETL process.

8. Let's query the table storage information from the metadata. Note that the metadata can take 2-3 hours to refresh, so it is best to run the following final steps after waiting 2-3 hours:

```
USE ROLE ACCOUNTADMIN;
SELECT * FROM C6_R4.INFORMATION_SCHEMA.TABLE_STORAGE_
METRICS
WHERE TABLE_CATALOG='C6_R4';
```

The LINEITEM_INTERIM_PROCESSING table shows ACTIVE_BYTES as **0**, but TIME_TRAVEL_BYTES is not 0. Although this table is being used for temporary purposes, it unnecessarily contributes to the storage costs by storing Time Travel data:

TABLE_CATALO	TABLE_SCHEMA	TABLE_NAME	ID	CLONE_GROUP	IS_TRANSIENT	ACTIVE_BYTES	TIME_TRAVEL_B	FAILSAFE_BYTE
C6_R4	PUBLIC	ORDER_REPORTING	1026	1026	NO	5632	0	33792
C6_R4	PUBLIC	LINEITEM_INTERIM_PROCESSI...	4	4	YES	0	245316096	0

Figure 6.18 – Data inserted into the temporary table

9. We can recreate the interim processing table by using the TRANSIENT keyword, which will ensure that the table does not store Time Travel data or Fail-safe data, therefore providing savings on the storage costs:

```
DROP TABLE lineitem_interim_processing;
CREATE TRANSIENT TABLE lineitem_interim_processing (
    L_ORDERKEY NUMBER(38,0),
    L_PARTKEY NUMBER(38,0),
    L_SUPPKEY NUMBER(38,0),
    L_LINENUMBER NUMBER(38,0),
    L_QUANTITY NUMBER(12,2),
    L_EXTENDEDPRICE NUMBER(12,2),
    L_DISCOUNT NUMBER(12,2),
    L_TAX NUMBER(12,2),
    L_RETURNFLAG VARCHAR(1),
    L_LINESTATUS VARCHAR(1),
    L_SHIPDATE DATE,
    L_COMMITDATE DATE,
    L_RECEIPTDATE DATE,
    L_SHIPINSTRUCT VARCHAR(25),
    L_SHIPMODE VARCHAR(10),
```

```
    L_COMMENT VARCHAR(44)
);
```

How it works...

There are three types of tables in Snowflake: **permanent**, **temporary**, and **transient**. By default, a new table is created as a permanent table, which means that it has the Time Travel and Fail-safe functionalities enabled. Both of these functionalities contribute to the storage. In the case of a temporary table used to store data temporarily, it is much better to create that table as a transient table so that Time Travel and Fail-safe are disabled for such tables.

It is advisable to keep a check on the tables in your Snowflake system. Suppose you spot tables with large amounts of bytes in the Time Travel and Fail-safe bytes columns but have a low number (or even 0) in the active bytes column. In that case, it is likely that the table is used as a temporary table and may be created as a transient or temporary table.

Projections in Snowflake for performance

Snowflake offers the concept of MVs for optimizing different access patterns. MVs allow disconnecting the table design from evolving access paths. This recipe shall provide you with guidance on using MVs, their limitations, and their implications.

Getting ready

This recipe shows how Snowflake MVs can be constructed from a table and how query latency can be reduced. Note that these steps can be run in either the Snowflake web UI or the SnowSQL command-line client.

How to do it...

Let's start by creating a table in a database, followed by generating a large dataset to demonstrate how MVs improve efficiency. The steps for this recipe are as follows:

1. We will start by creating a new database:

    ```
    CREATE DATABASE C6_R5;
    ```

    The database should be created successfully.

2. Moreover, we shall execute a configuration change for the following steps so that Snowflake does not use caching:

```
ALTER SESSION SET USE_CACHED_RESULT=FALSE;
```

3. Let's create a simple table called SENSOR_DATA to hold the demo data. The table will have data observed by a sensor, starting with the create timestamp (CREATE_TS) for each row, followed by the sensor identifier (SENSOR_ID), and the third column is a measurement taken by the sensor (SENSOR_READING):

```
CREATE OR REPLACE TABLE SENSOR_DATA(
    CREATE_TS BIGINT,
    SENSOR_ID BIGINT,
    SENSOR_READING INTEGER
);
```

The table should be created successfully.

4. Now that we have successfully created a table to hold our dataset, we can generate and insert demo data into the table. Let's generate 1 billion sensor observations that are randomly generated. CREATE_TS will be populated by a sequence automatically generated by the Snowflake system, using the SEQ8 function. The data type is BIGINT to allow large numbers to be stored. The next column is also a BIGINT data type, generated by the UNIFORM Snowflake function. The third column, SENSOR_READING, uses a definition similar to the previous column. To generate 1 billion rows, Snowflake's GENERATOR function has been used and has been passed a value of 1000000000 (1 billion) to its parameter. This would allow 1 billion rows to be generated with randomly generated data in parallel. *Please note that this step will take some time to execute*:

```
INSERT INTO SENSOR_DATA
SELECT
    (SEQ8())::BIGINT AS CREATE_TS
    ,UNIFORM(1,9999999,RANDOM(11111))::BIGINT SENSOR_ID
    ,UNIFORM(1,9999999,RANDOM(22222))::INTEGER SENSOR_
READING
FROM TABLE(GENERATOR(ROWCOUNT => 1000000000))
ORDER BY CREATE_TS;
```

As a result of the preceding step, a billion rows should be inserted with randomly generated data.

5. Let's now introduce the concept of clustering. **Clustering** is a well-known technique for enabling data distribution into small, *related* storage blocks. We can also say that the data is a cluster of values with respect to a particular column. Clustering generally involves sorting data; that is, each micro-partition will have sorted data. This helps get to a required micro-partition quickly, and sorting allows efficiently getting to an individual row within the micro-partition. Let's first enable clustering on the CREATE_TS column. The following command enables clustering using the values of this column. The CLUSTER BY clause is used for this:

```
ALTER TABLE SENSOR_DATA  CLUSTER BY (CREATE_TS);
```

> **Note**
> This command should complete almost immediately but note that the redistribution of data based on the new clustering key can take some time and occurs in the background.

6. Let's run a couple of queries on each of the columns to understand the issue:

```
SELECT
COUNT(*) CNT
,AVG(SENSOR_READING) MEAN_SENSOR_READING
FROM SENSOR_DATA WHERE CREATE_TS
BETWEEN 100000000 AND 100001000;
```

The output of the preceding code is as follows:

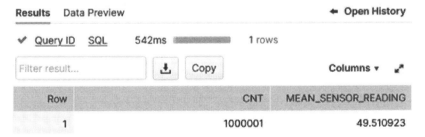

Figure 6.19 – Execution time for a query using the CREATE_TS (clustered) column

Here is another query to understand the issue:

```
SELECT COUNT(*) CNT, AVG(SENSOR_READING)  MEAN_SENSOR_
READING FROM SENSOR_DATA WHERE SENSOR_ID BETWEEN 100000
AND 101000;
```

The output of the preceding code is as follows:

Figure 6.20 – Execution time for a query using the SENSOR_ID (un-clustered) column

7. The preceding queries generate the same (or close to the same) number of records/ average readings, but the query runtimes are substantially different. The second query was more than 10,000 times slower. This provides us with insight that the table is not optimized for two different access patterns. To solve this, let's create an MV on our SENSOR_DATA table, then we shall include the three columns in the SENSOR_DATA table, but this time using SENSOR_ID for clustering data:

```
CREATE OR REPLACE MATERIALIZED VIEW MV_SENSOR_READING
(CREATE_TS, SENSOR_ID, SENSOR_READING)
CLUSTER BY (SENSOR_ID) AS
SELECT CREATE_TS, SENSOR_ID, SENSOR_READING
FROM SENSOR_DATA;
```

The MV should be created successfully as a result of the preceding query.

> **Note**
> Please note that the view creation will take some time.

8. Let's revisit the second query in *step 6* that did not perform well before. With improved clustering, we should see a reduction in execution time for the query when run against the newly created MV, MV_SENSOR_READING:

```
SELECT COUNT(*) CNT, AVG(SENSOR_READING)  MEAN_SENSOR_
READING
FROM MV_SENSOR_READING
WHERE SENSOR_ID BETWEEN 100000 AND 101000;
```

The output of the preceding code is as follows:

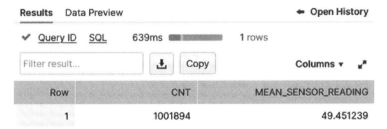

Figure 6.21 – Query execution is faster when using an MV

How it works...

Now that we have had a detailed look at the process for creating an MV for a table, let's look at the internal workings of an MV, shown in the following diagram. We can see how Snowflake manages it and ensures a dynamic link to the original table, as well as reflecting the changes consistently and in real time:

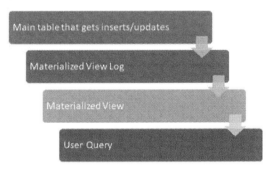

Figure 6.22 – MV internal workings

The link between a transactional table that needs to have an MV is maintained using a log. The log keeps track of the changes that happen to the source table and, in real time, runs the process to update the MV. This is done as consistent transactions and at scale. The logic or aggregation function defined in the MV is applied based on any changes in data in the MV source table.

There's more...

In the preceding example, we had a one-to-one corresponding MV created over our table, which was as good as creating a **CREATE TABLE AS SELECT (CTAS)** table from the original table. The benefit here is that a table created using the CTAS technique is not dynamically linked to the original table. As soon as a **Data Manipulation Language (DML)** operation is executed on the original table, the CTAS table or the derived table will be rendered stale and will not reflect the original table's changes. MVs, on the other hand, are updated systemically and automatically.

Another benefit is that Snowflake has smart routing or query tuning. The Snowflake query engine can intercept queries that are written against the main table, and if an MV is present for that table and the MV can answer the query, it automatically routes the query to the MV.

Another consideration in creating MVs is to use the elastic virtual warehouse sizing capability of Snowflake. This is done as MVs take time to create as data is redistributed and cached. To make the process faster, Snowflake's capability to resize virtual warehouses elastically should be used. In our case, we can add a step before and after the query provided in *step 6*:

```
ALTER WAREHOUSE <NAME> SET WAREHOUSE_SIZE=XXXLARGE;
CREATE OR REPLACE MATERIALIZED VIEW MV_SENSOR_READING
  (CREATE_TS, SENSOR_ID, SENSOR_READING)
CLUSTER BY (SENSOR_ID) AS
SELECT CREATE_TS, SENSOR_ID, SENSOR_READING
FROM SENSOR_DATA;
ALTER WAREHOUSE <NAME> SET WAREHOUSE_SIZE=MEDIUM;
```

Reviewing query plans to modify table clustering

Snowflake provides the option to configure clustering keys for tables so that larger tables can benefit from partition pruning. This recipe will analyze query plans in conjunction with table structures and identify whether a new clustering key will improve the query performance.

Getting ready

The steps in this recipe can be run either in the Snowflake web UI or the SnowSQL command-line client.

How to do it...

Let's start by creating and populating a table in Snowflake. We will simulate data being inserted into the table regularly, resulting in an increased size on disk and an increased number of partitions. The steps for this recipe are as follows:

1. Create a new database, followed by the creation of a table that will hold the transaction data:

```
CREATE DATABASE C6_R6;


CREATE TABLE TRANSACTIONS
(
   TXN_ID STRING,
   TXN_DATE DATE,
   CUSTOMER_ID STRING,
   QUANTITY DECIMAL(20),
   PRICE DECIMAL(30,2),
   COUNTRY_CD STRING
);
```

2. Next, we will populate this table with dummy data using the SQL given in the code block that follows. Note that we will run this step *8–10 times repeatedly* to ensure that a large amount of data is inserted into the TRANSACTIONS table and many micro-partitions are created. Also, note that each run adds 10 million rows to the table:

```
INSERT INTO TRANSACTIONS
SELECT
     UUID_STRING() AS TXN_ID
     ,DATEADD(DAY,UNIFORM(1, 500, RANDOM()) * -1,
        '2020-10-15') AS TXN_DATE
     ,UUID_STRING() AS CUSTOMER_ID
```

```
     ,UNIFORM(1, 10, RANDOM()) AS QUANTITY
     ,UNIFORM(1, 200, RANDOM()) AS PRICE
     ,RANDSTR(2,RANDOM()) AS COUNTRY_CD
FROM TABLE(GENERATOR(ROWCOUNT => 10000000));
```

3. Now that enough data has been populated, we will run a sample query simulating a report that needs to access the last 30 days of data and check the profile of this query:

```
SELECT * FROM TRANSACTIONS
WHERE TXN_DATE BETWEEN DATEADD(DAY, -31, '2020-10-15')
    AND '2020-10-15';
```

4. Once the preceding query is complete, check the profile of this query by clicking the query ID:

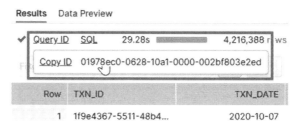

Figure 6.23 – Navigating to the query profile via the query ID

5. Clicking **Query ID** will take you to the query profile page. Click **Profile**, which will take you to the profile page, where on the right-hand side will be the **Profile Overview** pane, as shown in the following screenshot:

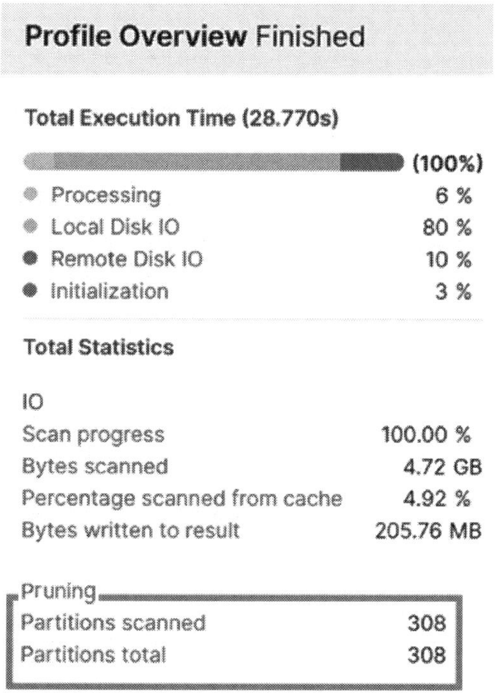

Profile Overview Finished

Total Execution Time (28.770s)

(100%)

- Processing   6 %
- Local Disk IO   80 %
- Remote Disk IO   10 %
- Initialization   3 %

Total Statistics

IO
Scan progress   100.00 %
Bytes scanned   4.72 GB
Percentage scanned from cache   4.92 %
Bytes written to result   205.76 MB

Pruning
Partitions scanned   308
Partitions total   308

Figure 6.24 – Query profile overview

You will observe that the number of total partitions and the number of partitions scanned is the same. This indicates that there is no partition pruning occurring, and there is a likelihood that a better clustering key will provide us with the desired partition pruning.

6. Since our query is filtering on TXN_DATE, we can change the clustering key to TXN_DATE. In production scenarios, you will need to analyze many queries to find the most common filter clause for large tables and use it in the clustering key. For our example, we will change the clustering key to TXN_DATE, as shown in the following code snippet:

```
ALTER TABLE TRANSACTIONS CLUSTER BY ( TXN_DATE );
```

The statement should immediately execute with a success message.

> **Note**
> The re-clustering is not immediate, and Snowflake might take some time to re-cluster the data; therefore, it is advisable to wait for some time before continuing with the next step.

7. Now that the re-clustering has been performed, we will rerun the same query and
    investigate whether the clustering key has improved performance:

```
SELECT * FROM TRANSACTIONS
WHERE TXN_DATE BETWEEN DATEADD(DAY, -31, '2020-10-15')
AND '2020-10-15';
```

When we look at the query profile of the re-executed query, we notice that the
number of partitions scanned has dramatically reduced, resulting in less data being
processed, and there is a much quicker query response:

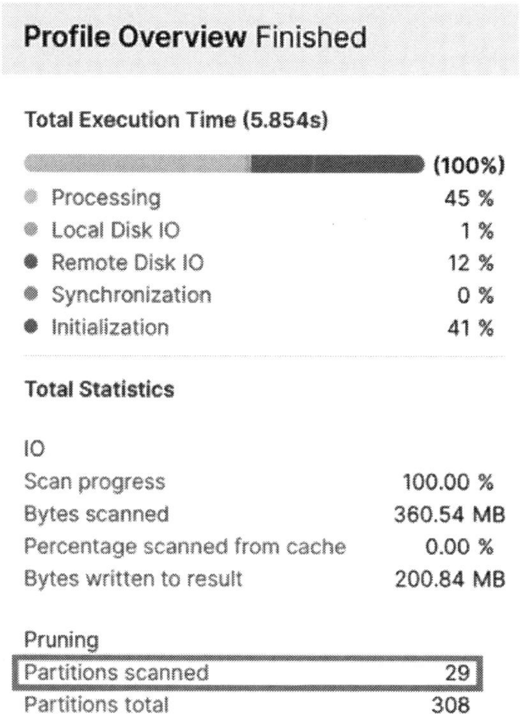

Profile Overview Finished

Total Execution Time (5.854s)

	(100%)
Processing	45 %
Local Disk IO	1 %
Remote Disk IO	12 %
Synchronization	0 %
Initialization	41 %

Total Statistics

IO

Scan progress	100.00 %
Bytes scanned	360.54 MB
Percentage scanned from cache	0.00 %
Bytes written to result	200.84 MB

Pruning

Partitions scanned	29
Partitions total	308

Figure 6.25 – Query profile overview after rerunning the query

The changed clustering key has resulted in only the required partitions being
scanned and therefore improves performance and reduces costs.

How it works...

Snowflake automatically partitions tables, where the partitions are added as new data added into a table. Over time, as data is added to the table, the partitions may not be contagious anymore, resulting in similar values for a given column to be distributed over several micro-partitions. In the scenario explained in the recipe, the last 30 days of data is distributed across all partitions, requiring a full table scan every time, even when a WHERE clause is provided. Re-clustering the table redistributes the data such that the data for a given date is combined into a few partitions. When the same query is rerun, now a small number of partitions are scanned, resulting in better query performance.

Optimizing virtual warehouse scale

This recipe will explore how we can expand the number of concurrent queries that a virtual warehouse can process and identify the optimal sizing for your virtual warehouses. This entails analyzing query usage for each virtual warehouse and identifying whether the warehouse can process an additional load of queries concurrently or is limited. If it is struggling to match the demand from the workload, we will see how we can resize the cluster or virtual warehouse to an optimal size from a processing and billing perspective.

Getting ready

In this recipe, we will use Snowflake's web UI to show how to use different tools to put a load on the warehouse. We intend to use benchmarking queries in this case, which are available with Snowflake. Secondly, we shall be exploring analytics provided within the web UI to help understand the workload and actions that we can take based on the analysis.

How to do it...

Let's start with the benchmarking queries and how to access those:

1. Open the web UI by logging in to your account by providing a username and password. As you can see, there is a tab opened that says **New Worksheet**. There is a plus (+) sign next to it and then a triangle pointing downward to its right:

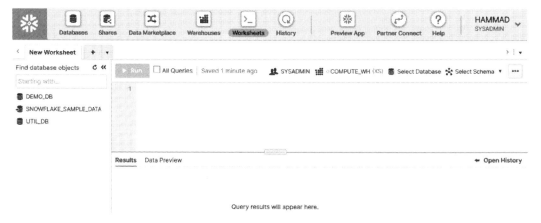

Figure 6.26 – New Worksheet page

2. Click the dropdown (the triangle pointing downward). The list will show you a menu. Then, select **Open Tutorials**. This should show you a pop-up window, as shown in the following screenshot. Select **Tutorial 2: Sample queries on TPC-DS data** from the menu and click **Open**:

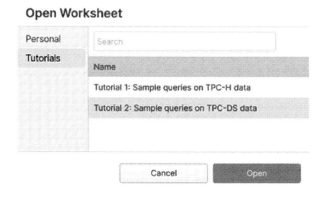

Figure 6.27 – Opening a worksheet

We should see a new tab added to the web UI now. The tab should show commented text starting with /* Tutorial 2:   Sample queries on TPC-DS .... After the comments end, there should be a statement starting with the use keyword:

```
use schema snowflake_sample_data.tpcds_sf10tcl;
-- or --  use schema snowflake_sample_data.tpcds_
sf100tcl;
```

3. To simulate a workload, we shall use an extra-small-sized virtual warehouse and execute the 99 queries one by one. This can be done by copying each query in the statements provided in the preceding step into new tabs for each query. The web UI should look as in the following screenshot, with the **Query 4** tab highlighted:

Figure 6.28 – Sample query

4. We shall start executing these queries in parallel. To do that, select the **Query 1** tab. Check the **All Queries** checkbox, and then click **Run (2)**. The number **2** inside the braces is the number of statements that will be executed:

Figure 6.29 – Executing the queries

We shall execute the first 10 queries from the TPC-DS tutorial.

5. Let's look at the workload monitoring. Click the **Warehouses** button, which will take you to the warehouse load monitoring window:

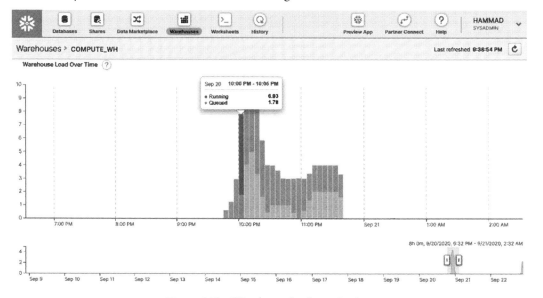

Figure 6.30 – Warehouse load monitoring

Each of the bars in the preceding screenshot shows the average number of queries running on the warehouse and the average number of queued queries during a 5-minute window. The window is represented by each bar. Let's zoom into the cluster of queries shown in the preceding screenshot:

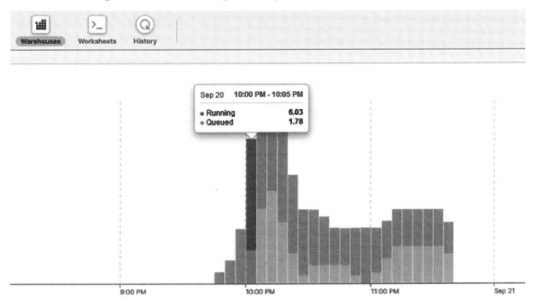

Figure 6.31 – Cluster of queries

From 10:00 P.M. to 10:05 P.M., the warehouse's load from running queries was **6.03** and **1.78** from queued queries. The number of queries queued is more or less proportional to the number of queries running in the warehouse. This shows that the vertical scale is adequate for the workload, and horizontal scaling (scaling out) is required. In such circumstances, it is recommended to use a multi-cluster warehouse. That would allow more queries to be admitted into execution, and fewer queries would need to wait in the queue.

6. The next step is to drill deep into one of the queries and see whether there is
    an opportunity for scaling up (also called vertical scaling). For that, Snowflake
    provides insight into the execution of individual queries. To do that, we shall click
    the **History** button in the web UI. This will take you to the list of queries that have
    executed, are in execution at that time, or are waiting for execution. In this case,
    we'll select a long-running query to explain what aspects of a query need to be
    analyzed. We'll select a running query for this example; look at the last row. Then,
    click on the value of the **Query ID** column. This should take the user to the details
    page for the query:

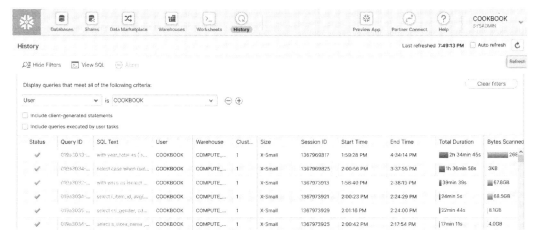

Figure 6.32 – History window

7. Let's zoom in. The query under investigation is Query 4 from the tutorial
    workload:

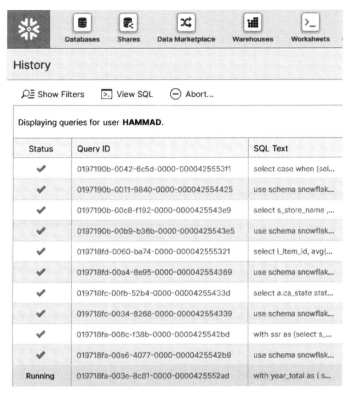

Figure 6.33 – Zoomed-in view of the history list

8. When we click the last query in the list, we shall be taken to statistics collected by the system around the execution of the query and resource consumption:

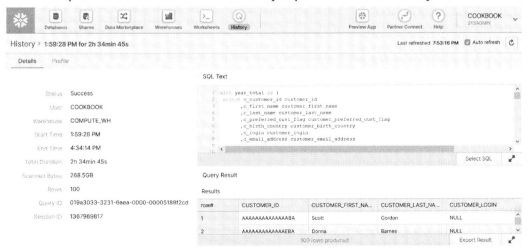

Figure 6.34 – Details page of the selected query

9. Let's click the **Profile** tab in this view. The view will change and show two frames. The one on the left will show the execution graph and different nodes. Each node represents a step in the execution. This shows the steps that took more resources/time. You can click and get statistics of individual steps.

The tab toward the right-hand side provides detailed statistics on the execution of the query. Let's zoom in to the costliest step (a **costly step** is one that itakes the longest time to execute):

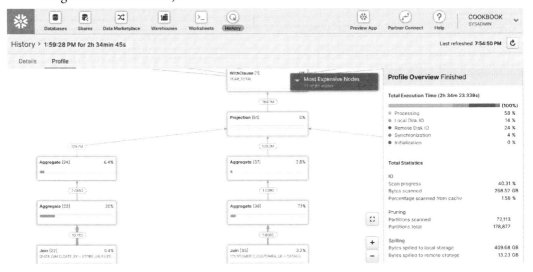

Figure 6.35 – Zoomed-in view of the most expensive node

The details of the step show that processing took 95% of the execution time. The other interesting aspect is captured under the heading of **Spilling**. Under **Statistics | Spilling**, the **Bytes spilled to local storage** caption means that the execution nodes could not fit data into memory. **Bytes spilled to remote storage**, the other metric, means that the amount of data was larger than what local storage could handle. **Bytes spilled to remote storage** is an expensive operation as it involves storing data in cloud storage. If you frequently encounter such query profiles, you can benefit in performance by scaling up the virtual warehouse, which means a larger warehouse size can be used for your workload.

How it works...

The preceding section has shown us how Snowflake enables a user (in a database administrator role) to do the following:

- Put a load on a virtual warehouse.

- Investigate the virtual warehouse for resource usage when loaded with queries.

Snowflake has different ways to handle the challenges of big data. It offers horizontal and vertical scalability. Admittance of a large number of queries for concurrent execution requires horizontal scaling. In that case, a multi-cluster warehouse needs to be configured. In this case, a valid question would be – how many nodes are required in the cluster? The answer would be the number of queries that are queued or are waiting. If we can see that half of the queries went into a waiting state, then the cluster needs to double its size. It is linearly scalable.

The other aspect of scaling is the memory available for processing. In *step 6* in the preceding section, we saw that when data being processed could not fit into memory, it spilled to disk. The amount of data spilled would provide insight into the gap between the required resources and provisioned resources. This gap leads to I/O operations that are slow. There are two levels of spillage, as we could see in this recipe.

The spill to the local disk involves shedding data to storage provisioned in the virtual warehouse. The impact of this phenomenon on the virtual warehouse is not simple. This storage to which data is spilling is slower than memory. Secondly, the operation involved requires additional effort on the part of the machine's compute resources, which would use the processing resource to transfer data from memory to disk.

The next level of disk spill involves storage that is not local to the processing unit. It is remote and is a shared resource available to the different compute nodes on the network. This is an even lower tier than disk storage available to the processing units. Secondly, now the network is involved as well, which further adds to latency in data transfer.

In this case, it is important to provision a virtual warehouse that can handle the data in memory, and local disk spill is limited. Remote storage should be avoided as much as possible as it is slow and adds to the billing of the node, as network I/O slows down the processing, requiring more time, and time is money in Snowflake's case.

7
Secure Data Sharing

Traditional warehouse solutions share data by extracting the data out and sending it over transport mechanisms such as FTP and email. A downside to this is that as soon as the data is extracted, it is already out of date. Snowflake overcomes this by providing a unique data-sharing solution that ensures reduced costs, reduced operational overhead, and always provides up-to-date data.

This chapter details how to share data with other Snowflake customers as well as non-Snowflake customers.

The following recipes will be covered in this chapter:

- Sharing a table with another Snowflake account
- Sharing data through a view with another Snowflake account
- Sharing a complete database with another Snowflake account and setting up future objects to be shareable
- Creating reader accounts and configuring them for non-Snowflake sharing
- Sharing an object with a non-Snowflake user
- Keeping costs in check when sharing data with non-Snowflake users

Technical requirements

This chapter requires access to a modern internet browser (Chrome, Edge, Firefox, or similar) and access to the internet to connect to your Snowflake instance in the cloud.

The code for this chapter can be found at `https://github.com/PacktPublishing/Snowflake-Cookbook/tree/master/Chapter07`.

Sharing a table with another Snowflake account

We will share a basic table with another Snowflake account through this recipe by creating a **share** and assigning the necessary privileges.

Getting ready

You will need to be connected to your Snowflake instance via the web UI or the SnowSQL client to execute this recipe. We will be acting as a data provider and sharing data with *another* Snowflake account, acting as the data consumer. Therefore, you will need to know the consumer Snowflake account and, more specifically, you will need to know the consumer account name.

Since we will be creating and consuming a share, which is an account level activity, `ACCOUNTADMIN`-level access is required on the Snowflake account acting as a provider and on the consumer Snowflake account.

How to do it...

We will be creating a table and populating that table with some sample data. We will share that table further in this recipe. The steps are as follows:

1. We will start by creating a new database, followed by the creation of a table that will hold some transaction data:

    ```
    CREATE DATABASE C7_R1;

    CREATE TABLE TRANSACTIONS
    (
        TXN_ID STRING,
        TXN_DATE DATE,
        CUSTOMER_ID STRING,
    ```

```
    QUANTITY DECIMAL(20),
    PRICE DECIMAL(30,2),
    COUNTRY_CD STRING
);
```

2. Next, we will populate this table with a thousand rows of dummy data using the following SQL command:

```
INSERT INTO TRANSACTIONS
SELECT
    UUID_STRING() AS TXN_ID
    ,DATEADD(DAY,UNIFORM(1, 500, RANDOM()) * -1, '2020-
10-15') AS TXN_DATE
    ,UUID_STRING() AS CUSTOMER_ID
    ,UNIFORM(1, 10, RANDOM()) AS QUANTITY
    ,UNIFORM(1, 200, RANDOM()) AS PRICE
    ,RANDSTR(2,RANDOM()) AS COUNTRY_CD
FROM TABLE(GENERATOR(ROWCOUNT => 1000));
```

You should see a thousand rows inserted into the table.

3. Next, we will create the share object through which we will share the table. You will need to use the ACCOUNTADMIN role to create the share. To do so, run the following SQL:

```
USE ROLE ACCOUNTADMIN;
CREATE SHARE share_trx_data;
```

4. Next, we need to provide various permissions to the newly created share object to ensure that the sharing works correctly. The first two permissions that we need to provide are the USAGE permissions on the database and the public schema in which our table is created. To do so, run the following SQL:

```
GRANT USAGE ON DATABASE C7_R1 TO SHARE share_trx_data;
GRANT USAGE ON SCHEMA C7_R1.public TO SHARE share_trx_
data;
```

The grants should succeed with a success message.

5. Finally, we will provide the SELECT permissions on the transaction table to the
    share object. Note that you can provide the SELECT permission to more than one
    table, which will result in each of the tables having permissions to then be shared.
    To do so, run the following SQL:

    ```
    GRANT SELECT ON TABLE C7_R1.public.transactions TO SHARE
    share_trx_data;
    ```

    The grant should succeed with a success message.

6. We have defined a share and added objects to the share by providing permissions
    on the objects to the share by this point. Now, we are ready to add the consumer to
    the share. To do so, we must first ascertain the account name of the consumer. The
    consuming party will generally provide the consumer account name. However, if
    you are using an additional Snowflake account acting as a consumer, you can find
    your account name from the URL of that Snowflake instance. The first numbers in
    the URL will be the consumer account name, as shown:

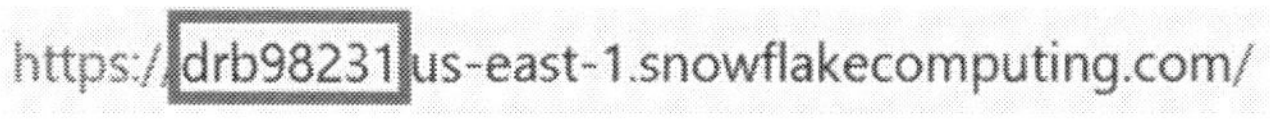

    https://drb98231.us-east-1.snowflakecomputing.com/

    Figure 7.1 – Ascertaining the account name from the Snowflake web UI URL

7. Let's now add the consumer to the share. Please ensure that you replace the
    placeholder text (consumer_account_name_here) with the appropriate
    consumer number. To do so, run the following SQL:

    ```
    ALTER SHARE share_trx_data ADD ACCOUNT=consumer_account_
    name_here;
    ```

    At this point, we have, as a data provider, successfully shared a table with a
    consumer. Our next steps are to log in *as the consumer* and create a database using
    the share so that the consuming account can read the table.

    > **Note**
    > Do note that for secure data sharing, either your consumer should exist in the
    > same region and cloud as the provider account, or data should be replicated to
    > the consumer region and cloud.

8. For the next steps, log in to the consumer account as an ACCOUNTADMIN role and configure the share to be usable, and the shared table can then be queried. First, we list all the shares and validate that the new share does appear in our system. To do so, run the following command:

```
USE ROLE ACCOUNTADMIN;
SHOW SHARES;
```

The query will execute with the following output:

↓ created_on	kind	name	database_name	to	owner
2021-02-07 02:1...	INBOUND	SHARE_TRX_DATA			
2019-09-18 16:4...	INBOUND	SNOWFLAKE.ACCOUNT_USAGE	SNOWFLAKE		
2019-08-19 17:2...	INBOUND	SFC_SAMPLES.SAMPLE_DATA	SNOWFLAKE_SAMPLE_DATA		

Figure 7.2 – List of shares available to the consumer

As you can see, there is an inbound share with the name of SHARE_TRX_DATA, which is the share object shared by the provider. However, there is no database attached to the share. A database must be attached to the share by the consumer before someone can query it.

9. Let's now run the DESCRIBE command on the share to view what is contained in the share. To do so, run the following SQL:

```
USE ROLE ACCOUNTADMIN;
DESC SHARE provider_account_name_here.SHARE_TRX_DATA;
```

The query will execute with the following output:

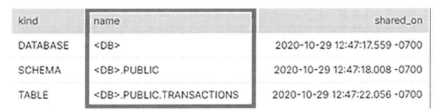

kind	name	shared_on
DATABASE	<DB>	2020-10-29 12:47:17.559 -0700
SCHEMA	<DB>.PUBLIC	2020-10-29 12:47:18.008 -0700
TABLE	<DB>.PUBLIC.TRANSACTIONS	2020-10-29 12:47:22.056 -0700

Figure 7.3 – Output of the describe share command

The output of running the DESCRIBE command shows that the share contains a database, that the database contains a schema called PUBLIC, and that there is a single table called TRANSACTIONS in that schema. Do note that the shared database's name is shown as <DB>, which is because you (as a consumer) have not attached any database to the share.

10. We will now create and attach a database to the share. To do so, execute the following SQL:

```
CREATE DATABASE SHR_TRANSACTIONS FROM SHARE provider_
account_name_here.SHARE_TRX_DATA;
```

11. Let's now rerun the DESCRIBE command on the share to validate that the database is attached to the share. To do so, run the following SQL:

```
USE ROLE ACCOUNTADMIN;
DESC SHARE provider_account_name_here.SHARE_TRX_DATA;
```

The query will execute with the following output:

kind	name	shared_on
DATABASE	SHR_TRANSACTIONS	2020-10-29 12:47:17.559 -0700
SCHEMA	SHR_TRANSACTIONS.PUBLIC	2020-10-29 12:47:18.008 -0700
TABLE	SHR_TRANSACTIONS.PUBLIC.TRANSA...	2020-10-29 12:47:22.056 -0700

Figure 7.4 – Validating whether the database is attached to the share

You will notice that the previous output from the DESCRIBE command showed <DB> as a placeholder. But after a database was created pointing to the share, the describe output clearly shows the attached database, which is SHR_TRANSACTIONS.

12. At this point, we (as consumers) can query the TRANSACTIONS table, just like how we would query any other table:

```
USE ROLE ACCOUNTADMIN;
SELECT * FROM SHR_TRANSACTIONS.PUBLIC.TRANSACTIONS;
```

You will be shown the data from the table, as shown:

TXN_ID	TXN_DATE	CUSTOMER_ID	QUANTITY	PRICE	COUNTRY_CD
ed58ec30-e033...	2019-12-16	385b7145-a53f-...	10	189.00	oJ
26764eb9-768d...	2020-03-25	bcc95cd8-e861...	1	149.00	a5
962427f1-510d-...	2020-08-31	ce705904-6fe1-...	2	93.00	EV

Figure 7.5 – Querying the TRANSACTIONS table as a data consumer

You can now grant access to this database and the table(s) to other roles so that the shared data is accessible by others in the consumer Snowflake account.

How it works...

The concept of sharing can best be understood through the diagram that follows, which describes the steps we took in this recipe. The transactions table exists in the Provider account within the C7_R1 database. The share object called share_trx_data contains the transactions table within. Think of that as a soft reference to the table since the table hasn't been copied or moved, but rather the share is merely pointing to the table:

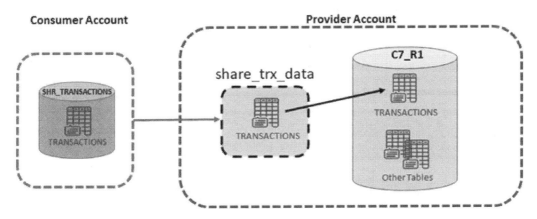

Figure 7.6 – Sharing in Snowflake illustrated

Once the share is created and has all the required objects, one or more consumer accounts can access the share, making the share available to them within their account. However, to use the shared data, the consumer account must create a database on top of the share, which is shown as the shr_transactions database on the consumer side. After a database is created pointing to the share, the tables inside the share can be queried like any other table.

Sharing data through a view with another Snowflake account

Through this recipe, we will share data through a secure view to another Snowflake account. We will create the secure view, create a share, and assign the necessary grants for the view and the share to function correctly. If you need to share data from multiple databases, creating a secure view and sharing it is the recommended option.

Getting ready

You will need to be connected to your Snowflake instance via the web UI or the SnowSQL client to execute this recipe. We will be acting as a data provider and sharing data with another Snowflake account, acting as the data consumer. Therefore, you will need to know the consumer Snowflake account and, more specifically, you will need to know the consumer account name.

Since we will be creating and consuming a share, which is an account level activity, ACCOUNTADMIN-level access is required on the Snowflake account acting as a provider and on the consumer Snowflake account.

How to do it...

We will start by creating two databases with one table each. We will populate the tables with some sample data. Further along in the recipe, we will create a secure view on these tables and share that view. The steps for this recipe are as follows:

1. We will start by creating a new database, followed by creating a table that will hold the customer name data:

```
CREATE DATABASE C7_R2_DB1;
CREATE TABLE CUSTOMER
(
    CUST_ID NUMBER,
    CUST_NAME STRING
);
```

The command should succeed with a success message stating that the CUSTOMER table was created successfully.

2. Next, we will populate this table with a thousand rows of dummy data using the SQL provided:

```
INSERT INTO CUSTOMER
SELECT
    SEQ8() AS CUST_ID,
    RANDSTR(10,RANDOM()) AS CUST_NAME
FROM TABLE(GENERATOR(ROWCOUNT => 1000));
```

You should see a thousand rows inserted into the table.

3. Next, we will create an additional database, followed by creating a table that will hold the customer address data:

```
CREATE DATABASE C7_R2_DB2;
CREATE TABLE CUSTOMER_ADDRESS
(
    CUST_ID NUMBER,
    CUST_ADDRESS STRING
);
```

The command should succeed with a success message stating that the CUSTOMER_ADDRESS table was created successfully.

4. Next, we will populate this table with a thousand rows of dummy data using the SQL provided:

```
INSERT INTO CUSTOMER_ADDRESS
SELECT
    SEQ8() AS CUST_ID,
    RANDSTR(50,RANDOM()) AS CUST_ADDRESS
FROM TABLE(GENERATOR(ROWCOUNT => 1000));
```

You should see a thousand rows inserted into the table.

5. Next, we will create a third database, which will contain our view. To do so, run the following SQL:

```
CREATE DATABASE VIEW_SHR_DB;
```

The command should succeed with a success message stating that the database was created successfully.

6. Let's now create the secure view, in which we will combine data from the CUSTOMER and CUSTOMER_ADDRESS tables. To do so, run the following SQL:

```
CREATE SECURE VIEW CUSTOMER_INFO AS
SELECT CUS.CUST_ID, CUS.CUST_NAME, CUS_ADD.CUST_ADDRESS
FROM C7_R2_DB1.PUBLIC.CUSTOMER CUS
INNER JOIN C7_R2_DB2.PUBLIC.CUSTOMER_ADDRESS CUS_ADD
ON CUS.CUST_ID = CUS_ADD.CUST_ID;
```

7. Let's now validate that the view works correctly. To do so, run the following SQL:

```
SELECT * FROM CUSTOMER_INFO;
```

You should see a hundred rows with random data returned as a result as shown:

CUST_ID	CUST_NAME	CUST_ADDRESS
0	jdmQH5GA1J	LXAYxsldzqseAt1S30TXsc1Qx23n0lyptbXpKoNkbVJogatg5V
1	scCydZ9tl3	gCY89nx7pLYG9rwRSslaxXLJkNexvnQ5DsuWzSkwslu9XBl9lC
2	AHCRo5Vg9S	zhbDyr4Od3ZHZHPRdgCtHv5OTkZsKyeYlejnHJgtHkauzrO4RR

Figure 7.7 – Validating the view

8. Next, we will create the SHARE object through which we will share the view. You will need to use the ACCOUNTADMIN role to create the share. To do so, run the following SQL:

```
USE ROLE ACCOUNTADMIN;
CREATE SHARE share_cust_data;
```

9. Next, we need to provide various permissions to the newly created share object to ensure that the sharing works correctly. The first two permissions that we need to provide are the USAGE permissions on the database and the public schema in which our view is created. To do so, run the following SQL:

```
GRANT USAGE ON DATABASE VIEW_SHR_DB TO SHARE share_cust_
data;
GRANT USAGE ON SCHEMA VIEW_SHR_DB.public TO SHARE share_
cust_data;
```

10. When sharing data from a secure view, we also need to provide the REFERENCE_ USAGE privileges on the databases that contain the tables underlying the view. To do so, run the following SQL:

```
GRANT REFERENCE_USAGE ON DATABASE C7_R2_DB1 TO SHARE
share_cust_data;
GRANT REFERENCE_USAGE ON DATABASE C7_R2_DB2 TO SHARE
share_cust_data;
```

11. Finally, we will provide the `SELECT` permissions on the `CUSTOMER_INFO` view to the `SHARE` object. To do so, run the following SQL:

```
GRANT SELECT ON TABLE VIEW_SHR_DB.public.CUSTOMER_INFO
TO SHARE share_cust_data;
```

12. By this point, we have created a view that combines data from two different databases. We have defined a share and added the view to the share by providing permissions on the view to the share. Now, we are ready to add the consumer to the share. To do so, we must first ascertain the account name of the consumer. The consuming party will generally provide the consumer account name. However, if you are acting as a consumer, you can find your account name from the URL you are using to access your Snowflake instance. The first numbers in the URL will be your account name, as shown in the following screenshot:

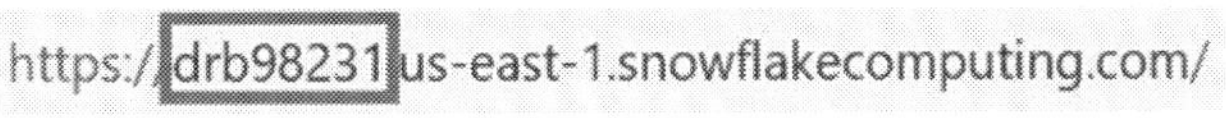

https:/ drb98231 us-east-1.snowflakecomputing.com/

Figure 7.8 – Ascertaining the account name from the Snowflake web UI URL

13. Let's now add the consumer to the share. Please ensure that you replace the following placeholder text with the appropriate consumer number. To do so, run the following SQL:

```
ALTER SHARE share_cust_data ADD ACCOUNT=consumer_account_
name_here;
```

At this point, we have, as a data provider, successfully shared a secure view with a consumer. Our next steps are to log in *as the consumer* and create a database using the share so that the consuming account can read the table.

> **Note**
> Do note that for secure data sharing, either your consumer should exist in the same region and cloud as the provider account, or data should be replicated to the consumer region and cloud.

14. For the next steps, log in to the consumer account as an `ACCOUNTADMIN` and configure the share to be usable, and the shared view can be queried. First, we list all the shares and validate that the new share does appear in our system. To do so, run the following command:

```
USE ROLE ACCOUNTADMIN;
SHOW SHARES;
```

The query will execute with the following output:

kind	name	database_name
INBOUND	SHARE_CUST_DATA	
INBOUND	SFC_SAMPLES.SAMPLE_DATA	SNOWFLAKE_SAMPL...
INBOUND	SNOWFLAKE.ACCOUNT_US...	SNOWFLAKE

Figure 7.9 – List of shares available to the consumer

As you can see, there is an inbound share with the name of `share_cust_data`, which is the share object shared by the provider. However, there is no database attached to the share. A database must be attached to the share by the consumer before someone can query it.

15. Let's run the `DESCRIBE` command on the share to view what is contained in the share. To do so, run the following SQL:

```
USE ROLE ACCOUNTADMIN;
DESC SHARE provider_account_name_here.SHARE_CUST_DATA;
```

The query will execute with the following output:

kind	name ↓
DATABASE	<DB>
SCHEMA	<DB>.PUBLIC
VIEW	<DB>.PUBLIC.CUSTOMER_INFO

Figure 7.10 – Output of the describe share command

The output of running the `DESCRIBE` command shows that the share contains a database, that the database contains a schema called `PUBLIC`, and that there is a single view called `CUSTOMER_INFO` in that schema. Do note that the shared database's name is shown as <DB>, which is because you (as a consumer) have not attached any database to the share.

16. We will now create and attach a database to the share. To do so, execute the following SQL:

```
CREATE DATABASE SHR_CUSTOMER FROM SHARE provider_account_
name_here.SHARE_CUST_DATA;
```

17. Let's now run the DESCRIBE command again on the share to validate that the database is attached to the share. To do so, run the following SQL:

```
USE ROLE ACCOUNTADMIN;
DESC SHARE provider_account_name_here.SHARE_CUST_DATA;
```

The query will execute with the following output:

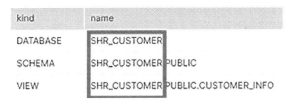

kind	name
DATABASE	SHR_CUSTOMER
SCHEMA	SHR_CUSTOMER.PUBLIC
VIEW	SHR_CUSTOMER.PUBLIC.CUSTOMER_INFO

Figure 7.11 – Validating that the database is attached to the share

You will notice that the previous output from the DESCRIBE command showed <DB> as a placeholder. But after a database was created pointing to the share, the describe output clearly shows the attached database, which in this case is SHR_CUSTOMER.

18. At this point, we (as consumers) can query the CUSTOMER_INFO view, just like how we would query any other table:

```
USE ROLE ACCOUNTADMIN;
SELECT * FROM SHR_CUSTOMER.PUBLIC.CUSTOMER_INFO;
```

You will be shown the data from the view, as shown:

CUST_ID	CUST_NAME	CUST_ADDRESS
0	jdmQH5GA1J	LXAYxsldzqseAt1S30TXsc1Qx23n0lyptbXpKoNkbVJogatg5V
1	scCydZ9tl3	gCY89nx7pLYG9rwRSslaxXLJkNexvnQ5DsuWzSkwslu9XBI9IC
2	AHCRo5Vg9S	zhbDyr4Od3ZHZHPRdgCtHv5OTkZsKyeYlejnHJgtHkauzrO4RR

Figure 7.12 – Querying the CUSTOMER_INFO view as a consumer

19. You can now grant access to this database and the view to other roles so that the shared data is accessible by others in the consumer Snowflake account.

How it works...

A variety of objects can be shared with a consumer through Snowflake data sharing, including sharing entire databases, entire schemas, individual tables, and views. Sharing a view is somewhat similar to how a table is shared; however, some additional steps are required when sharing data through a view.

A view that is created for sharing must be created as a **secure view**. A secure view removes some of the internal query optimizations, allowing users to view the data from the tables underlying the view. When sharing a view, the data from tables underlying the view shouldn't be exposed; therefore, a secure view is required for sharing.

Additionally, you must grant reference usage to the share object on the tables underlying the view so that the share can run the SQL in the view definition successfully.

Sharing a complete database with another Snowflake account and setting up future objects to be shareable

We will share a complete database through this recipe and include all the schemas, tables, and views within that database. We will also provide a method so that future objects in the database can be automatically shared.

Getting ready

You will need to be connected to your Snowflake instance via the web UI or the SnowSQL client to execute this recipe. We will be acting as a data provider and sharing data with another Snowflake account, acting as the data consumer. Therefore, you will need to know the consumer Snowflake account and, more specifically, you will need to know the consumer account name.

Since we will be creating and consuming a share, which is an account level activity, ACCOUNTADMIN-level access is required on the Snowflake account acting as a provider and on the consumer Snowflake account.

How to do it...

We will be creating a database with a single table contained in the database initially. We will share the database first and then create another table in the database. Then we will demonstrate how to share this new (and other future tables) by running a simple GRANT statement. The steps are as follows:

1. We will start by creating a new database, followed by the creation of a sample table:

```
USE ROLE ACCOUNTADMIN;
CREATE DATABASE C7_R3;
CREATE TABLE CUSTOMER
(
    CUST_ID NUMBER,
    CUST_NAME STRING
);
```

2. Next, we will create the SHARE object through which we will share the table. You will need to use the ACCOUNTADMIN role to create the share. To do so, run the following SQL:

```
USE ROLE ACCOUNTADMIN;
CREATE SHARE share_cust_database;
```

3. Next, we need to provide various permissions to the newly created share object to ensure that the sharing works correctly. The two permissions that we need to provide are the USAGE permissions on the database and the public schema in which our table is created. To do so, run the following SQL:

```
GRANT USAGE ON DATABASE C7_R3 TO SHARE share_cust_
database;
GRANT USAGE ON SCHEMA C7_R3.public TO SHARE share_cust_
database;
```

4. Next, we will provide the SELECT permissions on all existing tables to the share object. To do so, run the following SQL:

```
GRANT SELECT ON ALL TABLES IN SCHEMA C7_R3.public TO
SHARE share_cust_database;
```

5.   We have defined a share and added objects to the share by providing permissions on the objects to the share by this point. Now, we are ready to add the consumer to the share. To do so, we must first ascertain the account name of the consumer. The consuming party will generally provide the consumer account name. However, if you are acting as a consumer, you can find your account name from the URL you are using to access your Snowflake instance. The first numbers in the URL will be your account name, as shown in the following screenshot:

https://drb98231 us-east-1.snowflakecomputing.com/

Figure 7.13 – Ascertaining the account name from the Snowflake web UI URL

6.   Let's now add the consumer to the share. Please ensure that you replace the placeholder text with the appropriate consumer number. To do so, run the following SQL:

```
ALTER SHARE share_cust_database ADD ACCOUNT=consumer_
account_name_here;
```

At this point, we have, as a data provider, successfully shared a database and existing table(s) contained in that database with a consumer.

7.   Let's now run the DESCRIBE command on the share object to see what tables are being shared. To do so, run the following command:

```
DESC SHARE share_cust_database;
```

The query will execute with the following output:

kind	name
DATABASE	C7_R3
SCHEMA	C7_R3.PUBLIC
TABLE	C7_R3.PUBLIC.CUSTOMER

Figure 7.14 – List of objects contained in the share

You will notice a single table by the name of CUSTOMER, which is part of the share.

8. Now we will create an additional table in the shared database to demonstrate how to share future tables. To do so, run the following SQL:

```
USE C7_R3;
CREATE TABLE CUSTOMER_ADDRESS
(
    CUST_ID NUMBER,
    CUST_ADDRESS STRING
);
```

9. Now that we have added a new table to the shared database, let's check whether the new table is automatically shared. To do so, run the following command:

```
DESC SHARE share_cust_database;
```

The query will execute with the following output:

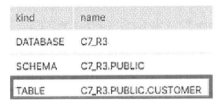

kind	name
DATABASE	C7_R3
SCHEMA	C7_R3.PUBLIC
TABLE	C7_R3.PUBLIC.CUSTOMER

Figure 7.15 – New table NOT added to the share

As you can see, there is still only a single table shared by the name of CUSTOMER and the CUSTOMER_ADDRESS table is not added to the share automatically:

1. To ensure that any newly created table(s) are added to the share, we need to provide the SELECT permissions on all existing tables in the database to the share object. To do so, run the following SQL:

```
GRANT SELECT ON ALL TABLES IN SCHEMA C7_R3.public TO
SHARE share_cust_database;
```

Note that this GRANT statement affected two objects. If there were more tables in the database, the count would accordingly be higher.

2. Let's again check whether the new table is now added to the share. To do so, run the following command:

```
DESC SHARE share_cust_database;
```

The query will execute with the following output:

kind	name
DATABASE	C7_R3
SCHEMA	C7_R3.PUBLIC
TABLE	C7_R3.PUBLIC.CUSTOMER
TABLE	C7_R3.PUBLIC.CUSTOMER_ADDRESS

Figure 7.16 – New table added to the share after privileges granted

You will now see that both tables are shared and will be available to the consumers of the share.

You can configure the statement in *step 10* to execute on a recurring schedule using Snowflake's tasks feature. This will ensure that any new tables in the database are automatically shared.

How it works...

Snowflake does not add newly added tables and views to a share object automatically. This is by design and likely done to ensure that new objects' security is not inadvertently compromised. Suppose you have requirements that all objects (existing and new) in a particular database should be shared with the consumers. In that case, you can run the GRANT SELECT ON ALL statement regularly to ensure that any new tables get shared. Alternatively, you can also use the Task functionality in Snowflake to schedule this statement's execution at regular intervals.

It is worth noting that Snowflake does provide a mechanism through which you can grant privileges on future objects in a database; however, that mechanism is not valid for share objects.

Creating reader accounts and configuring them for non-Snowflake sharing

Through this recipe, you will create a new reader account and configure the reader account to prepare it for sharing data with non-Snowflake customers.

Getting ready

You will need to be connected to your Snowflake instance via the web UI or the SnowSQL client to execute this recipe. We will act as a data provider and create a reader account subsequently used to share data with non-Snowflake users.

Since we will be creating a reader account, which is an account level activity, ACCOUNTADMIN-level access is required.

How to do it...

We will be utilizing the Snowflake web UI to create this new **Reader** account. The steps are as follows:

1. Ensure that you are logged in as a user who has access to the ACCOUNTADMIN role, and that you have changed the effective role to ACCOUNTADMIN in the top-right corner of the Snowflake web UI, as shown in the following screenshot:

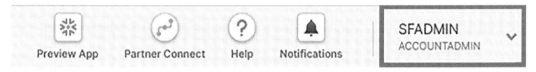

Figure 7.17 – Role selection in the top-right corner of the Snowflake web UI

2. Next, click the **Account** button on the top bar, as shown in the following screenshot:

Figure 7.18 – Clicking the Account button

3. Next, you will be shown a screen with several sub-tabs, as shown in the following screenshot. Click **Reader Accounts** and then click **Create Reader Account**:

Figure 7.19 – Creating a reader account

4. On the **Create Reader Account** page, enter the required details. The most important details on this page are the username and the password. Note that this username will be the ACCOUNTADMIN role for the newly created reader account and will be required to log in to the reader account and set up additional users. After adding the requisite detail, click **Create Account**:

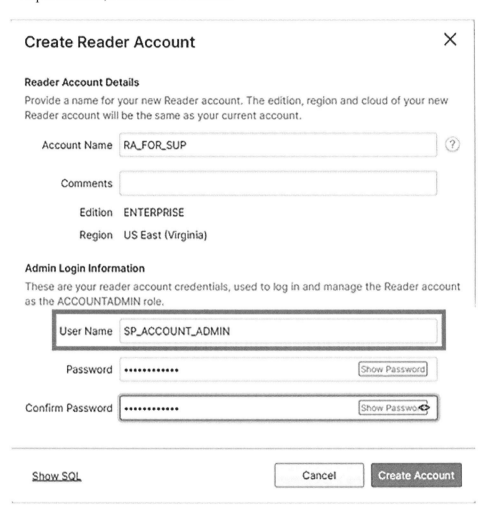

Figure 7.20 – Create Reader Account page

After waiting for around 30 seconds, you will be shown a congratulations message with the account URL and the locator (as shown in the following screenshot). Please note these values as you will need the account URL to access the reader account web UI, and you will need the locator for sharing:

Congratulations!   ✕

You have created a new reader account "TEST_R".

Account URL   https://lg09726.ap-southeast-2.snowflakecomputing.com

Locator   LG09726 ⦰

What's next?

○ Visit the secure shares page to create and provide access to your secure share.

○ Once you are able to access your reader account, log in and ensure it's ready for your data consumers.

Done

Figure 7.21 – Account URL and locator

Click on the account URL to access the reader account web UI and log in using the username we created in the previous step.

> **Note**
> Please note that it can take some time to provision a reader account, and until it is provisioned, you might get a 403 forbidden error message when trying to access it.

5. Upon login, you will be shown the following welcome screen. Please select **Dismiss** and follow the further steps given in this recipe. Alternatively, you can select **I'm a Data Provider** at this screen and follow the instructions provided by Snowflake:

Minimize ↗

Welcome to your reader account

Reader accounts allow you to prepare secure shares and explore shared data sets. To get started, tell us who you are:

I'm a Data Provider   I'm a Data Consumer

Dismiss

Figure 7.22 – Reader account welcome screen

6. A newly created reader account only contains a single user acting as the reader account's administrative user. In the same way as we set up a regular Snowflake account, we must create new users and other objects to configure the reader account properly. First, we will need to create a new user and grant them the SYSADMIN and SECURITYADMIN roles. This new user will act as the administrator for the reader account and will be able to create and manage objects and users as required. To do so, run the following SQL:

```
USE ROLE SECURITYADMIN;
CREATE USER SP_SYSADMIN PASSWORD='abc123' DEFAULT_ROLE =
SYSADMIN MUST_CHANGE_PASSWORD = TRUE;
```

You should see a message stating that the user was created successfully.

7. Now we will grant this new user the SYSADMIN and SECURITYADMIN roles so that the user can create new objects and new users within the reader account. To do so, run the following SQL:

```
GRANT ROLE SYSADMIN TO USER SP_SYSADMIN;
GRANT ROLE SECURITYADMIN TO USER SP_SYSADMIN;
```

You will see a success message stating that the statement was executed successfully. The SP_SYSADMIN user can now use both the SYSADMIN and SECURITYADMIN roles. Note that we reused the same user for both roles. If required, you can create separate users against each of these roles.

8. Now, the final steps are to create a virtual warehouse for the reader account since the reader account does not have a virtual warehouse by default. To create the virtual warehouse, run the following SQL:

```
USE ROLE ACCOUNTADMIN;
CREATE WAREHOUSE SP_VW WITH
WAREHOUSE_SIZE = 'SMALL' WAREHOUSE_TYPE = 'STANDARD'
AUTO_SUSPEND = 300 AUTO_RESUME = TRUE
INITIALLY_SUSPENDED = TRUE;
```

Note that we have created a small standard virtual warehouse to conserve costs. You can create a virtual warehouse as per your needs.

9. Since we are creating a virtual warehouse as the ACCOUNTADMIN role, we must grant other roles privileges to this virtual warehouse. Which roles you grant privileges to will be dependent on your requirements. In this case, we will grant USAGE privileges to the PUBLIC role so that any user in the reader account can use the virtual warehouse. We will also grant ALL privileges in the virtual warehouse to the SYSADMIN role so that the SYSADMIN role can manage the virtual warehouse. To do so, run the following SQL:

```
GRANT USAGE ON WAREHOUSE SP_VW TO ROLE PUBLIC;
GRANT ALL ON WAREHOUSE SP_VW TO ROLE SYSADMIN;
```

You will see a success message stating that the statements were executed successfully.

We have configured the reader account and created a new user with SYSADMIN and SECURITYADMIN privileges. We have created a new virtual warehouse that users in the reader account can use to run their queries. You can now share data from the provider account to the reader account as you would typically do with any other consumer account. You will follow that by creating users in the reader account who will be querying that shared data.

How it works...

Snowflake provides various methods for sharing data, including sharing with other Snowflake customers, and sharing with non-Snowflake customers. While sharing with another Snowflake customer is a straightforward process, it is slightly more involved for a non-Snowflake customer.

When sharing with a non-Snowflake customer, a method must allow them to log in and access the shared data. Snowflake enables access for non-Snowflake customers through **Reader** account(s), which you can consider as a child of your Snowflake account. A Reader account has its own URL through which it is accessed. By default, the Reader account has no virtual warehouses, databases, or users other than the administrative user created as part of the Reader account configuration process. Therefore, you must set up a new virtual warehouse in a Reader account and create users and roles if required. Note that a Reader account's computing costs are charged to the Snowflake account that created it, so monitor and restrict the compute usage in the Reader account.

Once the reader account is all set up, sharing data is relatively straightforward and simply requires the reader's account name. The account name is used in the sharing statement to enable sharing.

Sharing an object with a non-Snowflake user

Snowflake has support for sharing data with other Snowflake users and users who are not using Snowflake already. When sharing with a non-Snowflake user, a reader account must be created through which non-Snowflake users can access the shared data.

We will create a new reader account through this recipe, and then we will share a table and a view with the reader account and we will grant the required privileges.

Getting ready

You will need to be connected to your Snowflake instance via the web UI or the SnowSQL client to execute this recipe. We will act as a data provider and create a reader account that can be subsequently used to share data with non-Snowflake users.

Since we will be creating a reader account, which is an account level activity, ACCOUNTADMIN-level access is required.

How to do it...

To share data with a non-Snowflake user, the first step is to set up a reader account, with which we can then share the data. The steps for this recipe are as follows:

1. We will start by creating a new reader account. To do so, run the following SQL:

    ```
    USE ROLE ACCOUNTADMIN;
    CREATE MANAGED ACCOUNT SH_NON_SF_ACCOUNT TYPE=READER,
    ADMIN_NAME = 'READER_ADMIN',
    ADMIN_PASSWORD='<password_of_your_choice>';
    ```

    The command should succeed with the following message. Please make a note of the accountName and loginUrl values from the output:

Row	status
1	{"accountName": BE52113 "loginUrl": https://be52113.ap-southeast-2.snowflakecomputing.com }

Figure 7.23 – New reader account created

From the preceding output, BE52113 is the account identifier, and https://be52113.ap-southeast-2.snowflakecomputing.com is the URL through which you will be accessing the reader account.

2. Next, use a browser to navigate to the URL in the preceding step and log in using the username and password you supplied in *step 1*.

> **Note**
>
> Please note that it can take some time to provision a reader account, and until it is provisioned, you might get a 403 forbidden error message when trying to access it.

3. We will create a virtual warehouse for the reader account since the reader account does not have a virtual warehouse by default. To create the virtual warehouse, run the following SQL:

```
USE ROLE ACCOUNTADMIN;
CREATE WAREHOUSE SP_VW WITH
WAREHOUSE_SIZE = 'SMALL' WAREHOUSE_TYPE = 'STANDARD'
AUTO_SUSPEND = 300 AUTO_RESUME = TRUE
INITIALLY_SUSPENDED = TRUE;
```

Note that we have created a small standard virtual warehouse to conserve costs. You can create a virtual warehouse as per your needs.

4. Since we are creating a virtual warehouse as the ACCOUNTADMIN role, we must grant other role privileges to this virtual warehouse. Which roles you grant privileges to will be dependent on your requirements. In this case, we will grant USAGE privileges to the PUBLIC role so that any user in the reader account can use the virtual warehouse. We will also grant ALL privileges in the virtual warehouse to the SYSADMIN role so that the SYSADMIN role can manage the virtual warehouse. To do so, run the following SQL:

```
GRANT USAGE ON WAREHOUSE SP_VW TO ROLE PUBLIC;
GRANT ALL ON WAREHOUSE SP_VW TO ROLE SYSADMIN;
```

You will see a success message stating that the statements were executed successfully.

We have configured the reader account with a new virtual warehouse that users in the reader account can use to run their queries. Now, we will share data from the provider account to the reader account. To do so, log back in to the provider account.

5. We will now create a sample table in the provider account. To do so, run the following SQL:

```
CREATE DATABASE CUSTOMER_DATA;
CREATE TABLE STORE_SALES AS
SELECT * FROM SNOWFLAKE_SAMPLE_DATA.TPCDS_SF10TCL.STORE_
SALES
LIMIT 1000;
```

You will see a success message stating that the table was created successfully.

6. We will now create a secure view on top of the STORE_SALES table. Please note that it is not possible to share data through a standard view, and you must create a secure view if you need to share. To do so, run the following SQL:

```
USE DATABASE CUSTOMER_DATA;
CREATE OR REPLACE SECURE VIEW STORE_SALES_AGG
AS
SELECT SS_SOLD_DATE_SK,SUM(SS_NET_PROFIT) AS SS_NET_
PROFIT
FROM CUSTOMER_DATA.PUBLIC.STORE_SALES
GROUP BY 1;
```

7. Let's now create a share object. To do so, run the following SQL:

```
USE ROLE ACCOUNTADMIN;
CREATE SHARE share_sales_data;
```

You should see a success message stating that the share was created successfully.

8. Next, we will perform the necessary grants to include the objects in the share. To do so, run the following SQL:

```
GRANT USAGE ON DATABASE CUSTOMER_DATA TO SHARE share_
sales_data;
GRANT USAGE ON SCHEMA CUSTOMER_DATA.public TO SHARE
share_sales_data;
GRANT SELECT ON VIEW CUSTOMER_DATA.PUBLIC.STORE_SALES_AGG
TO SHARE share_sales_data;
```

Each of the preceding GRANT statements should execute successfully.

9. We will now share the data with the reader account. To do so, run the following SQL and use the `accountName` value that you noted in *step 1*:

```
ALTER SHARE share_sales_data ADD ACCOUNT=<reader_account_
name_here>;
```

You should see the preceding statement execute successfully.

10. Now, log back in to the reader account using the URL that you noted down in *step 1*. Once inside the reader account, we will create a new database from the share object. To do so, run the following SQL:

```
USE ROLE ACCOUNTADMIN;
CREATE DATABASE SALES FROM SHARE <provider_account_name_
here>.share_sales_data;
```

11. We should be able to select from the view in the database created from the share. To do so, run the following SQL:

```
SELECT * FROM SALES.PUBLIC.STORE_SALES_AGG;
```

This should run successfully with the following results:

SS_SOLD_DATE_SK	SS_NET_PROFIT
2451154	-928455.27

Figure 7.24 – Selecting from the shared secure view

With this last step, the process of sharing to a non-Snowflake user is complete.

How it works...

Snowflake provides various methods for sharing data, including sharing with other Snowflake customers, and sharing with non-Snowflake customers. While sharing with another Snowflake customer is a straightforward process, it is slightly more involved for a non-Snowflake customer.

When sharing with a non-Snowflake customer, you need a mechanism to allow them to log in to Snowflake. This is done by creating a new reader account, which, as the name suggests, is mainly for reading the shared data. A reader account can be thought of as a child account and, as such, it consumes the compute resources of its parent account. The reader account must be set up with a new virtual warehouse to allow the execution of queries.

Once the reader account is all set up, sharing data is relatively straightforward and simply requires the reader's account name. The account name is used in the sharing statement to enable sharing. In this recipe, we shared data through a view rather than a table. Snowflake doesn't support sharing data from a standard view, but instead requires the creation of a secure view.

Keeping costs in check when sharing data with non-Snowflake users

Snowflake allows data to be shared not only with other Snowflake users, but also with non-Snowflake users. When sharing with a non-Snowflake user, a reader account must be created through which non-Snowflake users gain access to the shared data. Because reader accounts share the parent account's compute resources, some limits must be introduced on the reader account to avoid a hefty compute bill.

Through this recipe, you will explore how to limit the compute costs associated with data sharing when data is shared with non-Snowflake customers, and the compute of the data provider is used.

Getting ready

You will need to be connected to your Snowflake instance via the web UI or the SnowSQL client to execute this recipe. We will act as a data provider and create a reader account that can be subsequently used to share data with non-Snowflake users.

Since we will be creating a reader account, which is an account level activity, ACCOUNTADMIN-level access is required.

How to do it...

To share data with a non-Snowflake user, the first step is to set up a reader account, with which we can then share the data. The steps for this recipe are as follows:

1. We will start by creating a new reader account. To do so, run the following SQL:

```
USE ROLE ACCOUNTADMIN;
CREATE MANAGED ACCOUNT A_NON_SF_ACCOUNT TYPE=READER,
ADMIN_NAME = 'READER_ADMIN',
ADMIN_PASSWORD='<password_of_your_choice>';
```

The command should succeed with the following message. Please make a note of the `accountName` and `loginUrl` values from the output:

Row	status
1	{"accountName": CP15526 "loginUrl": "https://cp15526.ap-southeast-2.snowflakecomputing.com"

Figure 7.25 – New reader account created

In the preceding output, `CP15526` is the account identifier, and `https://cp15526.ap-southeast-2.snowflakecomputing.com` is the URL through which you will be accessing the reader account.

2. Next, use a browser to navigate to the URL in the preceding step and log in as the username and password you supplied in *step 1*.

> **Note**
> Please note that it can take some time to provision a reader account, and until it is provisioned, you might get a 403 forbidden error message when trying to access it.

3. We will create a virtual warehouse for the reader account since the reader account does not have a virtual warehouse by default. To create the virtual warehouse, run the following SQL:

```
USE ROLE ACCOUNTADMIN;
CREATE WAREHOUSE SP_VW WITH
WAREHOUSE_SIZE = 'SMALL' WAREHOUSE_TYPE = 'STANDARD'
AUTO_SUSPEND = 300 AUTO_RESUME = TRUE
INITIALLY_SUSPENDED = TRUE;
```

Note that we have created a small standard virtual warehouse to conserve costs. You can create a virtual warehouse as per your needs.

4. We have configured the reader account with a new virtual warehouse that users in the reader account can use to run their queries. We will now set up some restrictions on the reader account so that it does not consume too much compute. To do so, log in to the Snowflake web UI and switch your role to ACCOUNTADMIN.

5. While logged in to the Snowflake web UI, make sure your role in the top-right corner is ACCOUNTADMIN. Select the **Account** button and then, in the sub-tabs, select the **Resource Monitors** tab, as shown in the following screenshot:

Figure 7.26 – Navigating to Resource Monitors in the Snowflake web UI

6. Click the **Create a Resource Monitor** button. You will be presented with the following screen for the creation of a resource monitor. Fill the screen with values that relate to your specific scenario. The following screenshot shows an example configuration:

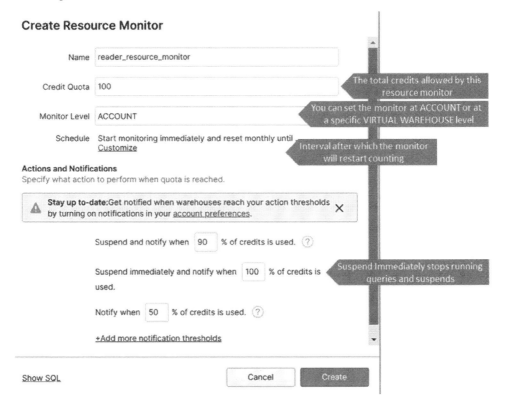

Figure 7.27 – Create Resource Monitor page

The critical configuration values to understand are that the resource monitor can be at the account level or a specific virtual warehouse level. Since we are trying to limit the processing in a reader account, it is advisable to create the monitor at the account level. Another important configuration value is the credit quota, which is the upper limit of credit that the resource monitor will allow. You can choose the actions to take as the resource monitor hits various thresholds. You can choose to suspend immediately, which will immediately abort running queries and suspend any virtual warehouses.

7. If you click on the customize link next to **Schedule**, you can select the interval after which the resource monitor will reset to zero, as shown:

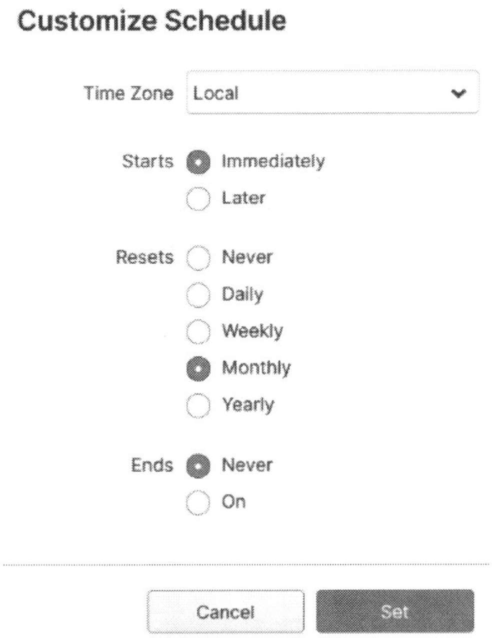

Customize Schedule

Time Zone	Local

Starts	● Immediately
	○ Later

Resets	○ Never
	○ Daily
	○ Weekly
	● Monthly
	○ Yearly

Ends	● Never
	○ On

Cancel   Set

Figure 7.28 – Customizing the resource monitor schedule

We have selected the monthly interval in our case. After providing all the configurations, click the **Set** button and then click **Create**.

8. You should see that the resource monitor has been created successfully and appears on the resource monitor screen, as shown:

Figure 7.29 – List of resource monitors

The resource monitor is now active and will be actively monitoring reader account credit usage. When the credit usage goes beyond the specified limit, it will suspend all virtual warehouses in the reader account.

How it works...

When sharing with a non-Snowflake customer, you need a mechanism to allow them to log in to Snowflake. This is done by creating a new reader account, which, as the name suggests, is mainly for reading the shared data. A reader account can be thought of as a child account, and as such, it consumes the compute resources of its parent account. Because it consumes the parent's compute resources (or those of the provider account), the provider account must track and control the reader account's compute usage or risk a hefty cost.

To limit the level of compute on a reader account, we used resource monitors. Resource monitors can be used on provider accounts as well as reader accounts. In this case, we have created a new account level monitor on the reader account, restricting the maximum compute to 100 credits. Once the reader account's total credit consumption approaches the maximum configured values, the resource monitor will suspend the virtual warehouses and stop them from being restarted.

8
Back to the Future with Time Travel

Dealing with data issues is never a pleasant job and especially so when you cannot determine when the data was changed or whether the data has been lost altogether. Snowflake provides an incredibly unique way of going back in time through the Time Travel feature. This chapter explores the various applications of the Time Travel feature and combines it with cloning to tackle common data loss and debugging issues.

The following topics will be covered in this chapter:

- Using Time Travel to return to the state of data at a particular time
- Using Time Travel to recover from the accidental loss of table data
- Identifying dropped databases, tables, and other objects and restoring them using Time Travel
- Using Time Travel in conjunction with cloning to improve debugging
- Using cloning to set up new environments based on the production environment rapidly

Technical requirements

This chapter requires access to a modern internet browser (Chrome, Edge, Firefox, and so on) and access to the internet to connect to your Snowflake instance in the cloud.

The code for this chapter can be found at the following GitHub URL: `https://github.com/PacktPublishing/Snowflake-Cookbook/tree/master/Chapter08`.

Using Time Travel to return to the state of data at a particular time

In this recipe, we will go back to a point in time for a table or a set of tables and query the data at that time using the Time Travel functionality.

Getting ready

You will need to be connected to your Snowflake instance via the web UI or the SnowSQL client to execute this recipe.

How to do it...

We will be creating a table and populating that table with some sample data. Further on in the recipe, we will run an update on this table and demonstrate how to recover to a point before the data was updated. The steps are as follows:

1. We will create a new database, followed by creating a table containing some sample customer data. We will be using sample data provided by Snowflake to populate this table. To do so, run the following SQL:

    ```
    CREATE DATABASE C8_R1;
    CREATE TABLE CUSTOMER AS
    SELECT * FROM SNOWFLAKE_SAMPLE_DATA.TPCDS_SF10TCL.
      CUSTOMER
    LIMIT 100000;
    ```

2. Let's validate that data has successfully been populated in the customer table. To do so, run the following SQL:

    ```
    SELECT * FROM CUSTOMER LIMIT 100;
    ```

You should see a result like what is shown:

C_CUSTOMER_	C_CUSTOMER_I	C_CURRENT_CD	C_CURRENT_HD	C_CURRENT_AD	C_FIRST_SHIPT	C_FIRST_SALES	C_SALUTATION	C_FIRST_NAME	C_LAST_NAME	C_PREFERRED_
18891201	AAAAAAAB...	1672603	1484	7455518	2451793	2451763	Miss	Edna	Figueroa	N
18891202	AAAAAAAA...	1664822	3607	10618745	2450648	2450618	Dr.	Helen	Estes	Y
18891203	AAAAAAAA...	909382	1243	18451857	2452041	2452011	Sir	William	Unger	N
18891204	AAAAAAAAE...	1833396	4666	13386336	2449280	2449250	Mr.	Charles	Reed	N

Figure 8.1 – Validating the customer table data

3. Make a note of the current time before running an update on the customer table. We will use this timestamp to see the data as it existed before our update:

```
SELECT CURRENT_TIMESTAMP;
```

You should see the result shown in the following screenshot. Copy the timestamp value somewhere as we will be using that later in the recipe:

Row	CURRENT_TIMESTAMP
1	2020-11-08 16:23:25.342 -0800

Figure 8.2 – Viewing the current timestamp

4. Let's now run UPDATE on the customer table. We will update the email address column for all rows. To do so, run the following SQL:

```
UPDATE CUSTOMER SET C_EMAIL_ADDRESS = 'john.doe@gmail.
com';
```

5. Validate that the email address column has indeed been updated for the whole table. To do so, run the following SQL:

```
SELECT DISTINCT C_EMAIL_ADDRESS FROM CUSTOMER;
```

You should see the result shown in the following screenshot:

Row	C_EMAIL_ADDRESS
1	john.doe@gmail.com

Figure 8.3 – A single distinct value for the email address after the update

6. We will now use Snowflake's Time Travel functionality to view the data as it existed before the update. We will use the timestamp and the AT syntax to travel back to how the table's data looked at or before a specific time. To do that, run the following SQL:

```
SELECT DISTINCT C_EMAIL_ADDRESS
FROM CUSTOMER AT
(TIMESTAMP => '2020-11-08 16:23:25.342 -0800'::timestamp_
tz);
```

You will see that almost 100,000 email addresses will be returned (rather than a single email address as in the previous step). The result will be like what is shown:

C_EMAIL_ADDRESS
Melinda.Mcdonald@S2y6OCshd.edu
Glenda.Gomez@Fyig2tnhFYdRf.edu
Mason.Roberts@iGC20e1MPvLR.edu
Bobby.Presley@L8QuISIHHc.org

Figure 8.4 – Email address data before the update was run

This indicates that we have been able to view the table's data through Time Travel as it existed before the update query was run.

7. If needed, you can now select all rows from the table and use them in various ways as per your requirements. To do that, run the following SQL:

```
SELECT *
FROM CUSTOMER AT
(TIMESTAMP => '2020-11-08 16:23:25.342 -0800'::timestamp_
tz);
```

8. The AT syntax in Time Travel is handy when you know the exact timestamp you would like to travel to. However, if you are not 100% sure when the update was made, you can use the BEFORE syntax and provide an approximate timestamp. To do so, run the following SQL:

```
SELECT DISTINCT C_EMAIL_ADDRESS
FROM CUSTOMER BEFORE
(TIMESTAMP => '2020-11-08 16:25:00.000 -0800'::timestamp_
tz);
```

Notice the timestamp we have provided at an approximate time at which we think the update query was executed. As a result of the SQL, you should see an output as shown in the following screenshot (note that you may see only one updated email address if your timestamp approximation is not correct; in that case, gradually remove 1 minute from the timestamp that you provided):

C_EMAIL_ADDRESS

Conrad.Samuels@KLbidv1dROr3z0E.com

Juana.Hahn@8J2HH2eEps.edu

Garrett.Roderick@iES5pM7NOCQ.edu

James.Jenkins@vmmD8NIGAyGEa.org

Figure 8.5 – Data before a particular timestamp

The preceding steps show how you can undo the effects of update statements by restoring the data to how it existed at a specific point in time.

How it works...

In this recipe, we used the AT and BEFORE syntax to retrieve historical data at or before a specific timestamp through a SQL extension referred to as **Time Travel**, which provides the capability to access data that has been historically changed or deleted. Time Travel enables users to access and restore changes to data in tables, schemas, and databases. The functionality even allows restoring complete databases and schemas after they may have been dropped.

Snowflake achieves this powerful feature by retaining a copy of changed or deleted data for a specified period. Snowflake tracks this copy of data through the metadata it maintains for each table and object. When a Time Travel query is executed, the Snowflake query engine can search through metadata to access and retrieve the historical data.

By default, when you make changes to a table's data, historical data is retained for 1 day. However, for Enterprise Edition and above versions of Snowflake, you can set the retention to be up to 90 days, therefore allowing you to undo changes up to 90 days in the past.

Using Time Travel to recover from the accidental loss of table data

This recipe will go through a scenario of accidental data loss after a delete query has been executed, affecting data in a table. We will demonstrate how we can recover data after it has been deleted accidentally.

Getting ready

You will need to be connected to your Snowflake instance via the web UI or the SnowSQL client to execute this recipe.

How to do it...

We will be creating a table and populating that table with some sample data. Further on in the recipe, we will run DELETE on this table and demonstrate how to recover to a point before the data was deleted. The steps for this recipe are as follows:

1. We will create a new database, followed by creating a table containing some sample customer data. We will be using sample data provided by Snowflake to populate this table. To do so, run the following SQL:

```
CREATE DATABASE C8_R2;
CREATE TABLE CUSTOMER AS
SELECT * FROM SNOWFLAKE_SAMPLE_DATA.TPCDS_SF10TCL.
    CUSTOMER
LIMIT 100000;
```

2. Let's validate that data has successfully been populated in the customer table. To do so, run the following SQL:

```
SELECT * FROM CUSTOMER LIMIT 100;
```

You should see a result like what is shown:

C_CUSTOMER_	C_CUSTOMER_I	C_CURRENT_CD	C_CURRENT_HD	C_CURRENT_AD	C_FIRST_SHIPT	C_FIRST_SALES	C_SALUTATION	C_FIRST_NAME	C_LAST_NAME	C_PREFERRED_
18891201	AAAAAAAAB...	1672603	1484	7455518	2451793	2451763	Miss	Edna	Figueroa	N
18891202	AAAAAAAA...	1664822	3607	10618745	2450648	2450618	Dr.	Helen	Estes	Y
18891203	AAAAAAAA...	909382	1243	18451857	2452041	2452011	Sir	William	Unger	N
18891204	AAAAAAAAE...	1833396	4686	13386336	2449280	2449250	Mr.	Charles	Reed	N

Figure 8.6 – Validating the data in the customer table

3. Let's now simulate an accidental `DELETE` on the customer table. To do so, run the following SQL:

```
DELETE FROM CUSTOMER;
```

The command should run successfully without any errors.

4. Validate that all rows from the table have been deleted. To do so, run the following SQL:

```
SELECT * FROM CUSTOMER;
```

No rows will be returned as a result of the preceding query.

5. We will first query the query history to identify which query deleted all the rows. To do so, run the following SQL:

```
SELECT QUERY_ID, QUERY_TEXT, DATABASE_NAME, SCHEMA_NAME,
    QUERY_TYPE
FROM TABLE(INFORMATION_SCHEMA.QUERY_HISTORY())
WHERE QUERY_TYPE = 'DELETE'
AND EXECUTION_STATUS = 'SUCCESS'
AND DATABASE_NAME = 'C8_R2';
```

The result set of this will be all `DELETE` queries that were executed successfully on the `C8_R2` database. An example result is shown in the screenshot that follows. Make a note of the value(s) in the `QUERY_ID` column as we will be using the value(s) in the next step:

QUERY_ID	QUERY_TEXT	DATABASE_NAME	SCHEMA_NAME	QUERY_TYPE
019825cd-0438-0033-0000-002fd30330bd	DELETE FROM CUSTOMER;	C8_R2	PUBLIC	DELETE

Figure 8.7 – Querying the query history

6. We will now use Snowflake's Time Travel functionality to view the data as it existed before the `DELETE` query was run. We will use the timestamp and the `BEFORE` syntax to travel back to how the table looked before the `DELETE` query was executed. To do that, run the following SQL:

```
SELECT *
FROM CUSTOMER BEFORE
    (STATEMENT => '019825cd-0438-0033-0000-002fd30330bd');
```

You will see that all 100,000 rows will be returned rather than an empty table. The result will be like what is shown here:

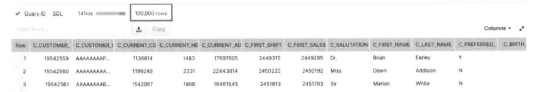

Figure 8.8 – Viewing the data before the DELETE query was run

This indicates that we have been able to view the table's data through Time Travel as it existed before the DELETE query was run.

> **Note:**
> Note that you should replace the query ID in the preceding statement with the query ID of the statement you would have run.

7. You can now undo the DELETE action by reinserting this data into the table by using Time Travel. To do that, run the following SQL:

```
INSERT INTO CUSTOMER
SELECT *
FROM CUSTOMER BEFORE
(STATEMENT => '019825cd-0438-0033-0000-002fd30330bd');
```

8. Validate that the data has indeed been restored by running the following SQL:

```
SELECT * FROM CUSTOMER;
```

You should see 100,000 rows returned as a result of the preceding query. The results are as shown:

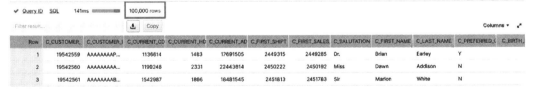

Figure 8.9 – Validating the restored data

The preceding steps show how an erroneous SQL statement's detrimental effects may be reversed easily by restoring the data as it existed before that statement was run.

How it works...

In this recipe, we used the STATEMENT syntax to retrieve deleted data as it existed before the specified DELETE query was executed. Using this approach, we can access and retrieve data that was deleted by a DELETE query or retrieve data that was changed through other queries such as an UPDATE query. The STATEMENT syntax allows you to provide a QUERY_ID value, and the data as it existed before that query was executed is retrieved.

Referred to as **Time Travel**, Snowflake achieves this powerful feature by retaining a copy of the modified or deleted data for a specified period of time. Snowflake tracks this data copy through the metadata it maintains for each table and object. When a Time Travel query is run, the Snowflake query engine can access and retrieve historical data via metadata.

Identifying dropped databases, tables, and other objects and restoring them using Time Travel

Time Travel can be used to recover tables, schemas, and even complete databases. In this recipe, we are given a scenario where a database and other objects have been deleted. We will identify what has been deleted and recover them back to the previous state.

Getting ready

You will need to be connected to your Snowflake instance via the web UI or the SnowSQL client to execute this recipe.

How to do it...

We will first create a database, then two schemas in that database, and some tables within those schemas. We will then gradually delete the tables, schemas, and eventually the complete database. Then we will try to recover them through the Time Travel feature:

1. We will start by creating a new database, followed by the creation of a schema. To do so, run the following SQL:

    ```
    CREATE DATABASE C8_R3;
    CREATE SCHEMA SCHEMA1;
    ```

2. Next, we will create a test table called CUSTOMER in this schema. We will be using sample data provided by Snowflake to populate this table. To do so, run the following SQL:

```
CREATE TABLE CUSTOMER AS
SELECT * FROM SNOWFLAKE_SAMPLE_DATA.TPCDS_SF10TCL.
   CUSTOMER
LIMIT 100000;
```

You should see a success message stating that the table was created successfully.

3. Next, we will create another test table called CUSTOMER_ADDRESS in this schema. Again, we will be using sample data provided by Snowflake to populate this table. To do so, run the following SQL:

```
CREATE TABLE CUSTOMER_ADDRESS AS
SELECT * FROM SNOWFLAKE_SAMPLE_DATA.TPCDS_SF10TCL.
CUSTOMER_ADDRESS
LIMIT 100000;
```

You should see a success message stating that the table was created successfully.

4. Next, we will create another schema by the name of SCHEMA2. To do so, run the following SQL:

```
USE DATABASE C8_R3;
CREATE SCHEMA SCHEMA2;
```

5. Next, we will create a test table call INVENTORY in this schema. We will be using sample data provided by Snowflake to populate this table. To do so, run the following SQL:

```
CREATE TABLE INVENTORY AS
SELECT * FROM SNOWFLAKE_SAMPLE_DATA.TPCDS_SF10TCL.
INVENTORY
LIMIT 100000;
```

You should see a success message stating that the table was created successfully.

If you expand the database tree on the left side of the Snowflake web UI, you should see the following structure of the database, schemas, and tables that we just created:

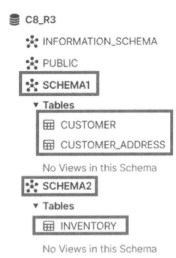

Figure 8.10 – Structure of the database, schemas, and tables just created

6. Let's now drop the customer table from the schema. To do so, run the following SQL:

```
USE SCHEMA SCHEMA1;
DROP TABLE CUSTOMER;
```

If you now expand and refresh the database tree on the left side of the Snowflake web UI, you should see that the customer table is now deleted, as shown:

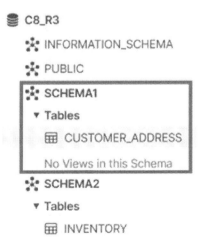

Figure 8.11 – Customer table deleted

7. If at any time you want to find out the tables that may have been dropped programmatically, you can run the following query to identify such tables:

```
USE ROLE ACCOUNTADMIN;
SELECT TABLE_CATALOG, TABLE_SCHEMA,TABLE_NAME,
  ID,CLONE_GROUP_ID, TABLE_CREATED, TABLE_DROPPED
  FROM INFORMATION_SCHEMA.TABLE_STORAGE_METRICS WHERE
  TABLE_CATALOG = 'C8_R3';
```

This should show you all the schemas and the tables within the C8_R3 database. The result is as shown:

Row	TABLE_CATALOG	TABLE_SCHEMA	TABLE_NAME	ID	CLONE_GROUP_ID	TABLE_CREATED	TABLE_DROPPED
1	C8_R3	SCHEMA2	INVENTORY	12	12	2020-11-09 18:43:...	NULL
2	C8_R3	SCHEMA1	CUSTOMER	2051	2051	2020-11-09 18:43:...	2020-11-09 18:44:...
3	C8_R3	SCHEMA1	CUSTOMER_ADD...	2053	2053	2020-11-09 18:43:...	NULL

Figure 8.12 – Schemas and tables in the C8_R3 database

Tables that have been dropped will have a non-null date value in the TABLE_DROPPED column.

8. Let's now restore the dropped table. To do so, simply run the following SQL:

```
USE SCHEMA SCHEMA1;
UNDROP TABLE CUSTOMER;
```

9. Validate that the table is indeed available now by running the following SQL:

```
SELECT COUNT(*) FROM CUSTOMER;
```

The query should succeed and should show 100,000 rows in the count column. This indicates that you can query the table, and the table has been restored successfully.

10. Let's now drop the whole SCHEMA1 schema. To do so, run the following SQL:

```
DROP SCHEMA SCHEMA1;
```

If you now expand and refresh the database tree on the left side of the Snowflake web UI, you should see that the SCHEMA1 schema is nowhere to be seen:

Figure 8.13 – Dropping the SCHEMA1 schema

11. Let's now restore the schema. To do so, run the following SQL:

```
UNDROP SCHEMA SCHEMA1;
```

If you now expand and refresh the database tree on the left side of the Snowflake web UI, you should see that the SCHEMA1 schema has reappeared along with its child tables:

Figure 8.14 – The SCHEMA1 schema restored

You can now query the tables in that schema as usual as the schema has been restored and is available for querying.

UNDROP is not limited to just tables and schemas. Like how we dropped and restored a schema, you can run UNDROP on complete databases to restore them after they have been deleted.

How it works...

In Snowflake, each table is maintained in the metadata within the cloud services layer. The table's actual data is maintained in object storage (S3, Azure Blob Storage, and so on). When a table is dropped in Snowflake, it is marked as deleted in the metadata, but the table's underlying data remains. When the UNDROP command is run on a dropped table, Snowflake changes the table's deleted status back to undeleted, in effect restoring the table immediately.

Using Time Travel in conjunction with cloning to improve debugging

Often, the debugging of data issues requires restoring data to a point and rerunning the process. It is typically required in traditional databases to make an actual copy of your production system's data. Additionally, if you require data as it existed at a specific time or in a specific state, it is almost impossible to achieve without significant effort. The Snowflake Time Travel feature combined with cloning simplifies that process. In this recipe, we will create a clone of a complete database at a point in time so that the development team can use the cloned version to validate and debug their code.

Getting ready

You will need to be connected to your Snowflake instance via the web UI or the SnowSQL client to execute this recipe.

How to do it...

We will be creating a database, two schemas, and then some tables within those schemas. We will then add some sample data in these tables, followed by inserting additional sample data into the tables. Then we will create a clone of this database. The steps are as follows:

1. We will create a new database called PRODUCTION_DB, which signifies that the database contains production data. We will also create a schema called SRC_DATA, which signifies that it contains raw data from the source systems. To do so, run the following SQL:

    ```
    CREATE DATABASE PRODUCTION_DB;
    CREATE SCHEMA SRC_DATA;
    ```

    The command should succeed with a success message.

2. Next, we will create a test table called INVENTORY in this schema. We will be using sample data provided by Snowflake to populate this table. To do so, run the following SQL:

```
CREATE TABLE INVENTORY AS
SELECT * FROM SNOWFLAKE_SAMPLE_DATA.TPCDS_SF10TCL.
INVENTORY
LIMIT 100000;
```

You should see a success message stating that the table was created successfully.

3. Next, we will create another test table called ITEM in this schema. Again, we will be using sample data provided by Snowflake to populate this table. To do so, run the following SQL:

```
CREATE TABLE ITEM AS
SELECT * FROM SNOWFLAKE_SAMPLE_DATA.TPCDS_SF10TCL.ITEM
LIMIT 100000;
```

You should see a success message stating that the table was created successfully.

4. Next, we will create another schema by the name of ACCESS_LAYER. To do so, run the following SQL:

```
USE DATABASE PRODUCTION_DB;
CREATE SCHEMA ACCESS_LAYER;
```

The commands should succeed with a success message.

5. Next, we will create a test table called STORE_SALES in this schema. We will be using sample data provided by Snowflake to populate this table. To do so, run the following SQL:

```
CREATE TABLE STORE_SALES AS
SELECT * FROM SNOWFLAKE_SAMPLE_DATA.TPCDS_SF10TCL.STORE_
SALES
LIMIT 100000;
```

You should see a success message stating that the table was created successfully.

6. If you expand the database tree on the Snowflake web UI's left side, you should see the following structure of the database, schemas, and tables that we just created:

Figure 8.15 – Database, schemas, and tables structure

7. We have created a database hierarchy like how it may exist in a production system. Let's now note the current time as we will need that information to clone our production database as it existed at a specific time. To do so, run the following SQL:

```
SELECT CURRENT_TIMESTAMP;
```

8. Let's also check the count of rows in each table so that when we clone the database in conjunction with Time Travel, we can demonstrate the database is cloned before additional data is added to the table. To do so, run the following SQL statements one by one and note the row counts of each table:

```
SELECT COUNT(*) FROM PRODUCTION_DB.SRC_DATA.INVENTORY;
SELECT COUNT(*) FROM PRODUCTION_DB.SRC_DATA.ITEM;
SELECT COUNT(*) FROM PRODUCTION_DB.ACCESS_LAYER.STORE_
    SALES;
```

You should see 100,000 rows in each table.

9. We will now insert more data into all the tables in our PRODUCTION_DB database, simulating how a regular ETL run may execute every day. To do so, run the following SQL statements several times:

```
INSERT INTO PRODUCTION_DB.SRC_DATA.INVENTORY
SELECT * FROM SNOWFLAKE_SAMPLE_DATA.TPCDS_SF10TCL.
INVENTORY
```

```
LIMIT 20000;


INSERT INTO PRODUCTION_DB.SRC_DATA.ITEM
SELECT * FROM SNOWFLAKE_SAMPLE_DATA.TPCDS_SF10TCL.ITEM
LIMIT 20000;


INSERT INTO PRODUCTION_DB.ACCESS_LAYER.STORE_SALES
SELECT * FROM SNOWFLAKE_SAMPLE_DATA.TPCDS_SF10TCL.STORE_
SALES
LIMIT 20000;
```

Running these statements will insert new rows into the tables in the PRODUCTION_
DB database and will increase the row count from the initial 100,000 rows we loaded
in those tables.

10. Let's now clone the PRODUCTION_DB database into the DEV_1 database, and while
doing so, we'll also go back to when the table only had the initial set of rows. To do
so, run the following SQL:

```
CREATE DATABASE DEV_1 CLONE PRODUCTION_DB AT(TIMESTAMP =>
'<replace with the timestamp from step#7>'::timestamp_
tz);
```

If you now expand and refresh the database tree on the left side of the Snowflake
web UI, you should see that the DEV_1 database has been created with the exact
structure of the PRODUCTION_DB database, as shown:

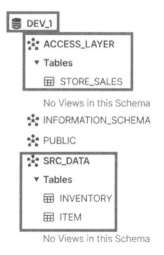

Figure 8.16 – DEV_1 database structure

11. Since we used Time Travel with cloning, the DEV_1 database is cloned from the PRODUCTION_DB database; however, it should contain only the 100,000 rows that were initially inserted into the tables. Let's validate that by running COUNT queries on the tables in the DEV_1 database. To do so, run the following SQL statements:

```
SELECT COUNT(*) FROM DEV_1.SRC_DATA.INVENTORY;
SELECT COUNT(*) FROM DEV_1.SRC_DATA.ITEM;
SELECT COUNT(*) FROM DEV_1.ACCESS_LAYER.STORE_SALES;
```

You should see 100,000 rows in each table.

12. Now you can perform your development and debugging activities on this cloned database. Any changes you make to the DEV_1 database will not impact anything in the PRODUCTION_DB database.

Using this cloning technique and Time Travel, you can make clones of a database as it existed at a point in time. Therefore, you get a more flexible method to develop and debug using production data without impacting the production data itself.

How it works...

In Snowflake, within the cloud services layer, information for each table is stored in the metadata. However, the table's actual data is stored in object storage (S3, Azure Blob Storage, and so on). The metadata for each table maintains references to the actual data in the object storage. This architecture allows Snowflake to track changes to a table transparent to the user; therefore, when you have updated a table, the data that existed before the update is retained for some time, allowing Snowflake to perform **Time Travel**.

Since references to actual data are maintained in the metadata, Snowflake can configure new tables and set up the metadata references to point to existing data, a phenomenon known as **cloning**. A cloned table and its parent table are in effect pointing to the same physical data. Snowflake also allows mixing **cloning** and **Time Travel**; as demonstrated in this recipe, you can create clones of objects as they existed at a point in time. This feature can be convenient when development teams are trying to debug production issues and may require the data to be in a state that it existed in on a particular day. You can simply clone the whole production database into a new database as of the required point in time without incurring any additional costs.

Using cloning to set up new environments based on the production environment rapidly

In traditional database and data warehousing, setting up a new development environment can be a lengthy and costly process. The process typically requires replicating the production structures in a new development database. Then some sample data in the production databases is copied over into the new development database. The process is time-consuming and error-prone since it involves running table DDLs in a new environment and then inserting the sample data. Creating one or several new environments based on an existing production environment is a straightforward process in Snowflake. In this recipe, we will explore how we can use the cloning capabilities to create new development environments in a matter of minutes.

Getting ready

You will need to be connected to your Snowflake instance via the web UI to execute this recipe.

How to do it...

We will be creating a database, two schemas in that database, and then a few different tables within those schemas. We will add some sample data in these tables, followed by inserting additional sample data into the tables. We will consider this database as the production database and clone this database into a new development database:

1. Let's start by creating a new database called PRD, which signifies that the database contains production data. We will also create three schemas called SRC_DATA, INTEGRATED_DATA, and REPORTING_DATA. To do so, run the following SQL:

```
CREATE DATABASE PRD;
CREATE SCHEMA SRC_DATA;
CREATE SCHEMA INTEGRATED_DATA;
CREATE SCHEMA REPORTING_DATA;
```

The commands should succeed with a success message.

2. Next, we will create a series of tables in these databases. To do so, run the following SQL statements:

```
USE SCHEMA SRC_DATA;
CREATE TABLE CUSTOMER AS
SELECT * FROM SNOWFLAKE_SAMPLE_DATA.TPCH_SF1.CUSTOMER;


USE SCHEMA SRC_DATA;
CREATE TABLE LINEITEM AS
SELECT * FROM SNOWFLAKE_SAMPLE_DATA.TPCH_SF1.LINEITEM;


USE SCHEMA INTEGRATED_DATA;
CREATE TABLE ORDERS AS
SELECT * FROM SNOWFLAKE_SAMPLE_DATA.TPCH_SF1.ORDERS;
```

Each of these should complete successfully.

3. We will also create a reporting view to demonstrate that views also get cloned. To do so, run the following SQL:

```
USE SCHEMA REPORTING_DATA;
CREATE VIEW REVENUE_REPORT AS
SELECT
L_RETURNFLAG,
L_LINESTATUS,
SUM(L_QUANTITY) AS SUM_QTY,
SUM(L_EXTENDEDPRICE) AS SUM_BASE_PRICE,
SUM(L_EXTENDEDPRICE * (1-L_DISCOUNT)) AS SUM_DISC_PRICE,
SUM(L_EXTENDEDPRICE * (1-L_DISCOUNT) * (1+L_TAX)) AS SUM_
CHARGE,
AVG(L_QUANTITY) AS AVG_QTY,
AVG(L_EXTENDEDPRICE) AS AVG_PRICE,
AVG(L_DISCOUNT) AS AVG_DISC,
COUNT(*) AS COUNT_ORDER
FROM PRD.SRC_DATA.LINEITEM
WHERE L_SHIPDATE <= DATEADD(DAY, -90, TO_DATE('1998-12-
01'))
GROUP BY L_RETURNFLAG,L_LINESTATUS;
```

You should see a success message stating that the view was created successfully.

4. If you expand the database tree on the left side of the Snowflake web UI, you should see the following structure of the database, schemas, and tables that we just created:

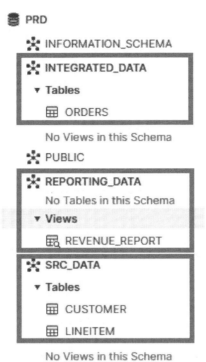

Figure 8.17 – Structure of database, schemas, and tables that we just created

5. We will now create a brand-new development environment for this PRD database, and we will create it with data. To do so, we will use Snowflake's clone functionality as shown here:

```
CREATE DATABASE DEV_DB_1 CLONE PRD;
```

6. Let's validate that the new environment has all the required objects. To do so, expand the database tree on the left side of the Snowflake web UI; you should see the following structure of database, schemas, tables, and views:

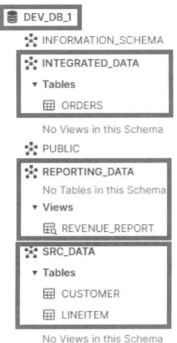

Figure 8.18 – Cloned schemas, tables, and views in the development database

You will observe that all tables and views are successfully cloned.

7. Let's validate that there is actual data in the cloned tables. To do so, run the following SQL statements:

```
SELECT COUNT(*) FROM DEV_DB_1.SRC_DATA.CUSTOMER;
```

8. Similarly, let's validate that there is actual data in the cloned views. To do so, run the following SQL statements:

```
SELECT COUNT(*) FROM DEV_DB_1.REPORTING_DATA.REVENUE_
REPORT;
```

9. At this point, we have successfully created a development environment out of a production environment. If we like, we can create as many clones of the PRD database as we want. We can even clone the DEV_DB_1 database further if needed.

10. Let's create a testing environment from the production environment. To do so, run the following SQL:

```
CREATE DATABASE TEST_1 CLONE PRD;
```

The database will be successfully created, and you can validate that it has all the required schemas, tables, and views created.

11. You can even create a new development environment from the existing development environment. To do so, run the following SQL:

```
CREATE DATABASE DEV_DB_2 CLONE DEV_DB_1;
```

The database will be successfully created, and you can validate that it has all the required schemas, tables, and views created.

How it works...

In Snowflake, each database, schema, and table is maintained in the cloud services layer's metadata. A table's actual data is maintained in object storage (that is, S3, Azure Blob Storage, and so on). This approach allows Snowflake to make clones of existing objects without requiring the actual copying of data. Each cloned object points to the same data in the object storage. Snowflake takes care of the fact that if data is updated in the original tables, it is not reflected in the cloned tables, and vice versa – if a query updates the cloned data in the development database, it doesn't impact the production database.

9
Advanced SQL Techniques

In this chapter, you'll learn how to use multiple advanced SQL techniques using the Snowflake data warehouse. These SQL techniques are essential from a data warehousing perspective, and include trend analysis, temporal analytics, managing sequences, unique counts, and managing processes as transactions.

The following recipes will be covered in this chapter:

- Managing timestamp data
- Shredding date data to extract calendar information
- Unique counts and Snowflake
- Managing transactions in Snowflake
- Ordered analytics over window frames
- Generating sequences in Snowflake

Let's get started!

Technical requirements

The recipes in this chapter work on Snowflake's web UI, as well as SnowSQL. The code for this chapter can be found at the following GitHub URL: `https://github.com/PacktPublishing/Snowflake-Cookbook/tree/master/Chapter09`.

Managing timestamp data

The recipe will provide you with an example of how files containing timestamp data should be managed using the timestamp functions available in Snowflake, as well as how formats are managed for the standard ISO format and non-standard formats. This recipe shall also provide you with some useful examples of how to avoid mixups that may occur if a source system provides inconsistent date and time data, or different zones are involved, as well as how to apply time zones using session.

Getting ready

Note that this recipe's steps can be run either in the Snowflake web UI or the SnowSQL command-line client.

How to do it...

Let's look at some practical examples of common date and time queries and calculations. We shall start with date and time data types, followed by timestamps. We shall investigate how time zones can be handled in Snowflake. In practical scenarios, data is received in text files, which will contain date and time data available as strings. Let's start by converting string values into date values, as shown in the following steps:

1. The data type for storing date values in columns in Snowflake tables is called DATE. A date is typically composed of the year, month, and the day of the month separated by hyphens (YYYY-MM-DD). Let's create a table, C9R1_DATE_TEST, where we will store a date value in a string. We shall use the to_date function to convert the string value into a valid formatted date. The function accepts a string value that must be converted and the format of the input string as parameters:

```
CREATE DATABASE C9_R1;
CREATE TABLE c9r1_date_test (date_id INTEGER, date_value DATE);
INSERT INTO c9r1_date_test (date_id, date_value)
Values
(1, to_date('2019-12-19','YYYY-MM-DD'));
```

2. The DATE data type is not limited to taking in just dates. It can take timestamp values as well. However, it will ignore the time component of the input:

```
INSERT INTO c9r1_date_test (date_id, date_value)
VALUES
(2, TO_TIMESTAMP('2019.12.21 04:00:00', 'YYYY.MM.DD
HH:MI:SS'));
```

3. Another variation is to use the to_date function but pass the time component only. It can take time values, but it assumes the value of January 1, 1970 for the date, thus completely ignoring the time value:

```
INSERT INTO c9r1_date_test (date_id, date_value)
VALUES
(3, TO_DATE ('08:00:00', 'HH:MI:SS'));
```

4. Let's now run a query so that we can select data in the table:

```
SELECT * FROM c9r1_date_test;
```

The result of the query is as follows:

DATE_ID	DATE_VALUE
1	2019-12-19
2	2019-12-21
3	1970-01-01

Figure 9.1 – Output of the query in step 4

The previous table shows that a timestamp value can be stored in a date type column. Here, Snowflake ignores the timestamp's time component. The third row shows that the date column will take the date value if nothing is provided.

5. Now, let's create a new table with a timestamp type column to demonstrate how Snowflake manages time zones:

```
CREATE TABLE c9r1_ts_test (ts_id INTEGER, ts_value
TIMESTAMP);
```

6. We shall now investigate the session object and how it can be used to manage time zones. The session holds various objects, where each object has a default value. To find out the values of all the objects in the session that are related to the time zone, run the following command:

```
SHOW PARAMETERS LIKE '%TIMEZONE%' IN SESSION;
```

7. The results are as follows:

Row	key	value	default	level	description	type
1	JDBC_FORMAT_DATE...	false	false		When true, ResultSet...	BOOLEAN
2	JDBC_USE_SESSION_...	false	false		When true, JDBC driv...	BOOLEAN
3	TIMEZONE	America/Los_Angeles	America/Los_Angeles		time zone	STRING

Figure 9.2 – Output of running a query on the session object

8. In the case of the **TIMEZONE** object stored in the session, the default value is **America/Los_Angeles**. This value can be changed by running the ALTER SESSION command. The string typed values that a **TIMEZONE** object can store can be obtained from IANA (https://www.iana.org).

9. To set the user-defined value for the time zone that will be used with our data, we can use the following statement:

```
ALTER SESSION SET TIMEZONE='Australia/Sydney';
```

10. The command should execute successfully.

11. Let's now rerun the command for the session to view the updated value:

```
SHOW PARAMETERS LIKE '%TIMEZONE%' IN SESSION;
```

12. The preceding statement shall generate the following output. Here, we can see that the **value** column has been updated, but the **default** value remains unchanged:

Row	key	value	default	level	description	type
1	JDBC_FORMAT_DATE...	false	false		When true, ResultSet...	BOOLEAN
2	JDBC_USE_SESSION_...	false	false		When true, JDBC driv...	BOOLEAN
3	TIMEZONE	Australia/Sydney	America/Los_Angeles	SESSION	time zone	STRING

Figure 9.3 – Output of the query in step 8

13. Now, let's insert a timestamp value:

```
INSERT INTO c9r1_ts_test (ts_id, ts_value)
VALUES (1, '2020-11-19 22:00:00.000');
```

14. Now, select the data from this table by running the following command:

```
SELECT * FROM c9r1_ts_test;
```

15. You should see the following results:

TS_ID	TS_VALUE
1	2020-11-19 22:00:00.000

Figure 9.4 – No change/interpretation of the time zone

16. Now, let's change another session parameter. We shall change how Snowflake manages timestamp data. For this, we shall be updating the value of the TIMESTAMP_TYPE_MAPPING parameter. Let's execute the following piece of code:

```
ALTER SESSION SET TIMESTAMP_TYPE_MAPPING = 'TIMESTAMP_
LTZ';
ALTER SESSION SET TIMEZONE = 'Australia/Sydney';
CREATE OR REPLACE TABLE c9r1_test_ts (ts TIMESTAMP);
INSERT INTO c9r1_test_ts VALUES ('2020-11-19
22:00:00.000');
SELECT ts FROM c9r1_test_ts;
```

The result will generate a column called **TS** in the table, as well as a value, as shown in the following screenshot:

Figure 9.5 – The time zone is shown, along with the time difference compared with GMT

17. Now, let's change how the timestamp value with a different time zone is handled. Let's execute the following piece of code. The difference this time is in the value being inserted. The timestamp value corresponds to the time zone for Australia/Perth (+0800 with regard to UTC):

```
CREATE OR REPLACE TABLE c9r1_test_ts (ts TIMESTAMP);
INSERT INTO c9r1_test_ts VALUES ('2020-11-19 22:00:00.000
+0800');
SELECT ts FROM c9r1_test_ts;
```

18. The output is shown in the following screenshot:

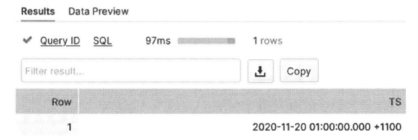

Figure 9.6 – Timestamp adjusted by + 3 hours due to a session time zone change

Here, we can see that Snowflake has converted the incoming timestamp into the one we configured in the session. The date value flipped to the next day to adjust the 3-hour difference between time zones.

How it works...

For date type columns, if a timestamp is inserted into a date column, the time part of the timestamp is dropped. If a time value is inserted into a date type column, it will result in the date column, while taking the value of January 1, 1970.

In the case of timestamps, Snowflake offers us an excellent way to manage time zones through the different session- and account-level parameters. These parameters can be viewed using the session object. To modify the value of the parameters, we can alter the session with specific values. It should be noted that the time zone can only be set at the time of creating a table and cannot be configured during load.

Shredding date data to extract Calendar information

In this recipe, you'll learn how the different functions that are available in Snowflake can help us extract parts of data, such as the day, day of the week, week of the year, name of the day, and important days in business reporting cycles, such as the last day of the month or the first day of the month. These capabilities are essential in data warehousing as most of the data uses time and date as dimensions. Along the way, this recipe shall introduce some pitfalls related to the start of the week configuration in Snowflake. You'll learn how to develop a utility calendar table with different columns related to the date.

Getting ready

Note that this recipe's steps can be run either in the Snowflake WebUI or the SnowSQL command-line client.

How to do it...

As part of this recipe, we shall start with a simple date generator. The generator function will be used to generate calendar dates for the calendar year (365 rows). This date field will be used to generate other fields in the table. Let's start by generating some dates:

1. First, we shall use the `seq4()` function to generate a list of numbers from 0 to 364. These numbers will be added to the first date of the year 2021. To generate 365 rows, we can use the following code, which uses the `GENERATOR()` function:

```
SELECT (to_date('2020-01-01') + seq4()) cal_dt
FROM TABLE(GENERATOR(ROWCOUNT => 365));
```

2. The output will be as follows. Here, we are showing the first five rows of the dataset, starting with January 1, 2021. The table has one column called **CAL_DT**. This column will be used in the subsequent steps as input to different extractor functions so that we can extract date parts:

Row	CAL_DT
1	2020-01-01
2	2020-01-02
3	2020-01-03
4	2020-01-04
5	2020-01-05

Figure 9.7 – Output of the query's execution in step 1

3. Now that we have the foundation set up, we can start adding functions so that we can extract date parts. In this step, we will extract the day, month, and year from the date using the DATE_PART() function:

```
SELECT (to_date('2020-01-01') + seq4()) cal_dt,
DATE_PART(day, cal_dt) as cal_dom, --day of month
DATE_PART(month, cal_dt) as cal_month, --month of year
DATE_PART(year, cal_dt) as cal_year --year
FROM TABLE(GENERATOR(ROWCOUNT => 365));
```

4. The result is as follows:

Row	CAL_DT	CAL_DOM	CAL_MONTH	CAL_YEAR
1	2020-01-01	1	1	2020
2	2020-01-02	2	1	2020
3	2020-01-03	3	1	2020
4	2020-01-04	4	1	2020
5	2020-01-05	5	1	2020
6	2020-01-06	6	1	2020
7	2020-01-07	7	1	2020
8	2020-01-08	8	1	2020

Figure 9.8 – Date components

5. Now that we have the basic parts of the date extracted, we can enhance it with more fields. We are going to add the first and last day of the month against each date in our dataset. We will add two columns, as shown in the following code:

```
SELECT
  (to_date('2021-01-01') + seq4()) cal_dt
  ,DATE_PART(day, cal_dt) as cal_dom --day of month
  ,DATE_PART(month, cal_dt) as cal_month --month of year
  ,DATE_PART(year, cal_dt) as cal_year --year
  ,DATE_TRUNC('month', CAL_DT) as cal_first_dom
  ,DATEADD('day', -1,
     DATEADD('month', 1,
     DATE_TRUNC('month', CAL_DT))) as cal_last_dom
  FROM TABLE(GENERATOR(ROWCOUNT => 365));
```

The output is as follows:

Row	CAL_DT	CAL_DOM	CAL_MONTH	CAL_YEAR	CAL_FIRST_DOM	CAL_LAST_DOM
1	2021-01-01	1	1	2021	2021-01-01	2021-01-31
2	2021-01-02	2	1	2021	2021-01-01	2021-01-31
3	2021-01-03	3	1	2021	2021-01-01	2021-01-31
4	2021-01-04	4	1	2021	2021-01-01	2021-01-31
5	2021-01-05	5	1	2021	2021-01-01	2021-01-31
6	2021-01-06	6	1	2021	2021-01-01	2021-01-31

Figure 9.9 – Last and first date of the month

The result set has two new columns; that is, cal_first_dom and cal_last_dom. Here, we can see that for January 2021, the values of cal_first_dom and cal_last_dom are 2021-01-01 and 2021-01-31, respectively. The DATE_TRUNC() function has been used with month as a parameter to get the first day of the month. For arriving at the last day of the month, we start by getting to the first day of the month, then add a month to the date, and then, finally, subtract a day to get to the last day of the date.

6. Now, let's add the English name of the month to the preceding dataset. We already have the month available in the CAL_MONTH column. We will use the DECODE function to get the English name of the month, as shown in the following code:

```
SELECT (to_date('2021-01-01') + seq4()) cal_dt,
DATE_PART(day, cal_dt) as cal_dom --day of month,
```

```
DATE_PART(month, cal_dt) as cal_month --month of year,
DATE_PART(year, cal_dt) as cal_year --yearSS,
DATE_TRUNC('month', CAL_DT) cal_first_dom,
DATEADD('day', -1,,
  DATEADD('month', 1,
  DATE_TRUNC('month', CAL_DT))) cal_last_dom
,DECODE(CAL_MONTH,
            1, 'January',
            2, 'February',
            3, 'March',
            4, 'April',
            5, 'May',
            6, 'June',
            7, 'July',
            8, 'August',
            9, 'September',
            10, 'October',
            11, 'November',
            12, 'December') as cal_month_name
FROM TABLE(GENERATOR(ROWCOUNT => 365));
```

Some partial output is shown in the following screenshot. Here, we can see some data rows corresponding to January and February 2021:

CAL_DT	CAL_DOM	CAL_MONTH	CAL_YEAR	CAL_FIRST_DOM	CAL_LAST_DOM	CAL_MONTH_NAME
2021-01-01	1	1	2021	2021-01-01	2021-01-31	January
2021-01-02	2	1	2021	2021-01-01	2021-01-31	January
2021-01-03	3	1	2021	2021-01-01	2021-01-31	January
2021-01-04	4	1	2021	2021-01-01	2021-01-31	January
2021-01-05	5	1	2021	2021-01-01	2021-01-31	January

Figure 9.10 – Using the DECODE() function to generate the month's name in English

We can map the numeric month to the name due to the DECODE function, which takes the month's numeric value and spits out the month's name. This has been made possible by the list of key-value pairs we provided to the decode function.

7. Now, let's add a column to our dataset that captures the quarter's end against each date. We will be using the DATE_TRUNC function, which will be passed alongside the 'quarter' parameter, to manage this. The process is like the one we used to arrive at the end of the month for each month. The following code shows the new CAL_QTR_END_DT column, which represents the last date of the quarter:

```
SELECT (to_date('2021-01-01') + seq4()) cal_dt
,DATE_PART(day, cal_dt) as cal_dom --day of month
,DATE_PART(month, cal_dt) as cal_month --month of year
,DATE_PART(year, cal_dt) as cal_year --yearSS
,DATE_TRUNC('month', CAL_DT) cal_first_dom
,DATEADD('day', -1,
    DATEADD('month', 1,
    DATE_TRUNC('month', CAL_DT))) cal_last_dom
,DECODE(CAL_MONTH,
            1, 'January',
            2, 'February',
            3, 'March',
            4, 'April',
            5, 'May',
            6, 'June',
            7, 'July',
            8, 'August',
            9, 'September',
            10, 'October',
            11, 'November',
            12, 'December') as cal_month_name
,DATEADD('day', -1,
    DATEADD('month', 3,
    DATE_TRUNC('quarter', CAL_DT))) as CAL_QTR_END_DT

FROM TABLE(GENERATOR(ROWCOUNT => 365));
```

The output of this query can be seen in the following screenshot:

CAL_DT	CAL_DOM	CAL_MONTH	CAL_YEAR	CAL_FIRST_DOM	CAL_LAST_DOM	CAL_MONTH_NAME	CAL_QTR_END_DT
2021-01-01	1	1	2021	2021-01-01	2021-01-31	January	2021-03-31
2021-01-02	2	1	2021	2021-01-01	2021-01-31	January	2021-03-31
2021-01-03	3	1	2021	2021-01-01	2021-01-31	January	2021-03-31
2021-01-04	4	1	2021	2021-01-01	2021-01-31	January	2021-03-31
2021-01-05	5	1	2021	2021-01-01	2021-01-31	January	2021-03-31

Figure 9.11 – Calendar generation for use in BI/Analytics

A new column has been added that shows the end of the quarters for March and April 2021. The end of quarter dates for the two months are March 31, 2021 and June 30, 2021.

Now that we have the SQL devised, the next step is to create a utility table with an appropriate name and then store the output in that table so that it can be used in an ETL process. The preceding SQL can also be extended as we can add important dates related to the fiscal calendar or any other calendar that's important to a business.

How it works...

In *step 1*, we used the generator function in the FROM clause, with the ROWCOUNT parameter passed a value of 365. This function will return a row set of 365 to the user. Then, we used the SEQ4() function, which allows a sequence of values to be used, starting with 0. The sequence function ensures that we increment its value when a new row is generated. Finally, adding the sequence value to the first date of 2021 allows each row to contain the next day of the year.

In *step 2*, we added extractors for the day of month, month, and year using the DATE_PART function.

In *step 3*, we used the DATE_TRUNC and DATEADD functions to manipulate the date to get to the values for the month's first and last days. Let's examine the process of calculating the last day of the month for January 1, 2021, as follows:

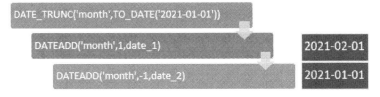

Figure 9.12 – Process for arriving at the last day of a month

In *step 4*, we used the DECODE function to map literal values to other literal values. In this case, the DECODE function has been provided with the names of the months that correspond to the numeric value of the month of the year. It is interesting to note that the DECODE function can take a variable number of parameters after the first parameter. Please note that to get the months' three-letter names, the DECODE function must be provided with key-value pairs such as DECODE(<param>, 1,'JAN',2,'FEB', …).

Unique counts and Snowflake

Estimating unique counts for rows in distributed systems is a compute-intensive process. Snowflake uses a distributed algorithm that is state of the art. This technique is different from those used in other databases. It is faster but, at the same time, approximate. The recipe shall show you how to use the uniqueness functions that are available in Snowflake.

Getting ready

Note that this recipe's steps can be run either in the Snowflake WebUI or the SnowSQL command-line client. An extra small warehouse will be used in the recipe.

How to do it...

As part of this recipe, we shall explore the different count functions/capabilities of Snowflake. We shall start with the typical count and distinct count functions and how different combinations can yield different results. Then, we shall explore the HyperLogLog algorithm implementation in Snowflake, which can efficiently approximate count over groups. This is recommended for use cases where accuracy can be traded for getting to the answer quickly. We shall make use of the existing dataset available within Snowflake. Let's get started:

1. First, let's perform a simple SELECT query on the Orders table, which is available in the SNOWFLAKE_DEMO_DB database and the TPCH_SF1000 schema. We shall query 1000 rows from the dataset:

```
select *
from "SNOWFLAKE_SAMPLE_DATA"."TPCH_SF1000"."ORDERS"
sample row (1000 rows);
```

The output can be seen in the following screenshot. Please note that it took 1 minute and 10 seconds for Snowflake to query the 1.5 billion rows in the table. Here, Snowflake has already queried the table; it has collected metadata and cached some data, which will help with subsequent queries:

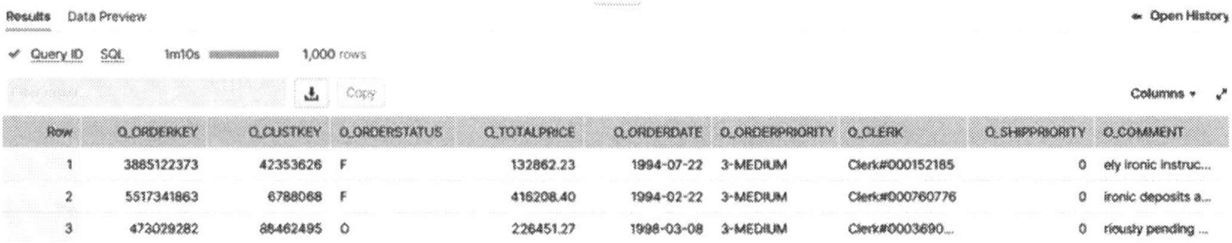

Row	O_ORDERKEY	O_CUSTKEY	O_ORDERSTATUS	O_TOTALPRICE	O_ORDERDATE	O_ORDERPRIORITY	O_CLERK	O_SHIPPRIORITY	O_COMMENT
1	3885122373	42353626	F	132862.23	1994-07-22	3-MEDIUM	Clerk#000152185	0	ely ironic instruc...
2	5517341863	6788068	F	416208.40	1994-02-22	3-MEDIUM	Clerk#000760776	0	ironic deposits a...
3	473029282	88462495	O	226451.27	1998-03-08	3-MEDIUM	Clerk#0003690...	0	riously pending ...

Figure 9.13 – Sample output

2. Next, we will execute a count on the `O_CUSTKEY` column while applying grouping to `O_ORDERPRIORITY`. The analytic that we are trying to calculate here is the popularity of order priority for customers. This does not mean we are looking for an interesting insight as we are dealing with synthetic data here:

```
select
O_ORDERPRIORITY
,count(O_CUSTKEY)
from "SNOWFLAKE_SAMPLE_DATA"."TPCH_SF1000"."ORDERS"
group by 1
order by 1;
```

We were able to get the result in almost 12 seconds, as shown in the following screenshot:

Row	O_ORDERPRIORITY	COUNT(O_CUSTKEY)
1	1-URGENT	300002709
2	2-HIGH	300005966
3	3-MEDIUM	299995087
4	4-NOT SPECIFIED	299993557
5	5-LOW	300002681

Figure 9.14 – Simple count results

3. Now, let's make things a bit difficult for Snowflake. We will calculate the same count but with a variation this time. Here, we will apply a `DISTINCT` function to the `O_CUSTKEY` column so that customers with repeat orders are counted once. However, to stop Snowflake from using results from its cache, we shall change one setting: we shall alter the session and set `USE_CACHED_RESULT` to `FALSE` first and then execute the query so that we do a distinct count over customers:

```
ALTER SESSION SET USE_CACHED_RESULT = FALSE;

SELECT O_ORDERPRIORITY
,count(DISTINCT O_CUSTKEY)
from "SNOWFLAKE_SAMPLE_DATA"."TPCH_SF1000"."ORDERS"
group by 1
order by 1;
```

The result can be seen in the following screenshot:

Figure 9.15 – Distinct count values

Please note that it took 1 minute and 58 seconds to get these five results on an extra small warehouse.

4. Now, let's try the same thing, but this time with the `APPROX_COUNT_DISTINCT` function on the `O_CUSTKEY` column, rather than with the `COUNT(DISTINCT …)` function we used in *step 3*:

```
select O_ORDERPRIORITY
,APPROX_COUNT_DISTINCT(O_CUSTKEY)
from "SNOWFLAKE_SAMPLE_DATA"."TPCH_SF100"."ORDERS"
```

```
group by 1
order by 1;
```

As expected, the result is similar to the previous step's outcome, but it is not the same, as shown in the following screenshot. Please note that the queries are being executed on an extra small virtual warehouse:

Row	O_ORDERPRIORITY	APPROX_COUNT_DISTINCT(O_CUSTKEY)
1	1-URGENT	97569695
2	2-HIGH	98219126
3	3-MEDIUM	97969543
4	4-NOT SPECIFIED	97856783
5	5-LOW	97596857

Figure 9.16 – Approximate counts

Let's look at the count for the **1-URGENT** category of **O_ORDERPRIORITY**. The count provided by the approximate method is around 97.5 million, while the result from the exact count was 97.8 million. This is an error of around 0.23 percent, while at the same time, the query execution time has come down to 17.29 seconds from almost 2 minutes. For use cases that do not require exact counts, it can be cost-effective to use an approximate method.

How it works...

The main item to understand in this recipe is the APPROX_COUNT_DISTINCT function. This function has another name in Snowflake – HLL. HLL stands for **HyperLogLog**. HyperLogLog is an algorithm that makes it easy to estimate the number of unique values within a large dataset. The mathematical term for this is **cardinality**. A set of 7 numbers, {3,6,2,5,6,1,7}, would have a cardinality of 6. It belongs to a class of algorithms called **probabilistic cardinality estimators**.

The HyperLogLog algorithm's basis is that the cardinality of a multiset of uniformly distributed random numbers can be estimated by calculating the maximum number of leading zeros in the binary representation of each number in the set. If the maximum number of leading zeros observed is nz, an estimate for the number of distinct elements in the set is 2nz.

Managing transactions in Snowflake

Snowflake is an ACID-compliant database system. ACID is an acronym for atomicity, consistency, isolation, and durability, a set of properties for database transactions that ensure that the data in a database remains valid during operations that change the data, regardless of errors and failures. This recipe will provide you with insights into how to use transactions in Snowflake. The different concepts around isolation will be covered in this recipe. Snowflake's limitations will also be explained, particularly around the scope of a transaction, how commits and rollbacks work, and how the session is important in managing transaction behavior.

Getting ready

Note that this recipe's steps can be run either in the Snowflake WebUI or the SnowSQL command-line client.

How to do it...

The recipe will start by introducing Snowflake constructs for enabling transactions. We shall investigate how transactions can be started, as well as how commits can be made or rolled back if an undesirable situation arises. We will use an example involving debits and credits in two tables, and we will use this as a transaction; that is, the credit and debit are balanced. Moreover, this recipe will involve a stored procedure that allows control over the transaction

Let's get started:

1. Let's create a database called CHAPTER9:

    ```
    CREATE DATABASE CHAPTER9;
    USE CHAPTER9;
    ```

2. Let's create two tables for this recipe. One table will be used to store debits in an account, while the other will store credits. The tables will be updated/inserted in a transaction:

    ```
    CREATE TABLE c9r4_credit (
    account int
    ,amount int
    ,payment_ts timestamp
    );
    ```

The preceding statement will create a table called `C9R4_CREDIT`. The table has one numeric column called `account` and another called `amount`.

3. Like the `C9R4_CREDIT` table, we will now create a table called `C9R4_DEBIT`:

```
CREATE TABLE c9r4_debit (
account int
,amount int
,payment_ts timestamp
);
```

Both tables we've created have a column called `payment_ts`. This column is of the timestamp type and will store timestamp data when it's inserted.

4. Now that we have created two tables that will be participating in a transaction, we shall introduce the stored procedure we'll be using. This stored procedure starts by inserting rows into the debit table. It then checks whether there are new rows in the debit table using the `payment_ts` value. If there are rows in the debit table that are absent in the credit table, it will insert the rows absent in the credit table from the debit table. We have introduced a random error in the stored procedure by using a random number generator to explain different scenarios. If the condition is true, then a delete operation is executed on a table that does not exist. This causes a failure in SQL. The error is placed after the inserts, which are part of the transaction. If that error is hit, the delete query statement is executed, and the stored procedure executes a rollback. That rollback will remove the row that was inserted into the debit and credit tables before the commit. We can then exit the stored procedure, which will show an error message that reads `Failed : Table not found …`:

```
create or replace procedure sp_adjust_credit
(PARAM_ACCT FLOAT,PARAM_AMT FLOAT)
    returns string
    language javascript
    as
    $$

    var ret_val = "";
    var sql_command_debit = "";
    var sql_command_credit = "";

    // INSERT data into the debit table
```

```
    sql_command_debit = "INSERT INTO CHAPTER9.PUBLIC.
C9R4_DEBIT VALUES (" + PARAM_ACCT + "," + PARAM_AMT +
",current_timestamp());";

    sql_command_credit = "insert into CHAPTER9.
    PUBLIC.C9R4_CREDIT select * from CHAPTER9.PUBLIC.
    C9R4_DEBIT where CHAPTER9.PUBLIC.C9R4_DEBIT.
    payment_ts > (select IFF(max(payment_ts) IS NULL,
    to_date ('1970-01-01'),max(payment_ts)) from
    CHAPTER9.PUBLIC.C9R4_CREDIT);";


    snowflake.execute( {sqlText: "BEGIN WORK;"} );
    // start transaction


    try {
            snowflake.execute ({sqlText: sql_command_
debit});


            if ((PARAM_ACCT % 2) === 0)
                snowflake.execute( {sqlText: "DELETE FROM
table_0123456789;"} ); // induce a fault


            snowflake.execute ({sqlText: sql_command_
credit});


            snowflake.execute({sqlText: "COMMIT
WORK;"});
            ret_val = "Succeeded";
        }catch (err) {
            snowflake.execute( {sqlText: "ROLLBACK
WORK;"} );
            return "Failed: " + err;   // Return a
success/error indicator.
        }
        return ret_val;
    $$;
```

5. We will use the previously stored `sp_adjust_credit()` procedure to atomically insert rows into the debit and credit tables we created in *steps 2 and 3*. A transaction will be managed within the stored procedure scope, as shown in the preceding code. The stored procedure has two `FLOAT` type arguments being passed in. These two arguments, `PARAM_ACCT` and `PARAM_AMT`, are supplied with the numbers representing the **Account Number** and **Amount** to be inserted into the **Credit Table**. Please note that JavaScript requires the parameters to be CAPITALIZED.

6. The numbers in the two arguments are supplied to the `INSERT` operation to be applied to the `C9R4_DEBIT` table. The next step involves creating some SQL statements for inserting data into the `C9R4_DEBIT` and `C9R4_CREDIT` tables. (Refer to lines 11 – 13 of the code for the stored procedure. Please note that the line numbers are based on the **Stored Procedure** code being opened in a text editor.)

7. Line 15 involves the beginning of the transaction. For a graceful exit in case of an error or fault (exception), a `TRY/CATCH` function is employed to manage the transaction's execution. Lines 18 and 23 execute the prepared inserts.

8. Line 20 captures a mechanism that generates an exception (for illustrating its behavior, not for practical use) while the inserts are executing. Line 21 contains the code that tries to delete records from a non-existing table, thus causing an exception. This would only happen when the account number is even. When this happens, control will be transferred to the `CATCH` section of the code (line 27), causing a ROLLBACK of the transaction and then returning an error message.

9. If the error is not induced, then a `COMMIT` function will be executed, and a normal return from the stored procedure will happen. The calling system shall receive a result saying "Succeeded". Upon executing the procedure, the following message should appear once the code has executed successfully:

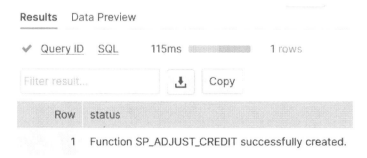

Figure 9.17 – Successfully deploying a stored procedure

10. Now that we have a good understanding of the stored procedure, let's insert some data into the tables by calling the following function. But before that, to gain better control of Snowflake's transactional behavior in stored procedures, we shall configure AUTOCOMMIT so that it's turned off:

```
ALTER SESSION SET AUTOCOMMIT = FALSE;
```

11. Next, let's call the stored procedure that handles the transaction and atomically insert some data into the credit and debit tables:

```
call sp_adjust_credit(1,100);
```

Here is the output of the preceding query:

Results   Data Preview

✔ Query ID   SQL   43ms ▬▬▬▬▬▬▬   1 rows

Filter result...   [↓]   Copy

Row	status
1	Statement executed successfully.

Figure 9.18 – Transaction successful

12. To confirm that the transaction was successful and that both tables – credit and debit – were inserted with exact numbers, let's execute some SELECT queries on the credit and debit tables:

```
SELECT * FROM c9r4_credit;
```

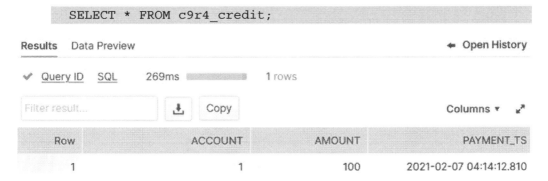

Results   Data Preview   ↞ Open History

✔ Query ID   SQL   269ms ▬▬▬▬▬▬▬   1 rows

Filter result...   [↓]   Copy   Columns ▾ ↗

Row	ACCOUNT	AMOUNT	PAYMENT_TS
1	1	100	2021-02-07 04:14:12.810

Figure 9.19 – Rows in the c9r4_credit table

Similarly, for the `c9r4_debit` table, we should get the following output:

Figure 9.20 – Rows in the c9r4_debit table

13. Now that we have data in the tables, let's simulate a transaction failure. We shall insert a record with the account number (`PARAM_ACCT`) equal to 2. This is an even number, thus causing the error mechanism to kick in, leading to transaction failure once the row has been inserted into the debit table:

```
call sp_adjust_credit(2,200);
```

14. The following screenshot shows that a failure was encountered, and the details of the error are provided. The failure was caused by the absence of the table that the delete operation had been executed on:

Figure 9.21 – Error resulting from a missing table

15. At this point, please execute the `SELECT` statements from *step 10*. The results will be the similar to the ones shown in *Figures 9.21* and *9.22*.

16. Finally, let's reconfigure the `AUTOCOMMIT` behavior so that it's turned on:

```
ALTER SESSION SET AUTOCOMMIT = TRUE;
```

How it works...

Transactions, in the case of Snowflake, are managed in a manner fairly similar to traditional databases. Snowflake allows us to combine multiple statements in a transaction block and commit or roll back the whole transaction block. In this recipe, we learned that a transaction can span over multiple SQL statements and can even be extended to stored procedures. Here, we have demonstrated how an error between a transaction can disrupt the transaction's execution. In real life, this error might be due to an operational failure that causes a SQL statement to fail. In such a scenario, the whole transaction block can be rolled back as a whole.

Ordered analytics over window frames

The recipe will provide you with insight into Snowflake's ability to run ordered or simple analytics over subsets of rows. Such analytics are typically used in marketing analytics applications, where moving average or cumulative functions are applied to data to identify trends. These capabilities help data scientists wrangle large datasets.

Getting ready

Note that this recipe's steps can be run either in the Snowflake WebUI or the SnowSQL command-line client. We shall be generating data that we intend to use in this recipe. The dataset will have three columns: `customer_id`, `deposit_dt`, and `deposit`. This data will capture deposits that have been made by a customer on a particular date.

How to do it...

Let's start by generating some sample data. We shall create a view with the logic to generate data:

1. The following query will be used to generate base data that will be used to implement a view. We will be using the CHAPTER9 database for this:

```
create database chapter9; // create if not exists
use chapter9;
create or replace view c9r5_vw as
select
    mod(seq4(),5) as customer_id
    ,(mod(uniform(1,100,random()),5) + 1)*100 as deposit
    ,dateadd(day, '-' || seq4(), current_date()) as
deposit_dt
```

```
from
  table
    (generator(rowcount => 365));
```

2. The view has the logic to generate 365 records. CUSTOMER_ID holds five unique values (0 to 4) that repeat for the records. The next column is DEPOSIT, and contains values from the set {100,200,300,400,500}. The third column is the date, starting with the current date, going back 365 days. The output of using a SELECT * function on the preceding view can be seen in the following screenshot:

Results   Data Preview

✔ Query ID   SQL   83ms ▬▬▬▬▬   365 rows

Filter result...   ⬇   Copy

Row	CUSTOMER_ID	DEPOSIT	DEPOSIT_DT
1	0	200	2020-11-24
2	1	100	2020-11-23
3	2	500	2020-11-22
4	3	100	2020-11-21
5	4	200	2020-11-20
6	0	100	2020-11-19

Figure 9.22 – Sample data representing transactions generated on different dates

3. Now that we have created a view, let's use this dataset to run a few window functions available in Snowflake. We shall highlight customers who made a single deposit amounting to more than the cumulative sum of their last two deposits:

```
SELECT
      customer_id,
      deposit_dt,
      deposit,
      deposit >
      COALESCE(SUM(deposit) OVER (
              PARTITION BY customer_id
              ORDER BY deposit_dt
              ROWS BETWEEN 2 PRECEDING AND 1
```

```
    PRECEDING)
          , 0) AS hi_deposit_alert
    FROM c9r5_vw
    ORDER BY
          customer_id, deposit_dt desc;
```

This query shall generate a column that will show TRUE or FALSE, depending on the fact that a customer made a deposit more than the sum of their last two deposits. The output is as follows:

Results   Data Preview

✔ Query ID   SQL   406ms ▒▒▒▒▒▒▒▒   365 rows

Filter result...   ⬇   Copy

Row	CUSTOMER_ID	DEPOSIT_DT	DEPOSIT	HI_DEPOSIT_ALERT
29	0	2020-07-07	500	TRUE
30	0	2020-07-02	300	TRUE
31	0	2020-06-27	100	FALSE
32	0	2020-06-22	100	FALSE
33	0	2020-06-17	200	FALSE

Figure 9.23 – Comparing each customer's deposit with the sum of their two preceding deposits

4. Here, we can see that for the given CUSTOMER_ID (0), the value of HI_DEPOSIT_ALERT is TRUE on DEPOSIT_DT = 2020-07-07. This is because the deposit that was made on that date was 500, which is greater than the sum of deposits of 300 and 100 that were made on 2020-07-02 and 2020-06-27, respectively. Similarly, the 300 deposit that was made on 2020-07-02 is greater than the sum of deposits of 100 that were made on 2020-06-27 and 2020-06-22.

5. We can use many other functions for the window ranges. Similarly, window ranges can have different configurations.

6. Let's change the window range and use the average rather than the sum. We shall specify a window that looks back at all the deposits that were made before the current row. We shall calculate the average deposit in that window and compare that with the current deposit to see whether it is a higher-than-normal deposit:

```
    SELECT
          customer_id,
          deposit_dt,
          deposit,
```

```
        COALESCE(AVG(deposit) OVER (
                  PARTITION BY customer_id
                  ORDER BY deposit_dt
                  ROWS BETWEEN UNBOUNDED PRECEDING AND 1
     PRECEDING)
         , 0) as past_average_deposit,
         deposit > past_average_deposit AS hi_deposit_alert
     FROM
         c9r5_vw

     WHERE CUSTOMER_ID = 3
     ORDER BY
         customer_id, deposit_dt desc;
```

The output is as follows:

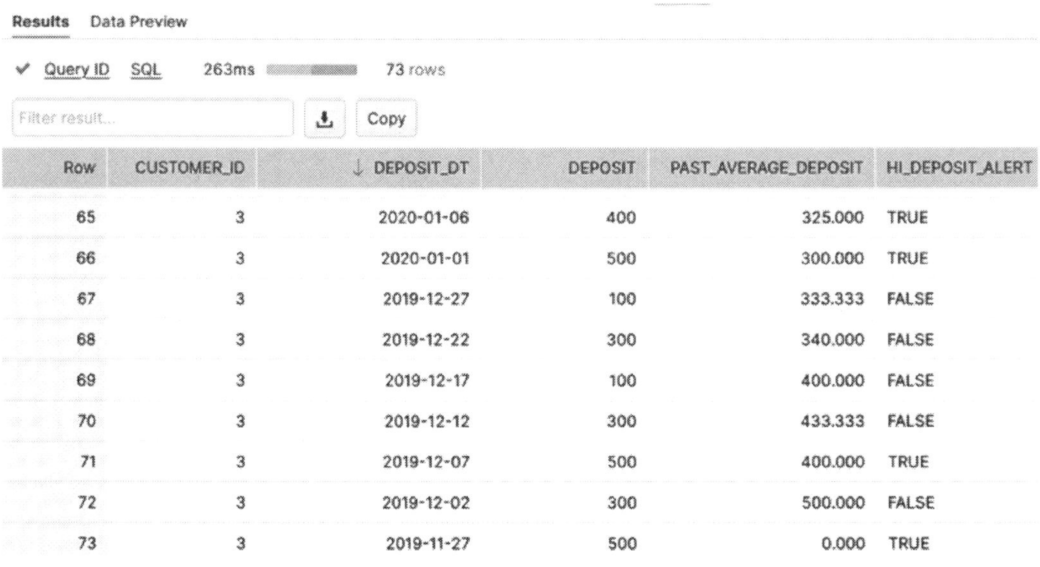

Results   Data Preview

✔ Query ID   SQL   263ms ▬▬▬▬▬▬   73 rows

[Filter result...]   ⬇   Copy

Row	CUSTOMER_ID	↓ DEPOSIT_DT	DEPOSIT	PAST_AVERAGE_DEPOSIT	HI_DEPOSIT_ALERT
65	3	2020-01-06	400	325.000	TRUE
66	3	2020-01-01	500	300.000	TRUE
67	3	2019-12-27	100	333.333	FALSE
68	3	2019-12-22	300	340.000	FALSE
69	3	2019-12-17	100	400.000	FALSE
70	3	2019-12-12	300	433.333	FALSE
71	3	2019-12-07	500	400.000	TRUE
72	3	2019-12-02	300	500.000	FALSE
73	3	2019-11-27	500	0.000	TRUE

Figure 9.24 – Comparing the current deposit to the average of all the previous deposits of a customer

We have also added a column that calculates the past average deposit for the customer with **CUSTOMER_ID = 3**. This is then compared with the current value of the deposit to generate an alert.

How it works...

Windowing functions in Snowflake allow you to aggregate and utilize information from rows other than the current row. Windowing functions can perform aggregations across other rows that are related to the current row in some manner. Unlike regular aggregations, the windowing functions do not group rows and reduce the number of output rows. The following table explains the concept of how windowing works:

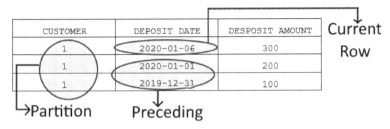

Figure 9.25 – Explanation of partition, grouping, and current row

The latest record for customer 1 is from the deposit date of 2020-01-06. If we need to look at the deposits from the last two records for the same customer, we can see that the latest deposit is equal to the sum of the previous two deposits, as explained in the preceding table.

Generating sequences in Snowflake

Sequence generation is a common practice in data warehousing that's required in different scenarios where row uniqueness is needed. This recipe will demonstrate what sequence value variations can be made with Snowflake sequences, while also demonstrating how to configure a column in a table so that it defaults to an auto-increment value.

Getting ready

Note that this recipe's steps can be run either in the Snowflake WebUI or the SnowSQL command-line client.

How to do it...

In this recipe, we shall be exploring the sequence creation process and the various parameters that control a sequence's behavior. Then, we will create and populate tables where their column values are based on values from sequences. Let's get started:

1. We will start by creating a database where we will create the objects for this recipe. Within this database, we will create a basic sequence object, as shown here:

```
CREATE DATABASE C9_R6;
CREATE SEQUENCE SEQ1;
```

2. The sequence should succeed and show the following message:

status

Sequence SEQ1 successfully created.

Figure 9.26 – SEQUENCE creation message given by Snowflake

3. Now, let's select a value from this newly created sequence. To do so, run the following SQL:

```
SELECT SEQ1.NEXTVAL;
```

4. You will see a value of 1 being returned, as shown here:

NEXTVAL

1

Figure 9.27 – Initializing a sequence

5. Now that the sequence has been incremented, if we perform the same SELECT statement again, we will get the next value in the sequence, which will be 2. Run the following SQL to check the next value:

```
SELECT SEQ1.NEXTVAL;
```

6. The result is shown in the following screenshot:

Figure 9.28 – The next value of the sequence on the second call

7. Let's try executing several `function` in a single statement to validate that the function always returns unique values, even if it's called several times during the same statement. To do so, run the following SQL:

```
SELECT SEQ1.NEXTVAL, SEQ1.NEXTVAL, SEQ1.NEXTVAL;
```

8. Depending on the sequence's value, you will see different values being printed for each column, as shown here:

NEXTVAL	NEXTVAL	NEXTVAL
3	4	5

Figure 9.29 – Series of calls made to the sequence and order of execution

9. Now, let's create a sequence that starts at 777 (instead of 1) and increments by 100 (rather than 1). To do so, run the following SQL:

```
CREATE SEQUENCE SEQ_SPECIAL
START WITH = 777
INCREMENT BY = 100;
```

10. The sequence should be created successfully, and you should see the following message:

status
Sequence SEQ_SPECIAL successfully created.

Figure 9.30 – Successful sequence creation

11. Let's test the preceding sequence by running the following SQL:

```
SELECT SEQ_SPECIAL.NEXTVAL, SEQ_SPECIAL.NEXTVAL, SEQ_
SPECIAL.NEXTVAL;
```

12. This command's output will show that this sequence starts at 777 and increments by 100, as shown here:

NEXTVAL	NEXTVAL	NEXTVAL
777	877	977

Figure 9.31 – Effect of INTERVAL on SEQUENCE

13. Sequences can also be used to populate incremental values in columns in a table. The following example shows how to create a new table and insert data into one of its columns using a sequence. Let's create the table first:

```
CREATE TABLE T1
(
   CUSTOMER_ID INTEGER,
   CUSTOMER_NAME STRING
);
```

14. We will follow that by creating a sequence that will be used for populating auto-increment values in the CUSTOMER_ID column:

```
CREATE SEQUENCE T1_SEQ;
```

15. We shall now use the sequence in the INSERT INTO statement to populate the data:

```
INSERT INTO T1
SELECT T1_SEQ.NEXTVAL,
        RANDSTR(10, RANDOM())
FROM
   TABLE
     (generator(rowcount => 500));
```

16. You will see that 500 rows have been inserted into this table. Now, let's perform a SELECT function on the table to view the inserted data. To do so, run the following SQL:

```
SELECT * FROM T1;
```

17. From the output, it is evident that the CUSTOMER_ID column has been populated with auto-increment values, as shown in the following screenshot:

CUSTOMER_ID	CUSTOMER_NAME
1	7AY4NU9wab
2	3LRjC3O8Dw
3	3YSHXySbQe
4	D75Bs7VYmy
5	gOiwOBlr6E
6	hAxBZMzTlp
7	RFMWN3oELp

Figure 9.32 – GENERATOR used with explicit calls to SEQUENCE

18. It is also possible to define the default value for a table column so that it's the sequence next value. To do so, run the following SQL:

```
CREATE SEQUENCE T2_SEQ;
CREATE TABLE T2
(
    CUSTOMER_ID INTEGER DEFAULT T2_SEQ.NEXTVAL,
    CUSTOMER_NAME STRING
);
```

19. The CREATE table should be created successfully.

20. Let's now insert some data into this table but omit CUSTOMER_ID while inserting. To do so, run the following SQL:

```
INSERT INTO T2 (CUSTOMER_NAME)
SELECT RANDSTR(10, RANDOM())
FROM
    TABLE
        (generator(rowcount => 500));
```

21. Notice that we have not provided a value for the CUSTOMER_ID column. The insert should succeed, with 500 rows being inserted.

22. Let's check the data in the table by running the following SQL:

```
SELECT * FROM T2;
```

23. The output is as follows:

CUSTOMER_ID	CUSTOMER_NAME
1	TSbkuwBz3L
2	eZt6nFWIPC
3	vlsS3Dv27d
4	iKoQ9aFCzz
5	rSWSdzr5sJ
6	tcy8rb7gGF

Figure 9.33 – GENERATOR used with an implicit SEQUENCE

24. As we can see, the CUSTOMER_ID column has automatically been assigned an incremental value since we set up the column default value to be NEXTVAL of the sequence.

How it works...

Sequences in Snowflake are used to produce unique numbers, which auto-increment according to a defined interval. Sequences can be used in a variety of manners and are guaranteed to be unique across multiple statements and sessions; that is, if the sequence is used in parallel, each execution of the sequence will produce a unique value that will not clash with the value in any other session or statement.

Sequences can be used in various use cases. A relatively common use case is allocating a primary key or auto-incrementing values to columns. In Snowflake, this is as simple as calling the NEXTVAL function on the sequence.

Please note that SEQUENCE in Snowflake, like other distributed databases, is not guaranteed to be gap-free.

10
Extending Snowflake Capabilities

This chapter provides techniques for extending Snowflake capabilities and integrating a Snowflake-based data warehouse to work with other technologies. The chapter guides you through the creation of **User-Defined Functions** (**UDFs**), which can help introduce functionality that may currently be missing in Snowflake. It also talks about the two different languages that UDFs support and the two different modes in which UDFs can exist, and offers a guide on connecting Snowflake with Apache Spark for data exchanges between Snowflake and Spark. Then, the chapter explores scenarios involving externalizing data processing to a Spark engine, which could help support existing Spark pipelines in the customer's ecosystem or as a cost optimization technique for ETL.

The following recipes will be covered in this chapter:

- Creating a Scalar user-defined function using SQL
- Creating a Table user-defined function using SQL
- Creating a Scalar user-defined function using JavaScript
- Creating a Table user-defined function using JavaScript
- Connecting Snowflake with Apache Spark
- Using Apache Spark to prepare data for storage on Snowflake

Technical requirements

This chapter requires access to a modern internet browser (Chrome, Microsoft Edge, Firefox, and so on) and access to the internet to connect your Snowflake instance to the cloud.

The code for this chapter can be found at the following GitHub URL:

```
https://github.com/PacktPublishing/Snowflake-Cookbook/tree/
master/Chapter10
```

Creating a Scalar user-defined function using SQL

Snowflake provides capabilities for creating UDFs that can extend the system and perform operations not available out of the box in Snowflake. Snowflake allows two languages for the creation of UDFs, SQL-based UDFs, and JavaScript-based UDFs. Either of the UDF types can return scalar or table results.

In this recipe, we will be walking you through the creation of SQL-based *Scalar* UDFs and demonstrating how to call the UDFs for various scenarios. A scalar UDF can return a single row of results consisting of a single column, which is essentially equivalent to returning a single value.

Getting ready

You will need to be connected to your Snowflake instance via the web UI or the SnowSQL client to execute this recipe.

How to do it...

We will be creating a series of UDFs to demonstrate the various SQL UDF capabilities provided by Snowflake. We will start by creating a relatively simple UDF and will slowly increase the complexity of the UDFs that we create. The basic syntax of creating a SQL function is straightforward and as follows:

```
CREATE FUNCTION <name> ( [ <arg_name> <arg_data_type> ] )
RETURNS <result_data_type>
AS '<function_definition_in_SQL>'
```

Using the previous syntax, we will create a new UDF and call the UDF in a SQL statement:

1. Let's start by creating a database in which we will create our SQL scalar UDFs. To do so, execute the following command:

```
CREATE DATABASE C10_R1;
```

2. Next, we will create a relatively simple UDF that squares the value that is provided as the input:

```
CREATE FUNCTION square(val float)
RETURNS float
AS
$$
    val * val
$$
;
```

The function should be created with a success message. Notice that the body of the function has been enclosed between the $$ symbols. You can use either the $$ symbols or enclose the function body between single quotes.

3. We can now test this function by calling it in a SELECT statement. To do so, run the following command:

```
SELECT square(5);
```

The statement will output the value 25 as expected.

4. Let's create a slightly more complicated function that can apply a tax percentage (10% in this case) and return us the profit after tax deduction. To do so, run the following command:

```
CREATE FUNCTION profit_after_tax(cost float, revenue
float)
RETURNS float
AS
$$
    (revenue - cost) * (1 - 0.1)
$$
;
```

The function should be created successfully.

5. Let's now call the function with a simple `SELECT` statement, shown as follows:

```
SELECT profit_after_tax(100,120);
```

The call returns **18** as a result, which indicates that the profit before tax was $20 and 10% was subtracted, to leave us with $18.

6. We can also call this UDF in several places in the SQL. This UDF can be used in the `SELECT` list or the `WHERE` clause and pretty much any place where a scalar value can be used, for example, joins. Let's call this UDF in the `SELECT` list and the `WHERE` clause as follows:

```
SELECT DD.D_DATE, SUM(profit_after_tax(SS_WHOLESALE_
    COST,SS_SALES_PRICE)) AS real_profit
FROM SNOWFLAKE_SAMPLE_DATA.TPCDS_SF10TCL.STORE_SALES SS
INNER JOIN SNOWFLAKE_SAMPLE_DATA.TPCDS_SF10TCL.DATE_DIM
    DD
ON SS.SS_SOLD_DATE_SK = DD.D_DATE_SK
WHERE DD.D_DATE BETWEEN '2003-01-01' AND '2003-12-31'
AND profit_after_tax(SS_WHOLESALE_COST,SS_SALES_PRICE)
    < -50
GROUP BY DD.D_DATE;
```

7. We are trying to return only those results in this query where the **profit_after_tax** was negative and less than -$50, which is the sales that made a significant loss. The results are shown as follows:

D_DATE	REAL_PROFIT
2003-01-01	-153011149.065
2003-01-02	-152977353.948

Figure 10.1 – Output of calling the profit_after_tax UDF

The preceding example demonstrated the creation and use of a simple scalar SQL UDF. Scalar UDFs can be used in most places in a SQL statement, including in `SELECT`, `WHERE`, and `GROUP BY` clauses.

How it works...

Snowflake provides the capability to create UDFs using the familiar SQL syntax. The more commonly occurring version of UDFs is scalar UDFs that return a single value. Almost all SQL operations can be performed within a UDF body, including arithmetic, calling other UDFs, and even aggregating data from a table.

Creating a Table user-defined function using SQL

Snowflake provides capabilities for creating UDFs that can be used to extend the system and perform operations that are not available out of the box in Snowflake. Snowflake allows two languages for the creation of UDFs, SQL-based UDFs and JavaScript-based UDFs. Either of the UDF types can return scalar or table results.

In this recipe, we will be walking you through the creation of SQL-based *Table* UDFs and demonstrating how to call the UDFs in various scenarios. A Table UDF can return multiple rows of data.

Getting ready

You will need to be connected to your Snowflake instance via the Web UI or the SnowSQL client to execute this recipe.

How to do it

We will be creating a series of UDFs to demonstrate the SQL *Table* UDF capabilities provided by Snowflake. We will start by exploring some of the existing Table UDFs provided by Snowflake and reviewing their output:

1. Let's start by creating a database in which we will create our SQL tabular UDFs. To do so, execute the following command:

```
CREATE DATABASE C10_R2;
USE DATABASE C10_R2;
USE SCHEMA PUBLIC;
```

2. Next, we will run an out-of-the-box table function provided by Snowflake to see how to call table functions and review the results returned by those functions. To do so, run the following command:

```
SELECT *
FROM TABLE(information_schema.query_history_by_session())
ORDER BY start_time;
```

The preceding query should show results like the following; however, do note that you will get different results depending on how many other queries you have run:

Row	QUERY_ID	QUERY_TEXT	DATABASE_NA	SCHEMA_NAME	QUER
1	019a4342-0...	CREATE DATABASE...	NULL	NULL	CREA
2	019a4342-0...	USE DATABASE C10...	C10_R2	PUBLIC	USE
3	019a4342-0...	USE SCHEMA PUBL...	C10_R2	PUBLIC	USE

Figure 10.2 – Output of the query_history_by_session table function

3. The vital aspect to note here is that we have just called a **table function**. Since a table function returns multiple rows and columns, the result we see in the previous step is in a relational table format.

4. It is also important to note that the call must be enclosed within a TABLE(<functionname>) statement when calling a table function.

5. Let's now create a relatively simple table function using SQL. The function will return the name of a location and the time zone that the location has.

The basic syntax of creating a SQL function is straightforward and as follows:

```
CREATE FUNCTION <name> ( [ <arg_name> <arg_data_type> ] )
RETURNS TABLE ( <output_col_name> <output_col_type> [,
<output_col_name> <output_col_type> ... ] )
AS '<function_definition_in_SQL>'
```

Using the previous syntax, we will create a new UDF and call the UDF in a SQL statement.

6. To keep things simple, we will use hardcoded values. Run the following SQL to create this function:

```
CREATE FUNCTION LocationTimeZone()
RETURNS TABLE(LocationName String, TimeZoneName String)
as
$$
    SELECT 'Sydney', 'GMT+11'
    UNION
    SELECT 'Auckland', 'GMT+13'
    UNION
    SELECT 'Islamabad', 'GMT+5'
    UNION
    SELECT 'London', 'GMT'
$$;
```

The function should be successfully created.

7. Let's now call this function. To do so, run the following SQL:

```
SELECT * FROM TABLE(LocationTimeZone());
```

You will see the following output produced:

Row	LOCATIONNAME	TIMEZONENAME
1	Sydney	GMT+11
2	Auckland	GMT+13
3	Islamabad	GMT+5
4	London	GMT

Figure 10.3 – Output from calling the Table UDF LocationTimeZone

8. Note that you can treat this output as any other relational table, so you can add WHERE clauses and select only particular columns. To do so, run the following SQL:

```
SELECT TimeZoneName FROM TABLE(LocationTimeZone())
WHERE LocationName = 'Sydney';
```

Predictably, the output has only the row for Sydney and has only one column in the result set.

9. We do not necessarily have to hardcode values in a table function. We can select from existing tables and even join tables within our function definition. Let's create such a table function that joins data from two tables to produce an output:

```
CREATE FUNCTION CustomerOrders()
RETURNS TABLE(CustomerName String, TotalSpent
Number(12,2))
as
$$
    SELECT C.C_NAME AS CustomerName, SUM(O.O_TOTALPRICE)
AS TotalSpent
    FROM SNOWFLAKE_SAMPLE_DATA.TPCH_SF1.ORDERS O
    INNER JOIN SNOWFLAKE_SAMPLE_DATA.TPCH_SF1.CUSTOMER C
    ON C.C_CUSTKEY = O.O_CUSTKEY
    GROUP BY C.C_NAME
$$;
```

The creation of the function should be successful.

10. Let's call this function to review the output. To do so, run the following SQL:

```
SELECT * FROM TABLE(CustomerOrders());
```

You will see an output like what is shown here, and the function will return around 100,000 rows:

Row	CUSTOMERNAME	TOTALSPENT
1	Customer#000044485	3480299.61
2	Customer#000055624	2442812.17
3	Customer#000041861	2262921.26
4	Customer#000003296	1392250.10
5	Customer#000000307	3866167.74

Figure 10.4 – Output from calling the CustomerOrders UDF

11. Let's assume that we want to get the `TotalSpent` value for only a single customer. We are going to alter the function so that it can take the customer name as a parameter. To do so, run the following command:

```
CREATE FUNCTION CustomerOrders(CustomerName String)
RETURNS TABLE(CustomerName String, TotalSpent
Number(12,2))
as
$$
    SELECT C.C_NAME AS CustomerName, SUM(O.O_TOTALPRICE)
AS TotalSpent
    FROM SNOWFLAKE_SAMPLE_DATA.TPCH_SF1.ORDERS O
    INNER JOIN SNOWFLAKE_SAMPLE_DATA.TPCH_SF1.CUSTOMER C
    ON C.C_CUSTKEY = O.O_CUSTKEY
    WHERE C.C_NAME = CustomerName
    GROUP BY C.C_NAME
$$;
```

The function should be created successfully.

12. Before we go any further, it is essential to understand that we have created two functions here. One function is called `CustomerOrders`, which does not take any parameters, and there's another with the same name, which accepts the name as a parameter. To demonstrate this, run the following SQL:

```
SHOW FUNCTIONS LIKE '%CustomerOrders%';
```

You will see the following output, which explains that there are two functions created:

created_on	name	schema_name	is_builtin	is_aggregate	is_ansi	min_num_argum	max_num_argu	arguments
2021-02-13 ...	CUSTOMER...	PUBLIC	N	N	N	0	0	CUSTOMERORDERS() RETURN
2021-02-13 ...	CUSTOMER...	PUBLIC	N	N	N	1	1	CUSTOMERORDERS(VARCHAR)

Figure 10.5 – Output from step 14 showing two UDFs with the same name

13. Let's now call the new function by passing in a customer name as a parameter:

```
SELECT * FROM TABLE(CustomerOrders('Customer#000062993'));
```

This should succeed, with a single row demonstrating that only the rows for the specified customer are returned.

The examples in this recipe demonstrated Snowflake's built-in Table functions and the creation of new `Table` UDFs. `Table` UDFs differ from Scalar UDFs in their return type, which is of the `Table` type in the case of Table UDFs.

How it works

Table functions are a powerful way of defining UDFs in Snowflake, with several existing system functions provided by Snowflake as table functions. You can find a list of Snowflake table functions at `https://docs.snowflake.com/en/sql-reference/functions-table.html`.

There are two aspects to be mindful of when creating and using table functions. A table function can return multiple rows and columns due to its invocation, and therefore, the results returned are in a relational format. A table function cannot be called in the same way a scalar function is called, but rather, it must be enclosed in a `TABLE()` statement to convert the results to be useable in your query.

Creating a Scalar user-defined function using JavaScript

In this recipe, we will be walking you through the creation of JavaScript-based *Scalar* UDFs and demonstrating the usage of JavaScript-based UDFs.

Getting ready

You will need to be connected to your Snowflake instance via the Web UI or the SnowSQL client to execute this recipe.

How to do it

We will be creating a series of UDFs to demonstrate the various JavaScript UDF capabilities provided by Snowflake. We will start by creating a simple UDF and will gradually increase the complexity of the UDFs that we create. The basic syntax for creating a JavaScript-based UDF is similar to the syntax for creating a SQL UDF, but with a slight difference. The difference is that if you do not specify the `LANGUAGE` attribute, a UDF will default to the SQL language. The syntax for a JavaScript-based UDF is as follows:

```
CREATE FUNCTION <name> ( [ <arg_name> <arg_data_type> ] )
RETURNS <result_data_type>
[ LANGUAGE JAVASCRIPT ]
AS <function_definition_in_SQL>
```

You can find the detailed syntax at `https://docs.snowflake.com/en/sql-reference/sql/create-function.html`.

We will use the preceding syntax to create a new scalar UDF that uses JavaScript as the language:

1. Let's start by creating a database in which we will create our JavaScript-based scalar UDF. To do so, execute the following command:

    ```
    CREATE DATABASE C10_R3;
    ```

2. Next, we will create a very simple UDF that squares the value that is provided as the input. Note that compared to a SQL UDF, we must capitalize the parameter name in the function definition when defining an input parameter in a JavaScript UDF. This can be seen in the following code, where the input parameter `val` is used in uppercase as VAL:

    ```
    CREATE FUNCTION square(val float)
    RETURNS float
    LANGUAGE JAVASCRIPT
    AS
       'return VAL * VAL;'
    ;
    ```

    This function should be created with a success message.

3. We can now test this function by calling it in a `SELECT` statement. To do so, run the following command:

    ```
    SELECT square(5);
    ```

    The statement will output the value `25` as expected.

4. We will now demonstrate how to create a recursive UDF using JavaScript. For the demonstration, we will be creating a simple factorial function that will recursively call itself to calculate the factorial of the input value:

    ```
    CREATE FUNCTION factorial(val float)
    RETURNS float
    LANGUAGE JAVASCRIPT
    AS
    $$
        if ( VAL == 1 ){
    ```

```
        return VAL;
    }
    else{
        return VAL * factorial(VAL -1);
    }
$$
;
```

The function creation should complete successfully.

5. Let's try out the factorial function by invoking the function in a SELECT statement, as follows:

```
SELECT factorial(5);
```

This should result in the value 120 being returned.

As demonstrated in the preceding examples, JavaScript-based UDFs can be relatively straightforward to implement; however, it is worth noting that they also provide more powerful features, such as recursion capabilities.

How it works

Like other databases, Snowflake provides the capability to create UDFs. Unlike many other databases, Snowflake also allows the creation of these UDFs in JavaScript. That opens up a whole world of possibilities when creating your UDFs.

The overall syntax for creating a Snowflake JavaScript-based UDF is like creating a SQL UDF; however, it is required to specify the language as JavaScript. A JavaScript UDF's execution happens within a restricted engine, limiting certain JavaScript functionalities such as system calls.

Creating a Table user-defined function using JavaScript

Snowflake provides capabilities for creating UDFs that can be used to extend the system and perform operations not available out of the box in Snowflake. Snowflake allows two languages for the creation of UDFs, SQL-based UDFs and JavaScript-based UDFs. Either of the UDF types can return scalar or table results.

In this recipe, we will create JavaScript-based Table UDFs and demonstrate how to call the UDFs for various scenarios.

Getting ready

You will need to be connected to your Snowflake instance via the Web UI or the SnowSQL client to execute this recipe.

How to do it

We will be creating a series of UDFs to demonstrate the Table SQL UDF capabilities provided by Snowflake. We will start by exploring some of the existing Table UDFs provided by Snowflake and reviewing their output. The basic syntax for creating a JavaScript table UDF is as follows:

```
CREATE FUNCTION <name> ( [ <arg_name> <arg_data_type> ] )
RETURNS TABLE ( <output_col_name> <output_col_type>
[, <output_col_name> <output_col_type> ... ] )
[ LANGUAGE JAVASCRIPT ]
AS <function_definition_in_SQL>
```

You can find the detailed syntax at https://docs.snowflake.com/en/sql-reference/sql/create-function.html.

1. Let's start by creating a database in which we will create our SQL tabular UDFs. To do so, execute the following command:

    ```
    CREATE DATABASE C10_R4;
    USE DATABASE C10_R4;
    USE SCHEMA PUBLIC;
    ```

2. Next, we will run an out-of-the-box table function provided by Snowflake to see how to call table functions and review the results returned by those functions. We will use the function to generate rows of random data – it is a handy function for various scenarios. The function is aptly called GENERATOR. Let's call this function to generate 10 rows of data. To do so, run the following command:

    ```
    SELECT seq4() AS incremental_id, random() AS a_random_
        number
    FROM TABLE(generator(rowcount => 10));
    ```

3. This should return 10 rows, as shown in the following screenshot:

Row	INCREMENTAL_ID	A_RANDOM_NUMBER
1	0	1319172314325829327
2	1	7287171906336155199
3	2	1471939173074368979
4	3	1446911816204395330
5	4	3570717189561876932
6	5	8748051370615372015
7	6	9163926763116258811
8	7	-166691577935958742
9	8	-1882923199411928270
10	9	-3889428872739052128

Figure 10.6 – Random data produced by the GENERATOR table function

4. The important aspect to note here is that we have just called a TABLE function. Since a TABLE function returns multiple rows and columns, the preceding result is in a relational table format. It is also important to note that the call must be enclosed within a TABLE(<functionname>) statement when calling a table function.

5. Let's now create a relatively simple table function using JavaScript. The function will return the two-letter ISO code for a country. To keep things simple, we will use hardcoded values for this initial example. Run the following SQL to create this function:

```
CREATE FUNCTION CountryISO()
RETURNS TABLE(CountryCode String, CountryName String)
LANGUAGE JAVASCRIPT
AS
$$
    {
    processRow: function f(row, rowWriter, context){
        rowWriter.writeRow({COUNTRYCODE: "AU",COUNTRYNAME:
            "Australia"});
        rowWriter.writeRow({COUNTRYCODE: "NZ",COUNTRYNAME:
```

```
        "New Zealand"});
        rowWriter.writeRow({COUNTRYCODE: "PK",COUNTRYNAME:
        "Pakistan"});
    }
  }
$$;
```

Snowflake interacts with user-defined table functions through callback functions during the execution of a query. The preceding code used the `processRow` callback function to process rows and return them to the function output. Please note that we simply wrote three rows in the same callback function. Depending on your requirement, you may be processing a single row per callback. You can see more details at the following link: `https://docs.snowflake.com/en/ sql-reference/udf-js-table-functions.html#object-callback- functions`.

6. Note that we have specified the language as JavaScript, and very importantly, we are using the uppercase `COUNTRYCODE` and `COUNTRYNAME` in the function definition. It is a requirement in Snowflake JavaScript UDFs that these are capitalized.

7. Let's now call this function. To do so, run the following SQL:

```
SELECT * FROM TABLE(CountryISO());
```

You will see the following output produced:

Row	COUNTRYCODE ↓	COUNTRYNAME
1	AU	Australia
2	NZ	New Zealand
3	PK	Pakistan

Figure 10.7 – Output from the CountryISO UDF

8. Note that you can treat this output as any other relational table, so you can add `WHERE` clauses and select only particular columns. To do so, run the following SQL:

```
SELECT COUNTRYCODE FROM TABLE(CountryISO()) WHERE
CountryCode = 'PK';
```

Predictably, the output has only the row for Pakistan and has only the COUNTRYCODE column.

9. We do not necessarily have to hardcode values in a table functio. Instead, we can select data from the existing table and process each row. Let's create such a JavaScript-based table function, which processes values for each row of a table and produces the count of characters for the input:

```
CREATE FUNCTION StringSize(input String)
RETURNS TABLE (Size FLOAT)
LANGUAGE JAVASCRIPT
AS
$$
{
    processRow: function f(row, rowWriter, context) {
        rowWriter.writeRow({SIZE: row.INPUT.length});
    }
}
$$;
```

The creation of the function should be successful with a success message.

10. Let's call this function to review the output. We can now call this function for a single value, which is not very useful; however, let's call it for a single value to demonstrate the concept:

```
SELECT * FROM TABLE(StringSize('TEST'));
```

As expected, you will see the value 4 returned as a result. But this is not especially useful, and we could have easily achieved the same results from a scalar function instead.

11. However, you can join this newly created table function with another table and have the `table` function process multiple rows. To do this, run the SQL as follows:

```
SELECT * FROM
SNOWFLAKE_SAMPLE_DATA.TPCH_SF1.NATION,
TABLE(StringSize(N_NAME));
```

The query produces the following output.

N_NATIONKEY	N_NAME	↓ N_REGIONK	N_COMMENT	SIZE
0	ALGERIA	0	haggle. carefully final deposi...	7
1	ARGENTINA	1	al foxes promise slyly accord...	9
2	BRAZIL	1	y alongside of the pending d...	6
3	CANADA	1	eas hang ironic, silent packa...	6
4	EGYPT	4	y above the carefully unusua...	5
5	ETHIOPIA	0	ven packages wake quickly. ...	8
6	FRANCE	3	refully final requests. regular,...	6

Figure 10.8 – Output from the StringSize UDF processing multiple rows

12. This approach of using table functions is particularly powerful and allows you to create exciting functionality. An example of a `table` function being used is the `FLATTEN` function provided out of the box by Snowflake. For examples of `FLATTEN`, head to `https://docs.snowflake.com/en/sql-reference/functions/flatten.html`.

In the preceding steps, the creation of a *table* function using the JavaScript language was discussed. We also demonstrated how a *table* function could be joined with a table and process multiple rows through that mechanism.

How it works

Table functions are a powerful way of defining UDFs in Snowflake. Several existing system functions provided by Snowflake are table functions. You can find a list of Snowflake table functions at `https://docs.snowflake.com/en/sql-reference/functions-table.html`.

Table functions created using the JavaScript language are particularly powerful and provide processing mechanics that are not typically possible using the standard SQL-based UDFs. The functions being written in JavaScript enable you to use variables and manipulate them as you would in any other programming language to create desired outputs in a much simpler manner.

Connecting Snowflake with Apache Spark

Spark is a general-purpose data processing engine that can connect with different technologies. This recipe walks you through downloading the drivers and performing the configuration required to connect Spark with Snowflake. For simplicity, we will be performing the configuration on a standalone version of Spark running on an on-premise machine, but these instructions are portable to Spark clusters running on cloud platforms as well.

Getting ready

You will need to be connected to your Snowflake instance via the Web UI or the SnowSQL client to execute this recipe.

> **Note**
>
> This recipe assumes that Spark is installed and configured on your machine or that you have access to a cloud-based Spark installation.

How to do it

We will locate the JDBC driver and the Snowflake connector for Spark and use them to configure Spark connectivity with Snowflake:

1. Our first step will be to identify the correct version of the Snowflake Connector for Spark. Snowflake supports different versions of Spark. At the time of writing this book, Snowflake had support for Spark 2.3, Spark 2.4, and Spark 3.0. To find out the Spark version you are using, run the following command on the command line or the terminal:

    ```
    spark-shell --version
    ```

    This will show you results like the following:

    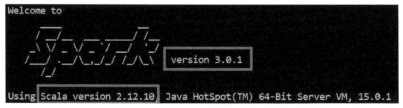

    Figure 10.9 – Output from the spark-shell-version command

2. Make a note of the Spark version and the Scala version shown in the output. In our case, we are using version 3.0.1 for Spark and the 2.12.10 Scala version.

3. Next, we will identify which version of the Snowflake Connector for Spark is most appropriate for us. While multiple versions of a connector may be supported, Snowflake recommends that you should always use the latest version of the connector that is appropriate for your version of Spark. To do so, navigate to `https://search.maven.org/` and search for `"spark-snowflake"`. Alternatively, you can navigate to the following URL with the search string in the URL itself, `https://search.maven.org/search?q=%22spark-snowflake%22`. You should see a result like what is shown here:

"spark-snowflake"						✕ Q
Group ID	Artifact ID	Latest Version		Updated	OSS Index	Download
net.snowflake	spark-snowflake_2.11	2.8.3-spark_2.4	(99+)	08-Dec-2020	☑	⬇
net.snowflake	spark-snowflake_2.12	2.8.3-spark_3.0	(23)	08-Dec-2020	☑	⬇
net.snowflake	spark-snowflake_2.10	2.5.3-spark_2.2	(56)	13-Sep-2019	☑	⬇

Figure 10.10 – List of Spark-related downloads in the Maven repository

4. In this list, each highlighted item means the following:

    a. `net.snowflake` is the **Group ID**, and we will use this when loading the Snowflake connector into Spark.

    b. `spark-snowflake_2.12` identifies a specific artifact, in this case, the Snowflake Connector for Spark. The name is postfixed with the Scala version, which in this case is 2.12. The artifact you choose from this list should match the Scala version identified in *step 1*.

    c. Finally, `2.8.3-spark_3.0`, identifies the Spark version that this connector supports. Note that the 2.8.3 in this name signifies the Snowflake connector version. It is advisable to choose the latest version for the connector.

5. Now that we have identified the Spark connector version we would like to use, we can start up `spark-shell` with the `-packages` command to load the correct connector. To do so, run the following on the command line:

```
spark-shell --packages net.snowflake:spark-
snowflake_2.12:2.8.3-spark_3.0
```

6. You will see `spark-shell` start and then see an output like what is shown in the following screenshot:

```
net.snowflake#spark-snowflake_2.12 added as a dependency
:: resolving dependencies :: org.apache.spark#spark-submit-parent-67ee4f32-a3da-4966-8103-f1b4e139b9af;1.0
        confs: [default]
        found net.snowflake#spark-snowflake_2.12;2.8.3-spark_3.0 in central
        found net.snowflake#snowflake-ingest-sdk;0.9.9 in central
        found net.snowflake#snowflake-jdbc;3.12.15 in central
:: resolution report :: resolve 171ms :: artifacts dl 29ms
        :: modules in use:
        net.snowflake#snowflake-ingest-sdk;0.9.9 from central in [default]
        net.snowflake#snowflake-jdbc;3.12.15 from central in [default]
        net.snowflake#spark-snowflake_2.12;2.8.3-spark_3.0 from central in [default]
        ---------------------------------------------------------------------
        |                  |            modules            ||   artifacts   |
        |       conf       | number| search|dwnlded|evicted|| number|dwnlded|
        ---------------------------------------------------------------------
        |     default      |   3   |   0   |   0   |   0   ||   3   |   0   |
        ---------------------------------------------------------------------
:: retrieving :: org.apache.spark#spark-submit-parent-67ee4f32-a3da-4966-8103-f1b4e139b9af
        confs: [default]
        0 artifacts copied, 3 already retrieved (0kB/39ms)
20/12/22 10:09:30 WARN NativeCodeLoader: Unable to load native-hadoop library for your platform... using builtin-java classe
s where applicable
Using Spark's default log4j profile: org/apache/spark/log4j-defaults.properties
Setting default log level to "WARN".
To adjust logging level use sc.setLogLevel(newLevel). For SparkR, use setLogLevel(newLevel).
Spark context Web UI available at http://host.docker.internal:4040
Spark context available as 'sc' (master = local[*], app id = local-1608592176845).
Spark session available as 'spark'.
Welcome to
      ____              __
     / __/__  ___ _____/ /__
    _\ \/ _ \/ _ `/ __/  '_/
   /___/ .__/\_,_/_/ /_/\_\   version 3.0.1
      /_/
```

Figure 10.11 – Output from the spark-shell startup

7. You can see that `spark-shell` is downloading the Snowflake Connector for spark and related dependencies. Once you see the **"Welcome to Spark"** message and no errors while resolving the dependencies, it means that `spark-shell` has successfully started with the Snowflake Connector for Spark.

8. We will now test that the connection works correctly. To do so, create a new text file called `test_sf_connect.scala` and paste the following code in that file. Please ensure that you replace the placeholders in the following code with your account information:

```
val SNOWFLAKE_SOURCE_NAME = "net.snowflake.spark.
snowflake"

// initialise the connectivity related variables
var snowflakeOptions = Map(
    "sfURL" -> "<replace_with_your_account_url>",
    "sfUser" -> "<replace_with_a_user_name>",
```

```
    "sfPassword" -> "<replace_with_password>",
    "sfDatabase" -> "SNOWFLAKE_SAMPLE_DATA",
    "sfSchema" -> "TPCH_SF1",
    "sfWarehouse" -> "<replace_with_the_virtual_
warehouse>"
)

//read and output a table
spark.read
    .format(SNOWFLAKE_SOURCE_NAME)
    .options(snowflakeOptions)
    .option("dbtable", "REGION")
    .load().show()
```

The preceding Spark script contains steps to connect to your Snowflake instance. Once a successful connection is established, it will attempt to query the REGION table from the TPCH_SF1 schema in the SNOWFLAKE_SAMPLE_DATA database.

9. Please note that the scala script in the previous code uses a basic authentication mechanism to reduce the complexity of this recipe. You can opt for other authentication mechanisms such as oAuth. The details for that can be found at https://docs.snowflake.com/en/user-guide/spark-connector-use.html#using-external-oauth.

10. Now, start spark-shell (if not already running) using the command provided in *step 3* of this section, and once spark-shell is ready, issue the following command. This command will load the script in the given file and execute it:

```
:load test_sf_connect.scala
```

11. Ensure that you start `spark-shell` in the directory where your `scala` file is or provide the full path to the `scala` file. As a result of the execution, you should see output like the following:

```
:load test_sf_connect.scala
Loading test_sf_connect.scala...
SNOWFLAKE_SOURCE_NAME: String = net.snowflake.spark.snowflake
snowflakeOptions: scala.collection.immutable.Map[String,String] = Map(sfSchema -> TPCH_SF1, sfPassword -> ,
sfUser -> , sfWarehouse -> COMPUTE_WH, sfDatabase -> SNOWFLAKE_SAMPLE_DATA, sfURL -> .snowflake
computing.com)
res0: org.apache.spark.sql.DataFrameReader = org.apache.spark.sql.DataFrameReader@a73b3c4
res1: org.apache.spark.sql.DataFrameReader = org.apache.spark.sql.DataFrameReader@a73b3c4
res2: org.apache.spark.sql.DataFrameReader = org.apache.spark.sql.DataFrameReader@a73b3c4
res3: org.apache.spark.sql.DataFrameReader = org.apache.spark.sql.DataFrameReader@a73b3c4
21/02/13 23:38:26 WARN DefaultJDBCWrapper$: JDBC 3.12.16 is being used. But the certified JDBC version 3.12.15 is recom
ended.
21/02/13 23:38:32 WARN DefaultJDBCWrapper$: JDBC 3.12.16 is being used. But the certified JDBC version 3.12.15 is recom
ended.
21/02/13 23:38:33 WARN DefaultJDBCWrapper$: JDBC 3.12.16 is being used. But the certified JDBC version 3.12.15 is recom
ended.
+-----------+-----------+-------------------+
|R_REGIONKEY|     R_NAME|          R_COMMENT|
+-----------+-----------+-------------------+
|          0|     AFRICA|lar deposits. bli...|
|          1|    AMERICA|hs use ironic, ev...|
|          2|       ASIA|ges. thinly even ...|
|          3|     EUROPE|ly final courts c...|
|          4|MIDDLE EAST|uickly special ac...|
+-----------+-----------+-------------------+
```

Figure 10.12 – Output from the test_sf_connect.scala sample Scala program

This indicates that the Snowflake Connector for Spark has successfully been configured, and we can connect to Snowflake and query a table through Spark.

This concludes our installation and configuration of the Spark Connector for Snowflake. The configuration's key aspect is identifying the correct version of Spark, Scala, and the Snowflake driver that you should use. Once the driver is configured, Snowflake can be queried from within Spark with ease.

How it works

Snowflake provides connectors for a variety of processing engines, including Spark. For Spark to connect to your Snowflake instance, you need to know two crucial aspects of your setup:

a) The version of Spark you are using; and

b) The version of Scala being used. Snowflake has drivers available that correspond to these versions. Once you know the version, start up Spark with the correct connector by passing the correct driver name during startup.

Using Apache Spark to prepare data for storage on Snowflake

This recipe provides you with an example of how Apache Spark and Snowflake partner to utilize the two systems' strengths. The recipe shows a scenario involving reading data from Snowflake into a Spark DataFrame and writing data back to Snowflake from a Spark DataFrame.

Getting ready

You will need to be connected to your Snowflake instance via the Web UI or the SnowSQL client to execute this recipe.

It is assumed that you have already configured the Snowflake Connector for Spark and can connect to the Snowflake instance successfully through Spark.

How to do it

We will be reading data from Snowflake sample tables and transforming the data before writing it back to Snowflake in a new table. The following code in the various steps should be added into a single `scala` file called `snowflake_transform.scala` since we will be calling that file from within `spark-shell`:

1. Let's start by creating a new database, which we will use to store our processing results from Spark. To do so, run the following SQL through the Snowflake web UI or SnowSQL:

```
USE ROLE SYSADMIN;
CREATE OR REPLACE DATABASE new_db;
```

2. Let's start by connecting to our Snowflake instances and validating that everything works. We will now test that the connection works correctly. Paste the following code in to the `snowflake_transform.scala` file. Please ensure that you replace the placeholders in the following code with your account information:

```
org.apache.spark.sql.DataFrameReader
import org.apache.spark.sql.DataFrame
import org.apache.spark.sql.SaveMode
val SNOWFLAKE_SOURCE_NAME = "net.snowflake.spark.
   snowflake"
```

```scala
// initialise the connectivity related variables
var snowflakeOptions = Map(
    "sfURL" -> "<replace_with_your_account_url>",
    "sfUser" -> "<replace_with_a_user_name>",
    "sfPassword" -> "<replace_with_password>",
    "sfDatabase" -> "NEW_DB",
    "sfSchema" -> "PUBLIC",
    "sfWarehouse" -> "<replace_with_the_virtual_
warehouse>"
)


// validate that connectivity works by querying a sample
table
//read and output a table
spark.read
    .format(SNOWFLAKE_SOURCE_NAME)
    .options(snowflakeOptions)
    .option("dbtable", "SNOWFLAKE_SAMPLE_DATA.TPCH_SF1.
         REGION")
    .load().show()
```

3. Now, run `spark-shell` and then run the following command:

```
:load snowflake_transform.scala
```

4. If the connection is successful, you will see the following results, which indicate that Spark successfully connected to your Snowflake instance and was able to query a sample table:

```
+-----------+-----------+--------------------+
|R_REGIONKEY|     R_NAME|           R_COMMENT|
+-----------+-----------+--------------------+
|          0|     AFRICA|lar deposits. bli...|
|          1|    AMERICA|hs use ironic, ev...|
|          2|       ASIA|ges. thinly even ...|
|          3|     EUROPE|ly final courts c...|
|          4|MIDDLE EAST|uickly special ac...|
+-----------+-----------+--------------------+
```

Figure 10.13 – Output from the test_sf_connect.scala sample Scala program signifying a successful connection

5. Please note that the preceding `scala` script uses a basic authentication mechanism to reduce the complexity in this recipe. You can opt for other authentication mechanisms, such as `oAuth`. The details for that can be found at `https://docs.snowflake.com/en/user-guide/spark-connector-use.html#using-external-oauth`.

6. Let's now run a query through Spark. The query will aggregate sales data from the sample database. To do so, append the following code snippet to your `scala` file:

```scala
val aggDFReader: DataFrameReader = spark.read
    .format("net.snowflake.spark.snowflake")
    .options(snowflakeOptions)
    .option("query", """SELECT C.C_MKTSEGMENT AS MARKET_
        SEGMENT, SUM(O_TOTALPRICE) AS REVENUE
                FROM SNOWFLAKE_SAMPLE_DATA.TPCH_SF1.ORDERS O
                LEFT OUTER JOIN SNOWFLAKE_SAMPLE_DATA.TPCH_
                    SF1.CUSTOMER C
                            ON O.O_CUSTKEY = C.C_CUSTKEY
                            GROUP BY C.C_MKTSEGMENT;""")

val aggDF: DataFrame = aggDFReader.load()
aggDF.show()
```

7. Now, run `spark-shell` and then run the following command:

```
:load snowflake_transform.scala
```

8. You should see the aggregated results from the query being displayed, as shown in the following screenshot:

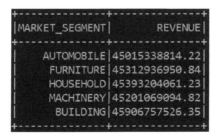

Figure 10.14 – Aggregated results output by the test_sf_connect.scala program

9. At this point, if you go into the Snowflake WebUI and click on the **History** tab and look for the query we just ran, you will find the query in the history, as follows:

Query ID	SQL Text
019a4771-...	SELECT * FROM (SELECT ("SUBQUERY_0"."MARKET_SEGMENT") AS "SUBQUERY_1_COL_0" , (CAST ("SUBQUERY_0"."REVENUE" AS VARCHAR)) AS "SUBQ...

Figure 10.15 – One of the queries initiated by the Snowflake Connector for Spark

10. Click the query text to view the complete text for the query, which will show you a query like what is shown in the following screenshot:

SQL Text

```
1  SELECT * FROM ( SELECT ( "SUBQUERY_0"."MARKET_SEGMENT" ) AS
   "SUBQUERY_1_COL_0" , ( CAST ( "SUBQUERY_0"."REVENUE" AS VARCHAR ) ) AS
   "SUBQUERY_1_COL_1" FROM ( SELECT * FROM ( ( SELECT C.C_MKTSEGMENT AS
   MARKET_SEGMENT, SUM(O_TOTALPRICE) AS REVENUE
2                         FROM SNOWFLAKE_SAMPLE_DATA.TPCH_SF1.ORDERS O
3                         LEFT OUTER JOIN
   SNOWFLAKE_SAMPLE_DATA.TPCH_SF1.CUSTOMER C
4                         ON O.O_CUSTKEY = C.C_CUSTKEY
5                         GROUP BY C.C_MKTSEGMENT ) ) AS
   "SF_CONNECTOR_QUERY_ALIAS" ) AS "SUBQUERY_0" ) AS "SUBQUERY_1" LIMIT 21
```

Figure 10.16 – SQL of an example query initiated by the Snowflake Connector for Spark

11. Now that we have our aggregate results, we are going to write them to a new table. To do so, append the following code snippet to your `scala` file:

```
aggDF.write
    .format("snowflake")
    .options(snowflakeOptions)
    .option("dbtable", "CUST_REV")
    .mode(SaveMode.Overwrite)
    .save()
```

12. Now, run `spark-shell` and then run the following command:

```
:load snowflake_transform.scala
```

The script should run without failure.

13. Now, via the Snowflake WebUI or SnowSQL, run the following command to validate that the table was successfully loaded:

```
SELECT * FROM new_db.PUBLIC.CUST_REV;
```

14. You should see five rows returned, as shown in the following screenshot:

Row	MARKET_SEGMENT	REVENUE
1	AUTOMOBILE	45015338814.22
2	MACHINERY	45201069094.82
3	BUILDING	45906757526.35
4	FURNITURE	45312936950.84
5	HOUSEHOLD	45393204061.23

Figure 10.17 – Output from the CUST_REV table

15. This indicates that the data was successfully loaded through Spark, using the Snowflake Connector for Spark.

16. Let's find out exactly what the Spark connector did. To do so, look at the query history via the Snowflake WebUI and look for the recent queries. The following list shows the history for an example run and is in reverse order, so the latest query is at the top and the earliest ones are toward the bottom:

Status	Query ID	SQL Text
✔	019a4779-...	alter table identifier(CUST_REV_staging_1426353982) rename to identifier(CUST_REV)
✘	019a4779-...	desc table identifier(CUST_REV)
✔	019a4779-...	copy into CUST_REV_staging_1426353982 FROM @spark_connector_load_stage_qAtKNIVqdt/gKg2Mbxz3N/ FILE_FORMAT = { TYPE=CSV FIELD_DELIMITER='|' ...
✔	019a4779-...	create table if not exists identifier(CUST_REV_staging_1426353982) ("MARKET_SEGMENT" STRING ,"REVENUE" DECIMAL(24,2))
✘	019a4779-...	desc table identifier(CUST_REV)
✔	019a4779-...	PUT file:///tmp/dummy_location_spark_connector_tmp/ @spark_connector_load_stage_qAtKNIVqdt
✔	019a4779-...	GET @spark_connector_load_stage_qAtKNIVqdt/ file:///tmp/dummy_location_spark_connector_tmp/
✔	019a4779-...	create temporary stage if not exists identifier(spark_connector_load_stage_qAtKNIVqdt)
✔	019a4779-...	alter session set timezone = 'Australia/Sydney', timestamp_ntz_output_format = 'YYYY-MM-DD HH24:MI:SS.FF3', timestamp_ltz_output_format = 'TZHTZM YYY...
✔	019a4779-...	SELECT * FROM ((SELECT C.C_MKTSEGMENT AS MARKET_SEGMENT, SUM(O_TOTALPRICE) AS REVENUE FROM SNOWFLAKE_SAMPLE_DATA.TPCH_SF1.OR...

Figure 10.18 – List of queries performed by the Snowflake Connector for Spark

17. From this list, we can see that the connector performed the following actions at a high level:

1. It created a temporary staging object where it loaded the data generated by Spark.

2. It created a table with the same name as our target table, but with _staging_ and a random number appended to it. The connecter issued the command to copy data from the temporary stage into this table.

3. Finally, it renamed the table to the target table name that we had supplied.

In the preceding steps, we went through the process of reading and writing data through Spark. The Snowflake Connector for Spark takes care of the heavy lifting and converts the read and write operations into several queries pushed down to Snowflake for execution.

How it works

The Snowflake Connector for Spark supports bi-directional data movement between Snowflake and your Spark cluster. You can read data from Snowflake as a DataFrame and write it back to Snowflake when required. For writing back, Snowflake uses the internal stage mechanism by default, through which data from Spark is written to a temporary internal stage first. The data is then copied from the internal stage into the target table using the standard `COPY` command. These steps are done transparently and under the covers, without requiring a Spark developer to worry about the underlying details.

Subscribe to our online digital library for full access to over 7,000 books and videos, as well as industry leading tools to help you plan your personal development and advance your career. For more information, please visit our website.

Why subscribe?

- Spend less time learning and more time coding with practical eBooks and Videos from over 4,000 industry professionals

- Improve your learning with Skill Plans built especially for you

- Get a free eBook or video every month

- Fully searchable for easy access to vital information

- Copy and paste, print, and bookmark content

Did you know that Packt offers eBook versions of every book published, with PDF and ePub files available? You can upgrade to the eBook version at packt.com and as a print book customer, you are entitled to a discount on the eBook copy. Get in touch with us at customercare@packtpub.com for more details.

At www.packt.com, you can also read a collection of free technical articles, sign up for a range of free newsletters, and receive exclusive discounts and offers on Packt books and eBooks.

Other Books You May Enjoy

If you enjoyed this book, you may be interested in these other books by Packt:

Data Engineering with Python

Paul Crickard

ISBN: 978-1-83921-418-9

- Understand how data engineering supports data science workflows

- Discover how to extract data from files and databases and then clean, transform, and enrich it

- Configure processors for handling different file formats as well as both relational and NoSQL databases

- Find out how to implement a data pipeline and dashboard to visualize results

- Use staging and validation to check data before landing in the warehouse

- Build real-time pipelines with staging areas that perform validation and handle failures

- Get to grips with deploying pipelines in the production environment

Learn Amazon SageMaker

Julien Simon

ISBN: 978-1-80020-891-9

- Create and automate end-to-end machine learning workflows on Amazon Web Services (AWS)
- Become well-versed with data annotation and preparation techniques
- Use AutoML features to build and train machine learning models with AutoPilot
- Create models using built-in algorithms and frameworks and your own code
- Train computer vision and NLP models using real-world examples
- Cover training techniques for scaling, model optimization, model debugging, and cost optimization
- Automate deployment tasks in a variety of configurations using SDK and several automation tools

Packt is searching for authors like you

If you're interested in becoming an author for Packt, please visit authors. packtpub.com and apply today. We have worked with thousands of developers and tech professionals, just like you, to help them share their insight with the global tech community. You can make a general application, apply for a specific hot topic that we are recruiting an author for, or submit your own idea.

Leave a review - let other readers know what you think

Please share your thoughts on this book with others by leaving a review on the site that you bought it from. If you purchased the book from Amazon, please leave us an honest review on this book's Amazon page. This is vital so that other potential readers can see and use your unbiased opinion to make purchasing decisions, we can understand what our customers think about our products, and our authors can see your feedback on the title that they have worked with Packt to create. It will only take a few minutes of your time, but is valuable to other potential customers, our authors, and Packt. Thank you!

Index

Printed in Great Britain
by Amazon

75472167R00188